PETER FLORIS

PETER FLORIS

HIS VOYAGE TO THE EAST INDIES IN THE GLOBE 1611-1615

EDITED BY

W. H. MORELAND

GYAN

Published by

GYAN

Gyan Publishing House
5, Ansari Road
Daryaganj, New Delhi-110002
Phone: 011-47034999, 9811692060
E-mail: books@gyanbooks.com

Distribution Network
gyanbooks.com
India, USA, Canada, UK, Australia

ISBN: 978-93-6280-163-0 (PB)
First Published, 1934

2nd Impression 2024

Printed at: Gyan Press, Delhi.

PETER FLORIS
Editor: W. H. MORELAND

PETER FLORIS

HIS VOYAGE TO THE EAST INDIES IN THE *GLOBE*

1611–1615

The Contemporary Translation of his Journal

Edited by

W. H. MORELAND, C.S.I., C.I.E.

LONDON

PRINTED FOR THE HAKLUYT SOCIETY

1934

PREFACE

THE reader will find in the Introduction such preliminary information as seems to be required regarding the personality of Peter Floris, and the objects of his voyage in the *Globe*. Here it will suffice to mention a few details of the lines on which the volume has been prepared.

The language and spelling of the manuscript are reproduced without adjustment, but the use of capital letters and italics has been modernised. Punctuation has presented some difficulty, mainly because the translator did not break up the long, rambling sentences which must have characterised the lost original, in common with so much of the Dutch commercial literature of the period; to break up his version now would involve occasional alterations in the wording, which would be contrary to the practice recognised by the Society, and all that has been found possible is to make the text easier to follow by the free use of colons and semi-colons. Square brackets have been used according to the ordinary practice to indicate either necessary insertions or brief explanations; parentheses, on the other hand, have a special and technical significance. It is clear that the manuscript was never finally revised, and it contains a number of alternative phrases written above the line, with no indication of the translator's preference for one over the other; in these cases I have selected the phrase which seems to be more appropriate, and, for convenience in printing, have placed the alternative alongside it in parentheses instead of above the line. The division into chapters, too, has been made for convenience; the manuscript is continuous.

In the foot-notes Indian words and names have been transliterated on the system followed in the *Imperial Gazetteer of India*; the vowels have the continental values, while the consonants are pronounced as in English, and, except that I have used *q* for one of the Arabic gutturals, no attempt is made to distinguish in cases where two or more Indian consonants are represented in English by a single character. Words belonging to other Asiatic languages are given as a rule in the form used by the authorities whom I have consulted, but in the case of Siamese words I have represented the aspirated consonants in the usual way, instead of by the method favoured by Mr W. A. R. Wood in his *History of Siam*, on which I have drawn so largely: for instance, I have written Phya where Mr Wood wrote P'ya. In order to save space, references in the foot-notes have been abbreviated; the full titles of the works so quoted will be found in the List of Authorities at the end of the volume.

The writer of the Journal was allusive as well as fond of detail, and I am indebted to a large number of scholars for generous help in elucidating the resulting obscurities of the text. Assistance on particular topics has been acknowledged in the foot-notes, but in this place it is my privilege to thank those who have allowed me to consult them on numerous questions relating to various departments of knowledge. Dr Krishnaswami Aiyangar, Sir Richard Burn, Sir Wolseley Haig and Mr C. E. A. W. Oldham have been my chief helpers on Indian matters; Professor D. G. E. Hall and Mr G. H. Luce on Burma; Dr H. G. Quaritch Wales on Siam; Mr C. J. Purnell on Japan; and Dr C. Otto Blagden on the Malay Peninsula. For information on points of Dutch language and history I have to thank Dr W. R. Bisschop and Professor P. Geyl, while Mr R. Bylsma has been most generous in tracing records of the period in the Rijksarchief at The Hague; and finally, Sir William Foster, the President of the Society, has given his invaluable assistance and advice at every stage from the preparation of the transcript of the Journal down to the revision of the last proof.

W. H. MORELAND

December, 1933

CONTENTS

INTRODUCTION . . . page xi

§ 1. The PLACE of the VOYAGE in COMMERCIAL HISTORY . . . xi
§ 2. The INCEPTION of the VOYAGE . . . xiii
§ 3. The TRADE CONDITIONS ENCOUNTERED . . . xix
§ 4. The POSITION in SIAM . . . xxvi
§ 5. The RESULTS of the VOYAGE . . . xxx
§ 6. The DUTCH CHIEF MERCHANTS . . . xxxvi
§ 7. PETER FLORIS, the MAN . . . liii
§ 8. The MANUSCRIPT . . . lxii

Note on Currency, Weights and Measures . . . lxix

THE JOURNAL

Chapter I. The Outward Voyage . . . 1
II. The Coromandel Coast . . . 8
III. Bantam . . . 22
IV. Patani . . . 30
V. Siam . . . 45
VI. Patani (*continued*) . . . 59
VII. Patani (*continued*) . . . 78
VIII. Patani (*continued*) . . . 91
IX. The Voyage to Masulipatam . . . 99
X. Masulipatam . . . 111
XI. Masulipatam (*continued*) . . . 124
XII. Bantam . . . 140

List of Authorities . . . 149

Index . . . 153

MAPS

The Course of the Voyage . . . *frontispiece*
The Southern Malay Peninsula . . . *to face page* 30
The Passage of the Straits . . . *to face page* 100

INTRODUCTION

§ I. The Place of the Voyage in Commercial History

The *Globe*, which made the seventh Voyage for the East India Company, was the first English vessel to engage in the trade of the Bay of Bengal and the Gulf of Siam; and consequently, the Journal of the voyage possesses the interest which attaches to all records of the experiences of pioneers. It has also a peculiar interest of its own, in that it enables us to realise, better perhaps than any record which has yet been published, the true inwardness of a prolonged trading voyage in the earliest days of the Company. It will be recalled that at first the Company had no capital of its own, nor did it engage in trade on behalf of the members as a body. When it decided that a Voyage should be undertaken, that is to say, that one or more ships should be sent out to the East, a subscription list was opened to provide the requisite capital, and the members who subscribed became the 'adventurers' for that particular Voyage, bearing the entire risk, and dividing the entire proceeds in proportion to the amounts they had subscribed.

Such a Voyage had necessarily to be self-contained, for when a ship had once left the English Channel, she could expect no help, except by accident, until she returned. There were, of course, no diplomatic or consular agents representing England in eastern seaports: the captain and merchants had to conduct their own diplomacy, and, on occasion, fight their own battles. The Company, again, had no permanent establishments in Asia, other than a not too efficient 'factory', that is, agency, at Bantam. The ship might perhaps get help from officers of other Voyages whom she might run across in eastern waters: it was equally possible that such a meeting might result in competition or intrigue, to the injury of both ventures. Casualties among staff and crew had to be provided for in the ship itself; commercial intelligence had to be picked up as occasion served; and carefully laid plans might have to be hurriedly revised in the light of political or economic changes, which occurred sometimes with disconcerting rapidity. All these features, and others, are illustrated in the Voyage of the *Globe*. By training and experience, if not actually by birth, the writer of the Journal was a Dutchman, and he possessed in some measure the national gift for elaborating details so as to present an artistic whole; from the written record we can follow not merely the course of the enterprise, but the workings of the writer's mind, from the day he left Gravesend, in January, 1611, until, more than four years later, he was ready to sail from Bantam to return to England.

The seventh Voyage belongs to what may be described as the second phase in the direct commercial intercourse between England and the East. Just at the outset, the East India Company followed the practice of the various Dutch ventures of the preceding years, and despatched its ships on an out-and-home voyage to the spice ports. Experience, however, proved very quickly that the spice trade, important as it was, could easily be overdone. Competition in the producing markets led to a heavy increase in cost: competition in the consuming regions led to heavy falls in price; and the large profits of the earliest ventures could not be maintained for long. Elimination of this injurious competition was one of the chief objects of the amalgamation of the various Dutch interests into the powerful Dutch East India Company, established in 1602; but there still remained the competition between Dutch and English, buying in the same eastern markets, and selling in the same regions of Europe. For both Companies alike, a policy of expansion was found to be essential: a larger variety of eastern goods had to be purchased, and new markets had to be explored, both for the provision of these goods and for the sale of European produce.

The rapid development in these directions can be traced in the commissions issued by the English Company for successive Voyages.[1] The commission issued in 1601 to Lancaster for the first Voyage contains no hint of expansion. The objective of the second Voyage, sent out in 1604, was still limited to the spice ports, but now endeavours were to be made to procure other

[1] *First Letter Book*, 4, 51, 114, 240, 295, 328.

commodities, such as silk, "wherewith theis parts of Christendome have not been gluted as with spices". The third and fourth Voyages, sent out in 1607 and 1608, were directed to explore new waters, and were concerned with the Red Sea and Western India as well as with the spice ports; the fifth, which was in fact an offshoot of the third, consisted of a single ship, which sailed in 1609 only for the spice ports; while the sixth was again concerned largely with Western India and the Red Sea.

So far, no vessel had been sent to the Bay of Bengal, but by the year 1607 the Directors of the Company had become alive to the possibilities of that region, and clause 44 of Keeling's commission for the third Voyage ordered that the factors to be left at Bantam should investigate the possibilities of such places "as Mesapatania [*i.e.*, Masulipatam] in the partes of Bengalla Cheremandall St. Thome or any other places fitt for trade...the omission of seekeinge out whereof all this while hath retourned to our greate losse, and to the benefit of the Hollanders, who have beene laborious and industrious therein". These instructions were repeated in the following year, but there is no record of anything having been done to comply with them; and in 1609 the position was that the Directors were alive to the possibilities of the Bay of Bengal, but had no precise information regarding it.

To conclude these preliminary observations, it may be noted that the system of separate Voyages wore out very quickly. The records of the change of policy are no longer extant, but it is known[1] that, some time in the year 1613, the Company decided on the formation of a Joint Stock, by which a succession of Voyages should be conducted as parts of an orderly whole; and the news of the inception of this third phase had reached Bantam when the *Globe* arrived there at the beginning of the year 1615.

§ 2. The INCEPTION of the VOYAGE

The movement which led to the despatch of the *Globe* was initiated by two Dutchmen, who for the present will be described as Peter Floris and Lucas Antheunis, the names under which

[1] See the Introduction to *Letters Received*, ii, where the subject is discussed at length.

they presented themselves in London; their identity and antecedents will be discussed in a later section. It is uncertain, however, whether Floris and Antheunis were the first, or the only, Dutchmen to offer their services to the English Company at this time.

In November, 1609, the Company was approached[1] by a Dutchman giving the name of Florence (*i.e.*, Florens, or Floris) Devyne, who stated that he had been employed on the Coromandel Coast, and proposed that, if the Company would send a small ship to those parts with a capital of 6000*l.* under his direction, he would guarantee them a return of three for one, and would be satisfied with the balance of profit as his remuneration. A committee was appointed to discuss this proposal with the projector, and a week later a letter, drafted by the Governor, was ordered to be sent to him in Holland. Here the story breaks off abruptly: the Governor's letter is not extant, and the Court Minutes, containing the records of the Company's proceedings, are missing for the period from January, 1610, to December, 1613. It is impossible therefore to say whether 'Florence Devyne' was identical with one of the two Dutchmen who inspired the despatch of the *Globe*, or was acting independently of them: no person of that name can be traced in the records of the Dutch factories on the Coromandel Coast, and the name was most probably a pseudonym. All that can be said is that in the autumn of 1609 the Company was considering a project for entering the Coromandel trade with the aid of Dutch experience.

For the action taken in the following year we are dependent, in the absence of the Court Minutes, on a series of documents preserved in a record which was printed in 1893, and is known variously as the 'Miscellaneous Court Book', 'The Register of Letters etc. of the Governor and Company of Merchants of London trading into the East Indies', and 'The First Letter Book of the East India Company'. What is probably the earliest of these documents in point of time, though it is the last of them in the book, is the note[2] of "A discourse delyvered to Mr

[1] *Court Minutes*, 18th and 25th November, 1609.

[2] *First Letter Book*, 427.

Governor, by Peter Floris and Lucas Antheumes [*sic*] of their pretended [*i.e.*, proposed] Voyage". The proposal was for a Voyage lasting nearly four years, to start in November, 1610, and visit successively the Coromandel Coast, Bantam, Patani and Siam, the Coromandel Coast again, Patani and Siam again, and finally to leave Bantam for England in December, 1613, or January, 1614.

This document is not dated. It is reasonable to infer that the discourse was delivered after 26th January, 1610, when the Court Minutes break off, for, if it had been earlier, there would probably have been some reference to it in that record. It may further be assumed that the discourse was an early incident in the negotiations, before the Voyage had been decided on, and consequently it must be several months earlier than January, 1611, by which time the required capital had been raised, the ship had been procured, and all necessary business transacted. The next document to be cited shows that a preliminary agreement regarding the Voyage had already been made on 27th March, 1610; and, if, as is probable, the discourse was earlier than this, its date would be February or early March.

The preliminary agreement was subsequently cancelled, and its terms are not on record. The next document is the agreement[1] which definitely laid down the conditions of the Voyage. It purports to have been made on 13th December, 1610, but its contents indicate that part of it must be much earlier, and we must infer that the date was left blank in the settled draft, and filled in only when all preparations had been made, and the time had come to sign and seal the fair copies. The principal indications of this fact are two. In the first place, the body of the agreement contemplated an investment of 12,000*l.* in all, but later clauses explain that owing to increased charges the capital had been raised to about 14,000*l.*: obviously the wording of the earlier part of the agreement belongs to the stage of estimation, while the addenda relate to ascertained facts. In the second place, the two projectors, Floris and Antheunis, misspelt in the document as Ploris and Athewmes, were allowed to invest 1500*l.* of the original capital—600*l.* in cash, and the balance "in

[1] *First Letter Book*, 363.

June or Julie next followinge the date of theis presentes". As the text stands, this second payment would have fallen due in the summer of 1611, when the *Globe* had been six months on her voyage; but the money was wanted for her equipment, and must have been paid in 1610, not 1611. The project must thus have been definitely settled before June, 1610, but after 27th March, the date of the preliminary agreement, in other words, some time in April or May.

The agreement provided that the two Dutch projectors and one Englishman, Robert Browne, who had been employed for some time as factor at Bantam, should act together as chief merchants in the business of the Voyage. Floris and Antheunis, but not Browne, were to have a commission on profits if they amounted to "*centum per centum*" or more, the rate rising from 4 to 10 per cent., according to the amount of the profit; they were to give their whole time, and their best powers, to the conduct of the business; and they were to furnish security, as was usually done, for the due performance of their duties, and also "for the deliveringe up in writeinge of a true and just accompt of all there proceedings in the said voyadge", a provision which doubtless accounts for the existence of this Journal.

Certain clauses dealing with the possibility of one or both of the projectors dying during the Voyage indicate that they were not to receive any salary, for the Company bound itself to pay to their executors or administrators the amount due as commission and the net proceeds of their investment, but no provision was made for their wages. According to the practice of the time their current expenses, on land as well as on the ship, would be defrayed out of the funds of the Voyage, but they would not receive the lump sum of accumulated wages which ordinary factors drew on the conclusion of their engagement; instead, they would receive whatever commission they had earned.

The next documents to be noticed are the commissions[1] for

[1] *First Letter Book*, 359 ff. for the Royal, and 369 ff. for the Company's, commission. These documents mark a departure from the usual practice of naming the same officers in both commissions, for the first was issued to Hippon alone, and the second to Hippon and the three chief merchants jointly; presumably it was considered undesirable to entrust aliens with the execution of martial law.

the Voyage. The Royal Commission, issued to Anthony Hippon, an experienced navigator who had been master of the *Dragon* on the third Voyage, and had now been chosen to be captain of the *Globe*, was in the usual form, enjoining the strict observance of international obligations, and empowering the captain to maintain discipline, and, in case of need, to apply "our Lawe called Lawe Martiall". Two commissions issued by the Company are on record, and a comparison of their contents bears out the suggestion made by the Editors of the *First Letter Book* that Floris and Antheunis may have been dissatisfied with the terms of the earlier document. These commissions bear no dates, but there is no doubt that the one which is placed second in the *Letter Book* was the operative document, for, unlike the first, it provided for the strengthening of the factory at Bantam, which the Journal shows was in fact done, while a memorandum,[1] written at Patani in the year 1613, quoted as the 9th article a clause which bore that number in the second commission, but did not appear in the first.

The main difference between the two commissions lies in the more precise definition of responsibility effected by the later one. Under it the chief merchants were to be entirely independent of the captain in all matters of trade, and were to have full control over the four factors appointed to the ship; under no circumstances could they be displaced during the voyage. The captain was to sail where the chief merchants directed, while anyone who even suggested a premature return was to be severely punished. On the other hand, the captain was to have full government over the ship and crew, and possibly it was in deference to Hippon's experience that several clauses dealing with details disappeared from the second commission. Provisions in regard to sanitation (clause 4 of the earlier document), records of the course (5), precautions during watering and the like (12, 13), care of empty casks (18), alterations in cabins (21), salutes (22), or avoidance of the Channel ports (28), may have been considered unnecessary in the circumstances; but it is a little surprising that among the omissions are two articles which were at this period common form—the prescription of morning

[1] *Letters Received*, i. 296.

and evening prayer, and the prohibition of blasphemy, theft, drunkenness, gambling, and other forms of misconduct. It would be futile to speculate as to the motive for these latter omissions, and all that need be said is that entries in the Journal show that prayers were in fact part of the daily routine, while drunkenness and gambling were, at the least, common.

The only unusual clause in the commission is the provision (16) that the captain and crew should defend and preserve the two Dutch merchants from their countrymen in the East, who, it was apprehended, "will seeke to doe them wronge and all the villanie they may". Happily no occasion seems to have arisen for putting this clause into operation; Floris, at least, was usually on excellent terms with the compatriots he met at Bantam, at Patani, and on the Coromandel Coast.

No details of the actual equipment for the Voyage have been preserved, but the agreement specified that the ship should be of about 400 tons, with a company of 80, including the merchants. A Dutch factor[1] described the *Globe* as about 170 last, or, say, 350 tons, and this figure may be taken as substantially accurate. The form in which the capital stock was sent out is not on record, but we may assume that the bulk of it was in reals of eight, while the Journal mentions incidentally that the cargo included some lead and some woollen cloth, but does not hint at the presence of any other goods. Nothing else is recorded of the preparations for the Voyage, but they were completed in time for the *Globe* to leave Gravesend on 5th January, 1610, according to the Old Style which Floris used for the occasion, corresponding to 15th January, 1611 (New Style).

Lastly, reference may be made to one other document. The Calendar of State Papers records[2] that on 27th November, 1610, royal permission was given for the East India Company "to admit into their society merchants strangers, aliens, or denizens to trade with them in common stock". The date and the circumstances indicate that the primary object of this grant must have been to regularise the position of the two Dutch merchants who contributed to the common stock employed in setting out

[1] *Golconda*, 63.

[2] *Cal. S.P.* ii. no. 495.

the *Globe*; and doubtless they were formally admitted to membership of the Company, though, in the absence of the Court Minutes, no record of the admission has survived.

§ 3. The Trade Conditions encountered

The first objective of the Voyage was the Coromandel Coast: the reason was that the countries to be visited farther east bought very little except cotton clothing, and the artisans on the Coast had for long specialised in the supply of these markets. A fuller account of the commercial activities of this part of India will be found in *Relations of Golconda* (Hakluyt Society, 1931); here it will suffice to indicate briefly the nature of the goods to be purchased, the methods of procuring them, and the influence of the administration on commercial transactions.

The cloth to be purchased may be classified as piece-goods and apparel. The former consisted of plain cotton cloth, usually bleached, but sometimes dyed red or blue, and sold either by the 'piece' of conventional size, or by the 'corge', that is, the score of pieces. Cloth of this kind had a large regular sale, but in the markets which the *Globe* was to serve the chief demand was for goods which could be brought into wear at once, and which may be called apparel, if we remember that no elaborate tailoring was involved in their preparation. The most important article was the skirt, then known in commerce as *tapé*, which consisted simply of a piece of cloth of correct size and pattern, worn by both sexes wrapped round the waist. There were also shawls or wraps for the shoulders, of the same general type, turbans for the head, and sashes or girdles for the waist.

For skirts and wraps in particular, the most important features were the style and pattern. In these matters the consuming markets were intensely conservative, each locality required its own familiar types, and even a slight divergence from the accepted standards might suffice to render the goods unsaleable. In some cases the patterns were produced by the use of coloured yarns, but for the markets with which we are concerned they were usually either printed or 'painted', to use the contemporary term. Printing with wooden blocks applied by hand was practised in many parts of India, and the product was known by the name of *chīnt*, now familiar in its English form as chintz; Gujarāt, on the west coast, was the principal exporter of these goods.

On the Coromandel Coast[1] the pattern was more usually produced, not with a block, but with an instrument described sometimes as a pen, and sometimes as a brush; and cloth which had been treated by this process was called by the Portuguese *pintado*, that is, 'painted'. English merchants followed this Portuguese usage, and described the goods as 'painted' cloth, or sometimes 'pintadoes', while the craftsmen who made them became 'painters'; and Dutch merchants of the period used the equivalent term *geschilderd* (from *schilderen*, to paint), though some modern writers prefer to substitute *gebatikt*, a participle formed from *batik*, which is the local name of a similar process still practised in Java. These 'painted' goods formed the bulk of the trade with which we are concerned.

Merchants had thus to be familiar with the precise forms and patterns of the goods demanded by the markets which they proposed to visit. They had also to know where to buy the goods they wanted, for there was a certain amount of specialisation in the commercial production of the Coast: weaving and bleaching, dyeing and 'painting', were practised in all centres, but some of them were more important than others for particular specialities. Thus the dyes obtainable in the northern centres, Masulipatam and Petapoli, were superior to those found farther south, and dyed pieces were ordinarily bought in them. On the other hand, some of the southern centres had specialised in the patterned cloths in demand for export, and Pulicat in particular had an old-established reputation for 'painted' goods for the markets farther east.[2]

[1] The fullest extant description of the processes employed on the Coast seems to be that which was recorded in 1742 by the Jesuit Father R. Cœurdoux, an English translation of which forms the Appendix to Mr MacIver Percival's *The Chintz Book* (London, 1923).

[2] See *The Book of Duarte Barbosa* (Hakluyt Society, 1921), ii. 132. The translation speaks of 'printed cotton cloths'; the phrase in the text is '*panos pintados dalgodam*' (painted cloths of cotton).

A somewhat similar statement of the position, made in the Introduction to *Relations of Golconda*, was questioned by a writer in the *English Historical Review* for April, 1932, who suggested that at this period Masulipatam was the chief source of 'painted' cloth of the finest quality, and that the speciality of the southern coast was rather cloth woven of dyed yarns. It may well be the case that the 'painted' products of the north were superior in artistic quality, but the export trade was not interested in such exquisite designs as, later in the century, were to become the rage in England: novelty and originality were ruled out by the conditions prevailing in the eastern markets, which insisted on meticulous reproduction of cheap, stereotyped designs; and in 'painting', as in other Indian crafts, the production of work of the finest quality must have depended mainly on the patronage of wealthy amateurs. A precise account of the position at this period has been compiled by Dr Terpstra[1] from the Dutch commercial records. The Dutch merchants, he tells us, looked primarily to the northern centres, Masulipatam and Petapoli, for bleached and dyed piece-goods, while Pulicat, in the south, was by far the most important source of the 'painted' cloth which they required; and, before they succeeded in establishing themselves in the town, they had arranged to import its products to Masulipatam for re-export thence.

These facts were naturally familiar to the chief merchants on board the *Globe*, two of whom had gained their practical experience in the Dutch factories on the Coast. The first call made by the vessel was consequently at Pulicat, to see if any business could be done; but the merchants learned to their surprise that a monopoly of its trade had recently been granted to the Dutch by the ruling King, the representative of the dynasty of Vijayanagar. They therefore sailed north, and established themselves in Petapoli and Masulipatam, the chief seaports of the kingdom of Golconda, where no similar obstacles existed, and where they were confident of obtaining a satisfactory cargo to order.

While the annual production on the Coast was very large, when judged by the standards of the time, the stocks available in the markets were ordinarily small, and a cargo of any size

[1] *De Indische Gids*, March, 1915, p. 335.

could not be procured out of hand. The artisans, who worked as individuals, were unprovided with capital, and were thus unable to manufacture for stock; the first thing for a buyer to do was to place orders, and give advances in cash; and, this having been done, the ship must wait until the goods ordered were delivered. One branch of the equipment required by a successful merchant was ability to manage this business, so that the goods should be made promptly, of the right quality, and at a reasonable price: a not less important qualification was ability to deal with the local authorities.

It may be said, not merely of Golconda, but of almost the whole Indian seaboard, that at this period foreign merchants were welcomed if they came prepared to pay cash for what they wanted, or provided with goods for which there was a demand; and the rulers of the various countries were anxious, broadly speaking, to foster sea-borne commerce. Customs duties were low, and complaints usually received a favourable hearing at the Courts; the difficulties which arose were created by the local, not the central, administration. In Golconda, the chief executive posts were held on the farming system, and fell usually to the highest bidder at an annual auction. The Governor, as he was called by Europeans, when he had once secured the farm, had in practice very wide powers, while any default in his payments to the treasury might involve the bastinado. The business of administration was thus highly speculative, and a Governor had the strongest possible motives for collecting every penny he could, without regard to the future of a region with which his connection might be merely temporary.

The troubles of foreign merchants in Golconda usually centred either in heavy local duties which were claimed in addition to the customs, or in demands for presents and forced loans to the Governor as a condition of his favour; and both these topics are adequately illustrated in the Journal of the *Globe*. Peter Floris, who, as will be explained later on, had lived for several years in Masulipatam, was well acquainted with these obstacles to profitable trade, and, though on this occasion he had somewhat the worst of a final dispute with the Governor, he was able to sail for Bantam on the first of February, 1612, after less than six months' stay on the Coast "withoute having made any penny in badde dettes, or leaving any remnants behynde us on shoare", with the ship fully laden, with plenty of time for the seasonal voyage, and well satisfied with the start which had been made.

Bantam, the second objective, which was reached on 26th April, was at this time the most important seaport in Java. It was one of the chief distributing centres for cotton goods, it offered large quantities of pepper for sale, and it was an entrepôt for silk, porcelain and other wares brought by the junks which came to purchase pepper for China. During the sixteenth century Java pepper had been sold only in Asia, and the prosperity of Bantam had been greatly increased by the advent of the Dutch and English, who were anxious to buy pepper for the European markets hitherto supplied by the Portuguese from the Malabar Coast of India. At first, the treatment accorded to the newcomers was liberal, but, the trade once established, demands on them tended to increase; and the Dutch were already considering the transfer of their principal activities to Jakatra, the next seaport to the east, where a few years later they were to establish their headquarters under the name of Batavia.

Floris found that the commercial conditions at Bantam were at the moment unfavourable, and after a few weeks' stay sailed for Patani, the next objective, leaving some cotton goods to be sold for account of the *Globe* by the factory, which, in accordance with his instructions, he had reinforced by George Chauncey, the youngest of his factors, and by a chest of reals. An uneventful voyage of three weeks brought him to his destination.

Geographically and culturally Patani was one of the northern Malay States, but at this period it was under the suzerainty of Siam, in which kingdom it has now been incorporated.[1] The boundaries of Siam cannot be defined with precision. The nucleus of the kingdom was the Menam valley, with the capital at Ayuthia, some way up the river. Round this nucleus lay a number of entities—Patani, Singora, Ligor, and other Malay States on the south-west and west, Tenasserim on the Bay of

[1] This account of Patani and Siam is based on *Schouten*, *van Vliet*, *Wood*, and *Anderson*, *passim*.

Bengal, Chiengmai on the north, Lanshan or Luang Prabang on the north-east, and Cambodia on the east and south-east—which, according to the varying views and capacities of the rulers, might be constituent provinces of a great empire, or sovereign states, paying, or withholding, tribute, as circumstances might determine. Commercially, it was all one region. The population was relatively large, the fertility of the soil enabled the people to live in some degree of comfort, and consequently the market for clothes was of very great importance. The principal exports were the dyewood known variously as brazil or sappan, several gums or resins, including lac, benzoin and gamboge, and skins and hides, which had a large market in Japan. Lead and tin were also available, while there was usually a surplus of rice to be had at low rates.

The ports in the Gulf of Siam were important also as entrepôts for the trade of China. Apart from the restricted privileges accorded to the Portuguese settlement at Macao, the Chinese seaboard was closed to foreigners, and consequently Chinese goods could be purchased only on neutral territory; at Patani, Singora and Ligor, as well as on the Menam, the arrival of the junks from China was, perhaps, the outstanding event of the commercial year, offering, as it did, the prospect of obtaining a supply of raw silk, silk fabrics, and porcelain, for transport to the markets further west.

It is a remarkable fact that, at the time when the *Globe* visited the Gulf of Siam, high hopes were entertained that these seaports might become entrepôts for the silk trade between China and Japan. This trade had increased greatly[1] during the past half century, but it was not open freely to the countries primarily concerned. No Japanese vessels could enter Chinese ports; a single Portuguese ship came annually to Japan from Macao carrying Canton silk, and a limited number of junks brought the product of Nanking to Nagasaki; the rest of the trade was conducted on neutral territory, Formosa, the Philippines, or elsewhere. Both Dutch and English hoped to obtain a share of this lucrative trade in the Gulf of Siam; and the early letters[2] from

[1] On this subject see *Takekoshi*, ii. ch. xliv.

[2] *Letters Received*, i. 316; ii. 5, 127, 205; v. 4, 46.

the English factory at Hirado, or Firando as the name was then written, insisted on the need for bringing silk thence. As a matter of fact, the Journal records that in July, 1612, the Dutch sent a consignment of silk and silk wares from Patani to Japan, and six months later Floris noted that silk and other Chinese goods were being sent to Japan from Siam also; but by May, 1613, he had apparently lost hope of the silk trade, and had recognised that skins must be the main export in that direction. The silk trade did not develop, probably because the other neutral entrepôts were more convenient for both Chinese and Japanese; and by the year 1617 the idea of it had been abandoned by the European merchants in Japan.

At Patani and in Siam, as elsewhere in this region, the ruler was the principal merchant of the country; he had the first call on all imports, and competition for them was in abeyance until he had made his choice; he monopolised all important articles of export; and, as a natural consequence, he controlled the supply of commercial capital. At Patani, Floris had the inevitable initial difficulties with the officials, with whose methods he was unfamiliar; but later on he dealt directly with the Queen, one of the pleasantest figures in the Asiatic literature of the period, and business was transacted in a straightforward way with very little friction.

In Siam, conditions were less satisfactory. Antheunis went there on the *Globe's* first trip in August, 1612, and, as it happened, the partners were not destined to meet again, for he was still at Ayuthia when Floris left Patani in October of the following year. It was not easy to do business with the commercial officials employed by the King of Siam, for goods might be taken on approval, kept for months, and eventually returned —"a pittifull case when Kings become merchants", as Floris observed. The King's reluctance to buy was, however, itself a symptom of the temporary disorganisation of the Siamese markets, due to a combination of commercial and political difficulties, which are explained at length in the Journal. As regards the former, it is sufficient to say here that the recent entry of the Dutch into markets previously monopolised by the Portuguese inevitably resulted in temporary dislocation of trade, and that the *Globe* was unfortunate in coming to Siam just when things were at their worst. The political difficulties present a more complex topic, which is discussed in the next section.

§ 4. The Position in Siam

The account offered by Floris of the political situation in Siam falls into two parts, the first of which was really irrelevant to his purpose. It would have been sufficient to describe the internal troubles of the year preceding the *Globe's* arrival, but before doing this he furnished a sketch of the relations between Siam and Burma for nearly half a century, a sketch which is necessarily imperfect, and not easily intelligible as it stands. The simplest course seems to be, first, to re-write his sketch in the light of the most recent authorities, leaving the discrepancies in details to be indicated in foot-notes to the text, and then to examine his account of the internal troubles, which is good historical material, and directly relevant to his purpose. It must not, however, be supposed that the last word has yet been said on the relations between Siam and Burma at this period. Much research has still to be done before the history of either country can be presented in a definitive form, and the sources on which I have chiefly relied—Mr G. E. Harvey's *History of Burma*, and Mr W. A. R. Wood's *History of Siam*—must be read as valuable contributions by pioneer workers in a region only partially explored.

At this period Burma, like Siam, is an indefinite term. The nucleus of the kingdom was the valley of the Irrawaddy, with three main centres of administration, Ava in the north, Toungoo in the centre, and Pegu, the capital, in the south. This region was inhabited by two races: to the north were the people properly called Burmese, to the south were the people hitherto usually known as Talaing, but now officially designated as Mon. Round this nucleus lay various entities. On the north-west, Arakan was definitely an independent kingdom, though deeply interested in Burmese affairs. On the north and north-east were various Shan States, which might be tributary or independent according to circumstances; while on the east Chiengmai, which has been reckoned in the preceding section as part of Siam, may also be regarded as a Burmese province, actual or potential. On the south-east, Martaban and Moulmein were usually, but not invariably, Burmese; and, further south, Tavoy and Tenasserim might be tributary to Burma or to Siam, according as the fortune of war decided.

The story told by Floris goes back to the reign of one of the most famous kings of Burma, Bayinnaung (1551–81), who, among other achievements, reduced Siam to the position of a vassal kingdom, and in 1569 placed Maha Thammaraja on the throne of Ayuthia. On the death of Bayinnaung, his loosely knit empire promptly began to disintegrate, and his successor, Nandabayin (1581–99), proved unable to hold it together. In 1584 Siam renounced her allegiance, and then followed the tragedy of Pegu which bulks so largely in the literature of the period. Nandabayin exhausted the resources of his kingdom in a series of unsuccessful invasions of Siam, which lasted until 1593. When his impotence became obvious, his enemies quickly gathered round him, and eventually he surrendered to his rebel Viceroy of Toungoo, who soon afterwards put him to death. The spoil of his capital, Pegu, was shared between Toungoo and Arakan, and the latter destroyed the city, leaving the neighbouring seaport of Syriam in the hands of Philip de Brito, a Portuguese adventurer in his service.

Siam was thus, for the time, relieved of anxiety on the west, and under 'the Black King', Naresuen, who had succeeded his father, Maha Thammaraja, in 1590, recovered rapidly in power and resources. On Naresuen's death in 1605, his brother Ekathotsarot became king, and ruled peaceably until 1610, when the internal troubles began which form the subject of the second portion of Floris' account. It may be worth while to add that the eclipse of Burma was not of long duration. A strong king emerged in the person of Anaukpetlun (1605–28), who repopulated Pegu, recovered its port of Syriam, and proceeded to extend the boundaries of his dominions. An attempt to regain Tenasserim was unsuccessful, but in 1614 Chiengmai was taken, and hostilities between Burma and Siam continued until 1618, when by treaty Chiengmai was restored to Siam in exchange for the latter's claim to Martaban.

The troubles in Siam itself originated in 1610, when a prominent man, whose name is given as Phya Naiwai, accused the Crown Prince of treason; the charge was believed by the King, and the young Prince either committed suicide or was executed. Shortly after this the King died, and was succeeded by another son named Intharaja, who is usually known as King Songtham. One of his first acts was to order the execution of Phya Naiwai, who, as it happened, had among his supporters a large band of Japanese. In retaliation for the death of their leader or master, the Japanese forced their way into the palace, imposed terms on the King, sacked the city, and withdrew unmolested with the booty.

The news of this trouble tempted the King of Luang Prabang to invade Siam; he was repulsed in April, 1612, a few months before the arrival of the *Globe*, but the whole country was still disturbed, and fresh invasions were anticipated from all sides.

The account of these affairs given by Floris agrees closely with that which is contained in Mr Wood's *History of Siam*: Mr Wood in fact accepted Floris as a credible witness. On the other hand, his accuracy was questioned by the late Sir Ernest Satow in his study of the intercourse between Japan and Siam in the seventeenth century (*Transactions of the Asiatic Society of Japan*, 1885, pp. 181 ff.). Satow pointed out[1] that Floris was contradicted, as regards dates in particular, by the Siamese chronicle known as the *Phongsawadan*, which he evidently regarded as the more trustworthy authority of the two, and he left Floris' reputation under a cloud. His view may have been tenable half a century ago, but the progress of research in the interval has finally disposed of it. Strictly speaking, the *Phongsawadan* is, as Satow recognised, not a chronicle at all, but a compilation made from uncertain materials after the original annals had been destroyed at the capture of Ayuthia by the Burmese in 1767; and critical study has established the facts, to use Mr Wood's words, that "starting from about the year 1370, almost every date given is wrong....Moreover the error is not uniform;

[1] Satow had not seen the full text of the Journal, but only the condensed version in Astley's Collection.

sometimes the dates given are wrong only by one or two years, sometimes by eighteen or twenty. The only conclusion to be drawn is that the compilers of the *Phongsawadan*, for some reason or other, invented a complete system of chronology for themselves, and this does not make us too ready to accept without question their authority as to facts".

The basis of Satow's criticism thus disappears, for it was on the discrepancies in dates that he chiefly relied, and the credit to be attached to Floris' account must be determined on other grounds. He was not actually an eye-witness, but he had before him the letters of his partner Antheunis, written from Ayuthia, and recounting events which had taken place there only a few months before the arrival of the *Globe*. In substance this is good evidence. Antheunis may have made mistakes as to details, but his position made it necessary for him to ascertain the main facts of the political situation, so far as they affected the markets; he had no motive for distorting those facts in his confidential correspondence with his partner; and the substantial accuracy of his description must be accepted.

Leaving then matters of detail to be noticed in the foot-notes to the text, the situation in broad outline was as follows. The information which Floris and Antheunis possessed regarding Siam related mainly to the halcyon period from about 1605 to 1608, when the country was peaceful and prosperous, and its constituent or allied kingdoms readily absorbed all the goods which the Coromandel Coast supplied. They made their plans in London on this basis, and provided goods on a suitable scale; but when the *Globe* reached Siam, they found the whole country disturbed by apprehensions of impending wars North and East and West, internal trade almost at a standstill, merchants unwilling to lay in stocks or transport goods to the regions where hostilities were expected, in a word no buyers for the exceptional quantities of goods which were now reaching the Siamese ports. The measures taken by Floris in this emergency are recounted at length in the Journal, and need not be recapitulated.

§ 5. The Results of the Voyage

The conditions prevailing in the Siamese markets led to a substantial modification in the plans for the Voyage. The original intention had been to make two trips between India and Siam, but the return to Masulipatam was unavoidably delayed, and eventually the second trip was abandoned. The *Globe* spent more than a year in Siamese waters, sailing twice between Patani and the Menam, and another year on the Coromandel Coast, where she was sheathed and refitted; it was late in 1614 before she was at last able to sail from Masulipatam for Bantam; and, after completing her lading there, she started for home in March, 1615 (New Style), and was off the Lizard in August, having been thus 4½ years in all at sea, or about a year more than was originally contemplated. Incidentally it may be noted that the course from Patani to Masulipatam lay through the Straits of Singapore and Malacca; and apparently the *Globe* was the first English vessel to accomplish this task, for the *James*, which had attempted it earlier in the year, had been forced to return to Bantam.

Commercially, the Voyage was a success. The detailed accounts are not now in existence, but a memorandum[1] which was prepared from them for the Company's use stated that "the seventh Voyage's capitall was 15,632*l* and the advance thereon was 218 per cent"; the capital had thus been increased substantially above the revised figure—"14,000*l* or thereabouts"—mentioned in the agreement for the Voyage. The words "the advance thereon" indicate that the total return, including the original capital, was just under 50,000*l*., or, in the phraseology of the time, more than three for one, a satisfactory figure, which, however, must be interpreted with due regard to the circumstances. Numerous entries in the Court Minutes show that the rate of interest ruling in London at this period for commercial loans was 9 or 10 per cent., while the 'adventurers' bore the entire risk of loss, a heavy liability when the whole venture was carried in a single ship, and they could hope for no return whatever for four or five years from the date of their investment.

[1] *Calendar of the Court Minutes of the East India Company*, 1650–4, p. 360.

It may be said then that the members who had subscribed in the middle of 1610 would not have been adequately remunerated by a return of two for one at the end of 1615, at least in the opinion of the Directors, who in that year declared[1] a "project of two for one" after 24 months "to be noe greate matter".

The entire return could not, of course, be made so early, for time was required to market the goods and collect the price of those which were sold on credit, while portions of the capital had been left at Bantam and with Antheunis in Siam, and a final distribution could not be made until after his return. Gaps in the Court Minutes make it impossible to say when the divisions were actually ordered, and consequently the real rate of profit cannot be calculated; our knowledge is limited to the following facts.[2] A few days after the return of the *Globe*, the 'auditors', or, as we should now say, accountants, reported that three capitals might be 'delivered'. This of course was not an actual division, but an expedient for marketing the large stock of pepper which had been brought by the *Globe* and by the *James*, her consort on the homeward voyage; adventurers who were in a hurry to realise could take out pepper, at fixed prices, up to the limit stated by the auditors, and the value of this pepper would be adjusted against their accounts when the formal divisions were made later on. No such division had been made up to 10th November, 1615, after which there is a gap of nearly two years in the Court Minutes. In July, 1618, the Governor announced a division, apparently the third, of one capital on the Voyage; and in November of that year, after Antheunis had returned, it appeared that the capital left in his hands would yield very little profit, so that on the whole Voyage the adventurers were not expected to get more than three for one. No record has been found of the final division, but it may be inferred that three capitals in all were returned between November, 1615, and July, 1618, and that some time later the Voyage was wound up by a final division of 18 per cent., thus giving the total 'advance' of 218 per cent. recorded in the account which has already been quoted.

[1] *Court Minutes*, 17th October, 1615.

[2] *Court Minutes*, 5th September, 1615; 3rd July, and 24th November, 1618.

The profit, such as it was, was obtained at the cost of heavy, but perhaps not unusual, mortality. The number of the original crew is not formally recorded, but on the figures given in the agreement for the Voyage it would be about 75 men, excluding the merchants and factors; and it may be noted that there is no reference to the presence of a surgeon on board. At first the ship was healthy, but at Bantam, always a dangerous port, the crew were infected with dysentery, and 20 men in all had been lost by the time she left Patani for Siam. Later in the year five men were drowned in a storm, so that, by the end of 1612, the number of the crew had fallen to about 50. The Journal makes no mention of any deaths during the next two years, and in October, 1613, there were still 46 men; but we know from other sources[1] that at least six died while the ship was being sheathed, and when she reached Bantam in January, 1615, there were only 38 men on board, not enough for the homeward voyage. A redistribution of the crews of the English ships then in harbour was accordingly made, and 50 men in all were allotted to the *Globe*.

Losses among the staff were relatively heavier. Hippon, the captain, fell a victim to the outbreak of dysentery, and died at Patani in July, 1612. Under the contingent nominations made by the Directors, he was succeeded by Thomas Essington, the senior of the four factors. Essington died at Narasapur in May, 1614, of "a suddayne heate", presumably heat-stroke, though his death was attributed locally to witchcraft. The nominations made by the Directors were already exhausted, and there was no one on the spot, except Floris himself, to assume command. He was unwilling to do so formally, but the records of the punishments he inflicted show that he in fact acted as captain until, at Bantam, Edward Christian was transferred from the *Osiander* to the *Globe*.

As an expert navigator, Hippon had had no sailing master, and the staff of master's mates were apparently not very efficient, for Floris, in recording the death of the most competent of them,

[1] *Letters Received*, ii. 115, 279, 284; iii. 130. In all, we have the names of 51 persons who sailed on the *Globe*—31 in the Journal, and 20 others in *Letters Received*.

added "the reste, God Hee knoweth, are but so and so". John Johnson, the senior master's mate, was appointed master on Hippon's death; and the Journal recounts at length the events which led to his displacement in favour of John Skinner, who, though a drunkard and a gambler, retained the position until, in the redistribution effected at Bantam, he was transferred to the *Osiander*, Nathaniel Salmon replacing him on the *Globe*.

Of the three principal merchants, Browne was already ill when the ship reached the Coromandel Coast, and he died at Masulipatam in September, 1611. No successor was appointed, which is somewhat remarkable, since the last clause of the commission[1] mentioned that a sealed nomination to his post was contained in "a Boxe No. 3", the preceding boxes having contained the nominations to the post of captain; there is nothing to show that the third box was ever opened. Antheunis, as has been said above, remained in Siam when the *Globe* left Patani; he was able to leave the Gulf in October, 1615, and came to Masulipatam as senior factor on the *Solomon*. He held charge of the factory there until the latter half of 1617, when he left for Bantam, and reached England in September, 1618.[2] His subsequent career is referred to in a later section. Floris himself returned on the *Globe*, but died a few weeks after his arrival in London, as will be related further on.

It was in the matter of factors that the inadequacy of the staff became most apparent. At the outset there were four in all, out of whom one was to be left at Bantam. The second, Symon Evans, was dead in May, 1612; the fourth, George Chauncey, remained at Bantam; the first, Thomas Essington, became captain, as has been mentioned above; there was left only Adam Denton. He worked at Patani and in Siam, and came back with the *Globe* to Masulipatam. There an exchange was effected, and Denton joined the *James*, while Chauncey, who had come on the *James* from Bantam, returned to the *Globe*. From Bantam Denton was sent back to Patani as chief of the factory, travelled thence with Antheunis to Masulipatam, and succeeded him in charge of the factory there, a position which he retained until

[1] *First Letter Book*, 388.

[2] *Letters Received*, iv. 28; *Court Minutes*, 8th September, 1618.

the middle of 1618. Eventually he returned to England in 1621.[1] Floris had intended to appoint Chauncey to be captain of the *Globe* for the homeward voyage, but these plans were altered, and from Bantam he was sent to Macassar as chief of the factory. He abandoned his post there on hearing rumours of a Spanish attack, and died at Patani in the autumn of 1615.[2]

The staff of factors was strengthened on two occasions. On the first visit to Bantam, John Persons, or Parsons, was appointed; his previous position on the *Globe* is not recorded, but seeing that the commission for the Voyage authorised the employment in case of need of "the purser or his mate, or both", and that the purser is otherwise accounted for, it may be inferred that he was purser's mate. As a factor he proved a failure; Floris left him at Bantam, and in 1615 he served on the *Thomas* during her voyage to Achin.[3] His name has not been found in later records. The purser, Robert Littlewood, was left as factor at Patani when the *Globe* sailed for Masulipatam, but he was in very bad health, and it was decided to join in the commission William Ebert, a cousin of Floris, who was not in the service of the Company, and had apparently come out as a private assistant, for Floris was very unwilling to spare him for this work. Littlewood died next year on the voyage to Bantam. Ebert rejoined the *Globe* there, and came home with his cousin. He offered to conduct another voyage for the Company,[4] but his plans were considered to be unsound; he was one of the 'overseers' under Floris' will, and until June, 1619, he attended the Company's office in connection with the accounts of the Voyage, a service for which he was granted "30 peeces as a gratification and remembrance of their bountye". Seeing that the 'peece', or unite, was at this time worth about a guinea, the remuneration cannot be regarded as liberal, but it may be presumed that Ebert benefited from the estate of his cousin, and consequently was

[1] *Letters Received*, ii. 44; iii. 315; iv. 304; v. p. xxvi; vi. p. xxxi. A very long letter from Denton to the Directors will be found in ii. 112 ff.

[2] *Letters Received*, iii. 134, 181, 319; iv. 29.

[3] *Letters Received*, iii. 59, 123–7.

[4] *Court Minutes*, 17th October, 1615; 9th November, 1617; 8th and 25th June, 1619.

working in his own interest as well as for the Company. A proposal to employ him further was 'distasted' owing to his nationality, and his name disappears at this point from the Company's records.

Turning to the wider aspects of the Voyage, it may be said at once that the visit to the Gulf of Siam proved to be an episode only: trade did not develop satisfactorily, and the factories were abandoned in the year 1623. In the Bay of Bengal, on the other hand, the connections established by Floris and Antheunis have lasted almost without interruption to the present day; the decision to open a permanent factory at Masulipatam was taken in 1615, the year after the *Globe* left, and received effect in the following January, when the *Solomon* arrived with Antheunis on board.[1] It was from Masulipatam that, ten years later, three factors started for Armagon, where the first English fortress in India was built; and, at the end of the next decade, Armagon gave way to what is now the city of Madras. It was from Masulipatam, again, that the first English ships sailed northwards to the Hūglī, to establish factories in Orissa and Bengal; and the Voyage of the *Globe* thus stands out as one of the foundations of the history of British India.[2]

In another aspect, the results of the Voyage were unfortunate, for it contributed materially to the growth of that ill feeling between Dutch and English which culminated in open warfare between the two Companies. When the *Globe* left London, the Dutch were already determined to monopolise the trade of the Spice Islands and the Farther East, and were, it seems, prepared to allow the English a predominant position in the Arabian Sea, and the maintenance of their factory at Bantam. The establishment of the English in the Gulf of Siam, followed closely by their appearance in Japan, showed that they were not prepared to leave the Far East to the Dutch; while their entry into the Coromandel trade was perhaps even more significant, because there, and only there, they could obtain at first hand the commodities in most demand in the Spice Islands. The feelings

[1] *Letters Received*, iii. pp. xxiv, 170, 178; iv. 28 ff.

[2] *English Factories*, iii. p. xlii; iv. p. xxx; vi. p. xxxvi.

excited among the Dutch by these developments can easily be imagined, but the process of imagination is unnecessary, because the facts are on record: as Jan Pietersz Coen, the protagonist of the Dutch, and perhaps the strongest man of his time in Asia, wrote in the year 1615,[1] "they [the English] followed us from Jakatra to Jambi, Patani, Siam and Japan"; and a continuance of the new situation would have meant the overthrow of the commercial policy on which the Dutch had determined.

To say this, however, is not to condemn the English Company for the new developments. There was a definite clash of policies, because the English claimed, and claimed with justice, a share in what the Dutch were determined to monopolise. Statesmanship on both sides could probably have effected a satisfactory adjustment, but in fact the statesmen failed to do so.[2] It would be going beyond the scope of this volume to tell once again the story of the war between the Companies[3] which lasted from 1617 to 1620: so much has been said merely to make it plain that among the antecedents of the war a prominent place must be assigned to the Voyage of the *Globe*.

§ 6. The Dutch Chief Merchants

We have now to discuss the identity and antecedents of the two Dutchmen who, as we have seen in § 2, approached the English Company as Peter Floris and Lucas Antheunis. The inference already drawn from the Dutch records by earlier writers[4] that Floris was the Pieter Willemsz van Elbing[5] who served the Dutch Company as junior factor at Masulipatam from 1605 (or earlier) to 1608 is amply confirmed by incidental remarks in the

[1] *MacLeod*, i. 184.

[2] The negotiations can be followed in *Cal. S.P.* ii and iii.

[3] See *English Factories*, i. pp. xxxviii ff.

[4] Foster in *Letters Received*, iii. 318; and Terpstra in *De Indische Gids*, March, 1915, p. 349.

[5] The second name is a patronymic, such as was commonly used in Holland at this period. The contemporary spelling of such names was usually *-ssen*; later it became *-szoon*, abbreviated first to *-sz.*, and more recently to *-sz* without the final stop. The third name is of a type which may be called a 'place-label', used originally to distinguish between persons of the same name, but frequently developing into a surname in the strict sense.

Journal, and the only uncertainties relate to his earlier career, and to his movements between May, 1608, and his arrival in London.

The decisive Dutch record is a private letter[1] written in October, 1615, by Gerard Reynst, the Governor-General, to his brother-in-law at Amsterdam. A translation of the relevant portion of this letter follows:

> Pr. Willemsz van Elbingh left here [Bantam] for England in March last, richly laden with [details of cargo omitted], all brought from the Coast. He wrote that he wished he had been able to speak to me, to communicate to me some secrets which would have been of use to the Company, but which could not be put on paper. Now the Directors will see what injury has been done to them by letting this person leave their employment: but apparently we cannot have any smart, sensible and honest men in our service. I shall be glad to hear of his safe arrival in due course. I wish he would re-engage himself to the Company for three or four years: through him they would learn all secrets and designs, which would be exceedingly important for them. But if he wants to change, the English will not let him go, yea, they would rather double his salary.

The reference here is certainly to the *Globe*, the only English ship answering the description which sailed from Bantam in March, 1615 (the actual date was 21st February, 1614, Old Style, corresponding to 3rd March); and obviously the man in question was well known to both writer and recipient of the letter. The only Pieter Willemsz known as a merchant in the records of this period is the one who served at Masulipatam as stated above; and the surname 'van Elbingh', given by Reynst, definitely identifies him with Floris, whose brother Hans used it regularly, as will be explained below.

The relevant passages in the Journal are as follows. When the *Globe* reached Masulipatam in August, 1611, Floris and two other factors on landing "were wel receyved and muche viseted of my olde acquainted friendes"; obviously the writer knew the place well, and did not come to it as a stranger. Again, the outstanding events in the service of Pieter Willemsz for the Dutch Company at Masulipatam were his visit to the Golconda Court in 1606, and his voyage to Arakan in 1608.[2] In the first,

[1] *Bouwstoffen*, i. 109.

[2] *Terpstra*, 40, 57.

the officers deputed were two, Paul van Soldt and Pieter Willemsz: in the second, two men only were sent to Arakan, Pieter Willemsz and Jan Gerritsz Ruyll: so that Pieter Willemsz was the only Dutch factor who, up to 1608, had been in both places. Writing on the 7th August, 1614, of the great flood which broke the bridge near Golconda, Floris observed: "Yf anybody shoulde have tolde mee this 7 yeares ago I shoulde hardly have believed it, for then I was uppon this bridge and behelde it with admiration". Floris had thus been in Golconda. Again, in the Journal for 11th November, 1612, Floris mentions that the King of Arakan took "certaine portions of the treasure of Pegu, the white elephant and the Kings daughter of Pegu, both which I have seene in Arracam *anno* 1608". Floris then had been to Arakan as well as Golconda, and his identity with Pieter Willemsz is quite certain.

The question of Floris' movements between 1608 and 1610 is bound up with the similar question regarding Antheunis, and may be postponed for the present, so that the two can be discussed together. Regarding his early history, the establishment of the Dutch on the Coromandel Coast has been studied exhaustively by Dr Terpstra, who was unable to find[1] any record of Dutch ships or men on the Coast before the arrival of the pinnace *Delft* in 1605, though he referred to an earlier voyage alleged by Valentyn. There is no journal or other record of the proceedings on land after the *Delft's* arrival. We know only that the pinnace appeared off Masulipatam in the spring of 1605; that Pieter Ysaacx Eyloff remained there as senior factor in charge of a small party; and that the pinnace, leaving the coast in May, returned to Bantam in August. No list of the party left at Masulipatam is on record, but Terpstra noted[2] that the name of Pieter Willemsz is not to be found on the muster-roll of the pinnace, and we can scarcely suppose that he came on her as a stowaway.

Next year the *Delft* returned from Bantam to the Coast, calling at Achin, and for this voyage we have the journal[3] kept

[1] *Terpstra*, 27 and *n*. [2] *Terpstra*, 35 *n*.

[3] *Begin ende Voortgangh*, van der Hagen's Voyage, 41 ff.: the quotation is from p. 57.

by Paul van Soldt, now the senior factor on board. On reaching Achin in March, 1606, they found a ship belonging to the King of Golconda lying ready to start on her return voyage, and we read that "On this ship had come Assalan, a Jew, despatched by Pieter Willemsz, junior factor at Masulipatam, with a consignment of iron, which was for account of the *restanten* [remnants]". Hence, Pieter Willemsz was certainly at Masulipatam in the autumn of 1605, when the King's ship would have left that port. Further, this consignment was clearly not on account of Eyloff's party; if it had been, it would have been made in his name as senior factor. Again, the word *restanten* is significant. Ordinarily it means in the records the goods or debts which were left over when the main business of a venture was wound up: as Floris wrote when he was leaving Masulipatam, on 7th February, 1612, "having imbarqued ourselves withoute having made any penny in badde dettes, or leaving any remnants behynde us on shoare". In the autumn of 1605 the time had not come for Eyloff's party to dispose of their 'remnants'.

All these facts point to the conclusion that Pieter Willemsz did not come on the *Delft*, but was already in Masulipatam on an independent venture when Eyloff arrived. Probably he sent the bulk of his capital to Bantam on the return voyage of 1605, when the pinnace carried a lading of cotton goods; he then sent his 'remnants' to Achin; and, having thus wound up the independent venture, worked in his rank of junior factor under Eyloff, the senior factor on the spot. He was certainly working under Eyloff when the *Delft* arrived for the second time in May, 1606.

This view is borne out by an entry in Floris' Journal for 7th August, 1614. Describing the floods in the low country, he wrote: "The water was att the leaste 1½ faddem above the common highwaye, a matter altogether incredible, and yf I had not seene it myselfe I coulde not have believed it, because of the knowledge which I have had of the countrye these 11 yeares". This mention of 11 years is obviously precise, not a round figure, as "ten years" might have been, and it shows that the writer had known the Coast since 1603, two years before the first arrival of the *Delft*.

This brings us to the passage in Valentyn,[1] which Terpstra mentioned in a note, but did not examine in detail. It may be premised that, for this early period, Valentyn is most untrustworthy. Terpstra's verdict[2] on him is to the effect that either his sources were exceedingly inaccurate, or his interpretation of them was wholly perverse; and consequently his unsupported statements scarcely suffice even to raise a presumption. In this case, however, Valentyn was summarising, as usual, inaccurately, facts on record in the printed journal[3] of Warwijk's Voyage of 1602, a document which was not quoted by Terpstra in this connection. This journal shows that Sebalt de Weert, who was Warwijk's Vice-Admiral, was sent with a squadron of the fleet to Ceylon by way of Achin, where, in March, 1603, he bought a pinnace to be employed on the Coromandel Coast. After de Weert's murder in Ceylon, the council of the squadron discussed, on 9th June, the disposal of the ships, and decided that the *Eendracht*, the *Hollandia*, and the pinnace should sail for Negapatam and Bengal. A month later, on 10th July, these plans were altered. The council, in view of the facts that they had achieved nothing during their stay off Ceylon, and had been seven months without news of the Admiral, agreed "to send one ship [not named] to the Coromandel Coast and to cruise to Bengal"; and that the rest of the squadron should proceed from Ceylon to Achin.

These entries are important as showing that in the first half of 1603 a voyage to the Coromandel Coast was seriously contemplated, but it does not appear to have been actually undertaken, as Valentyn asserted was the case. The squadron left Ceylon on 31st July, and reached Achin on 17th August, whence part of it proceeded through the Straits of Malacca to Patani. The *Eendracht* left Achin for Europe on 29th August, while the *Hollandia* and the pinnace went through the Straits, so it is certain that none of the vessels originally selected sailed for Coromandel; and all the other ships of the squadron appear to be accounted for elsewhere.

[1] *Valentyn*, Coromandel, 57.

[2] *Terpstra*, 6.

[3] *Begin ende Voortgangh*, Warwijk's Voyage, 13 ff.

It may be remarked that, from internal evidence, either the journal of this voyage was neglected during July, or, more probably, it was condensed at this point by the compiler of *Begin ende Voortgangh*; it ought to contain either a record of the ship which sailed for Coromandel, or in the alternative a decision not to send one, but in fact there is nothing of the kind.

Thus there is no record of a Dutch ship going to the Coromandel Coast in 1603, but there are good grounds for thinking that Pieter Willemsz arrived there before the end of the year. We must infer that he went on a native vessel from Achin. The desire of the Dutch to send a mission to the Coast is established by the entries in the journal already quoted: the facts given in the same journal suggest that eventually a ship was not sent from Ceylon; it would be a natural and reasonable course for the factors at Achin, anxious for a supply of goods from the Coast, and disappointed at this failure to despatch a ship, to send a factor on one of the vessels trading on that route in the ordinary course. The same expedient had already been adopted two years before[1] in the case of Gujarāt; and its adoption for the shorter journey to the East Coast would not be matter for surprise. No records have been traced showing the business transacted by the Dutch at Achin about this time, and without such records the question of fact cannot be finally decided; but there is no difficulty in the way of believing that Pieter Willemsz was sent from Achin to the Coast in the autumn of 1603. In that case, the probabilities are that he had come to the East on one of the various fleets which sailed from different ports in Holland before the establishment of the United Dutch Company in 1602; the records of these fleets are so fragmentary that the absence of any previous reference to him is no matter for surprise.

Some further facts regarding the activities of Pieter Willemsz at this time have been gathered from a source to which my attention was directed by Sir William Foster, a collection of early Malay manuscripts in the Cambridge University Library;[2] two

[1] H. Terpstra, *Opkomst der Wester-Kwartieren*, The Hague, 1918, p. 17.

[2] These MSS were first described by Dr van Ronkel in *Bijdragen tot de Taal-, Land-, en Volkenkunde van Nederlandsch-Indië*, series 6, part 2, pp. 1 ff. In the Library the 'History of Josef' bears the press-mark dd. 5. 37; the other two are in a miscellaneous volume, marked gg. 6. 40.

of these bear his name, and a third, which is anonymous, may be confidently attributed to him on the evidence of handwriting. The first is a copy of a Malay 'History of Josef', written presumably as an exercise in the language, and concluding with a note in Dutch, which may be rendered "*Finis* of the History of Josef, written in October, 1604, by Pr. Willemss". The second is a Malay-Dutch Vocabulary, begun, but not carried far, with the heading in Dutch, "Storehouse, wherein are collected various words in Dutch and Malay, arranged, each [word] in its place, by chapters; the Malay is written in Arabic characters; by Pieter Willemss van Elbinck, 1st June, 1604. In Achin". The third document is a copy of the Telugu alphabet, with a large number of syllables transliterated into Dutch, and was described by Professor Kern as "a very jewel of phonology for those times".

From the second document it is clear that Pieter Willemsz was in Achin on 1st June, 1604, and the course of the seasons justifies the inference that he was there, at any rate, from April or May, till about October. It is clear further that during this time he was making a serious study of the Malay language,[1] and it is probable that he had already mastered the phonology of Telugu, the language spoken in Masulipatam. In the absence then of any records of the Achin factory, we may infer that he was sent thence on a trading voyage to Masulipatam in the autumn of 1603, returned to Achin in the following spring, spent the summer there, and made a second voyage to Masulipatam in the autumn of 1604, remaining on the Coast until the arrival of the *Delft* early in 1605.

[1] In the article cited in the last note, Dr van Ronkel suggested that possibly Pieter Willemsz was procuring MSS for the Dutch scholar Erpenius, from whose collection these documents passed to Cambridge. It is impossible, however, to suppose that the fragment of a vocabulary had this origin, and the most probable view is that Willemsz wrote these documents for his own use, and that his executors, finding them among his papers, handed them over to Erpenius. The vocabulary is just the sort of thing which a student might start, but not continue for long; it consists of two 'chapters', quite incomplete, and a third containing merely a few Dutch words, with no Malay equivalents; the remaining 'chapters' were not begun. It is a curious fact that in the paging of the 'History of Josef' the digits are written in the reverse order; clearly, while the student knew the digits, he had not mastered the Arabic system of notation.

Incidentally it may be noted that these documents furnish some interesting details regarding their writer. For one thing, they show that on occasion he used the surname van Elbinck, or Elbing, which is applied regularly to his brother Hans. For another, they contain the only known specimens of his handwriting; and, meagre as these are, they show that he used particular forms of letters like *r* and *v* which could easily be misread in the manner I have suggested in various foot-notes to the text. Unfortunately, these specimens comprise scarcely any digits, but they establish the fact that his 1 could be easily mistaken for 2, a point which has a material bearing on the interpretation of one or two passages in the Journal. His knowledge of Malay and Telugu, again, fits in with the absence of any reference to interpreters in those languages. We hear, indeed, of a 'great *lingua*' at Masulipatam, but he was employed in communicating with the officials, and was obviously a Persian interpreter; and apparently Pieter Willemsz was able to deal personally with the Telugu-speaking merchants on the Coromandel Coast, as well as with the Malay speakers at Patani, obviously a valuable qualification for his task.

It is possible then to reconstruct with reasonable probability the story of Pieter Willemsz from the time when he left Achin for Masulipatam. Of his life before the year 1603 we know practically nothing. Such information as has been gathered regarding the family to which he belonged relates primarily to his brother, Hans Willemsz van Elbing, who is mentioned in the first entry of the Journal, and appears occasionally in the Court Minutes. From records preserved in the Gemeente Archief, or Common Record Office, of the City of Amsterdam, and communicated in generous detail by Mr A. de Bussy, the Archivaris, it appears that Hans was born in the year 1580 at Elbing, an important commercial centre in East Prussia, not far from Danzig. In 1593 he came to Amsterdam, where he married in 1608, his parents being then dead, and where he lived as a merchant until 1654, the surname van Elbing being regularly used of him in the records. In a will which he drew up in 1619, he left a legacy to a half-brother named Jaques Florissen, then living at Elbing.

From these data we may infer that, some time before 1580, the father, Willem, had married the widow of a resident of Elbing named Floris, a fact which incidentally explains how Pieter came to choose the surname Floris for use in England. Willem brought his family to Amsterdam in 1593, probably leaving his stepson at Elbing. Pieter went out to the East somewhere about 1600, while Hans remained in Amsterdam, either carrying on his father's business or starting in business for himself. The family was not really rich, for in the marriage-articles of 1608 the bridegroom, Hans, brought in 9000 guilders, or, say, 750*l.*, while the bride's portion was less than 600*l.*; but doubtless their position was improved substantially when Hans received the bulk of Pieter's estate, which amounted in all to about 4000*l.*, and there is nothing in the records to suggest that he was other than prosperous from 1620 onwards.

It is not clear from these records whether Pieter was older than Hans or younger. If he was younger, he would have been only 22, or less, in 1603, somewhat too young to be chosen for the independent venture to the Coromandel Coast; more probably then, he was the elder, and was perhaps about 25 at that date, somewhat over 30 when he joined the East India Company in London, and less than 40 at the time of his death.

The nationality of the two brothers is not established conclusively by the fact that they were born at Elbing, for at that time Dutchmen were active in the commerce of East Prussia, and it may well be that Willem had gone there from Holland to make a living, and that the move to Amsterdam was in fact a return home. Pieter certainly regarded himself as a Dutchman, for in the Journal he wrote of Holland as his 'patria', a common Dutch expression at this period, while in a letter[1] written in the year 1611 he described himself as a Netherlander, and the language of the original Journal indicates that he wrote in Dutch for preference. It is true that Sir Henry Middleton, who must have met him, or at least heard of him, frequently at the Company's office in the spring of 1610, called him a Dantiscan,[2] that is to say, a native of East Prussia, of which Danzig was the commercial centre; but this expression can be explained, as

[1] *Letters Received*, i. 136. [2] *Purchas*, I. iii. 271.

Sir William Foster has suggested, by the fact that Dutchmen were already unpopular with the adherents of the Company, and it is quite possible that, in order to facilitate the negotiations for the Voyage, Floris may have laid stress on the fact that he was not born in Holland. It is clear, at any rate, that, whatever the father's nationality may have been, the sons were Dutchmen for all practical purposes.

The records contain nothing to suggest that Floris was ever married, and, if he had left a widow or children, the Court Minutes for the period following his death would almost certainly have contained some mention of them; but in fact we read[1] only of the efforts of his brother, Hans, to accelerate the realisation of the estate, the bulk of which presumably passed to him.

We must now turn to the other chief merchant, Lucas Antheunis; his case presents certain obscurities, and such facts as are available have to be examined in some detail. To begin with the name. Antheunis, or more strictly Antheunisz, is a not uncommon patronymic, denoting 'son of Anthony'. Lucas, on the other hand, is decidedly rare. In a list[2] of over 700 Dutchmen who served in the East about this time, there are only two other men called Lucas, whereas there are 60 Pieters and over 100 Jans; the name may therefore be a clue to identity.

During his service with the English Company, Antheunis is mentioned by no other name, though the spelling of course varies, and we find such English forms as Anthonison. He was also known as Antheunis by the Dutch at Bantam,[3] when he visited that port in 1617 on his way home from India. On the Coromandel Coast, however, he had borne another name while in Dutch service. It has already been recorded that he returned to Masulipatam early in 1616 as senior factor on the *Solomon*: in April of that year, Samuel Kindt, the Dutch senior factor at Masulipatam, in a letter[4] to the Directors of his Company,

[1] *Court Minutes*, 27th October, 1615; 4th November, 1617.

[2] The full index in *MacLeod*, ii.

[3] *Ijzerman*, 75.

[4] Letter of 15th April, 1616, *Overgekomen Brieven, etc.* in the Rijksarchief.

wrote that on 11th January an English ship named the *Solomon* had arrived at Masulipatam, with "Your Excellencies' retired servant named Lucas Jansen" as senior factor. When this letter was written, Kindt and Antheunis had been living in the same town for three months, and it is impossible to suppose that they did not know each other's names; Kindt definitely recognised Antheunis as Lucas Janssen, a former servant of the Dutch Company.

Now Lucas Janssen was a name well known on the Coast.[1] Janssen arrived on the *Groote Sonne*, a vessel belonging to Matelieff's fleet, which left the Straits of Malacca in January, 1607, and, after calling at Achin, reached Petapoli on 1st April. Janssen was appointed to succeed Dirck van Leeuwen as senior factor at Petapoli, and entered into an engagement to serve in that capacity for two years; he was, however, ignorant of the trade in cotton goods, and van Leeuwen was persuaded to remain and teach him the business. The two men worked together at Petapoli for 15 months, and left the Coast on the *Eendracht* in June, 1608, reaching Bantam in the following October. Janssen's signature appears on a paper recorded there[2] on 5th November, after which his name disappears from the published records.

If these facts stood alone, the case would be simple. Janssen had served on the Coast at the same time as Pieter Willemsz (Floris), and must have known him fairly well. They left the Coast in the same year, and probably, as will be shown later, on the same ship, disappeared from the Dutch records, and appeared in London as Floris and Antheunis, each keeping his Christian name, but assuming a new surname. When they returned to the Coast in 1611, they naturally went to their old stations, Antheunis to Petapoli and Floris to Masulipatam. Floris, as we have seen, was welcomed by his old acquaintances, and we may be certain that Antheunis too was welcomed, or at least recognised, when he landed at Petapoli, and continued to be known among the Indian merchants by the name, Janssen, which was already familiar to them. Kindt, who was a later arrival at Masulipatam, would hear the original name mentioned

[1] *Terpstra*, 52–65. [2] *De Jonge, Opkomst*, iii. 287.

on Antheunis' return in 1616, and report it duly for the information of his superiors. It would then be necessary for the present purpose only to ascertain the antecedents of this Lucas Janssen, and it may be said at once that no information regarding him has come to light, previous to his appearance on the *Groote Sonne* at Petapoli.

On the other hand, a Lucas Antheunis is mentioned twice in earlier records. In the year 1601, Lucas Antheunis, of Rotterdam, went out to the East as a factor in the service of one of the Dutch Companies then trading independently, and in 1602 he was posted to Achin.[1] Nothing more is known of his movements: but in 1606, when Admiral Matelieff was attacking Malacca, certain Dutch prisoners of the Portuguese regained their freedom,[2] among them a factor named Lucas Antheunis, of Rotterdam, who at the end of the year was appointed junior factor on the *Groote Sonne*. There is nothing in the records to prove that this was the man who four years before had been posted to Achin; but taking into consideration the rarity of the name, the comparatively small number of Dutchmen then in those parts, and the other circumstances of the case, it is much more probable that this was the same man than that there were two men of the same name from the same city, and we may reasonably infer with Ijzerman, in his biographical note[3] on Antheunis, that the Achin factor had somehow or other fallen into the hands of the Portuguese.

The *Groote Sonne*, as we have seen, sailed from Malacca to Achin, and thence to the Coromandel Coast, where she landed Lucas Janssen to be employed as senior factor; and this Lucas Janssen subsequently became known as Lucas Antheunis, the name which had been borne by the junior factor on the ship. No discussion of this curious position has been found in the literature. Terpstra contented himself with noting[4] that Lucas Janssen was apparently also named Lucas Anthonissen: Ijzerman, who did not refer to Kindt's letter identifying Antheunis with Janssen, left Antheunis on the *Groote Sonne* in January,

[1] *De Jonge, Opkomst*, ii. 496.

[2] *Begin ende Voortgangh*, Matelieff's Voyage, 184.

[3] *Ijzerman*, 165 ff.

[4] *Terpstra*, 53 n.

1607, and picked him up again in London in 1610. Two hypothetical explanations appear to be possible. (1) Antheunis may have changed his name to Janssen while on the *Groote Sonne*. It is conceivable that he might not wish to be known as a former Portuguese prisoner, in a region where the Portuguese were still powerful, his capture may have been the result of want of courage, or some discreditable conduct on his part, or there may have been some other circumstances leading him to wish to start work in the new locality under a new name. (2) In the alternative, the original Antheunis may have died, and Janssen, when in want of a pseudonym for use in London, may have taken the name of his former shipmate, thus retaining his Christian name, as Floris retained his.

The decision between these hypotheses rests, so far, on a chance phrase in a single document. The *Eendracht*, on which van Leeuwen and Janssen sailed for Bantam, carried also Lodewyck Ysaacx Eyloff, who had been in charge of the factory at Masulipatam for a year during the absence of his better-known brother, Pieter. At Bantam Lodewyck submitted a report[1] regarding the trade of the Coast, and in corroboration of certain facts relating to the year 1607–8, he referred to the invoices sent from Petapoli to Bantam "by Dirck van Leeuwen and Luyckas Anthonissen". Here the reference can only be to Janssen, who, along with van Leeuwen, was in charge of the Petapoli factory during that year, and, as such, was responsible for the invoices of the goods despatched from thence; and it follows that the man who was known in the records of the Coast as Janssen, was known to Lodewyck as Anthonissen, that is, Antheunis. Had Janssen decided to take the pseudonym Antheunis in order to conceal his movements from the Dutch in Europe, he certainly would not have let the fact be known among the Dutch at Bantam; and, on the incomplete evidence which has been found, it is much more probable that this individual's real name was Antheunis, and that he took the patronymic Janssen, the commonest in the language, for temporary use while on the Coast. This name, having been used in the Coast

[1] *Informatie aengaende de Negotye op de Cust van Cormandel*.... MS in the Rijksarchief, *f*. 9.

records, would be familiar in the Company's offices in Holland, whereas they would have no recent knowledge of any factor called Antheunis; and reversion to his true name would thus conceal from the Company the fact that the Antheunis who was in London was the man who had so lately been in charge of their factory at Petapoli. The most probable view then is that Antheunis of the *Globe* was the Lucas Antheunis, of Rotterdam, who went out to the East in the year 1601.

The task remains of bridging the gap between 1608 and 1610. The last appearance of Antheunis under the name of Janssen is, as we have seen, at Bantam in November, 1608. The latest date we have for Pieter Willemsz (Floris) is 25th May, 1608, when he delivered his report[1] on Arakan to the Council at Masulipatam; his name does not recur in the local records, and Valentyn's statement that he became senior factor there is certainly incorrect, as Terpstra showed,[2] for that post was held continuously by Pieter Ysaacx Eyloff from 1608 until his death in 1610. Seeing that Floris and Antheunis were in the East on these dates, and in London in the early months of 1610, the only ships by which they could have travelled[3] were the *Ter Veere*, *Bantam* and *Ceylon*, which left Bantam in November, 1608, and arrived in Holland in August, 1609. Antheunis' time is thus fully accounted for, and we must infer that Floris left the Coast along with him on the *Eendracht*, because there is no record of any later sailing which would have enabled him to catch the homeward fleet at Bantam.

The records are silent as to the circumstances in which the two factors left the service of the Dutch Company. The ordinary practice of the period was to engage a factor for either two or three years, and at the end of the engagement the question of re-employment was one for negotiation. We may assume that Floris had entered into an engagement with Pieter Ysaacx at Masulipatam in the year 1605, and in that case his time would ordinarily have expired in 1608 at latest. Antheunis, as we have seen, was engaged to serve in Petapoli for two years in April,

[1] *De Jonge*, *Opkomst*, iii. 187. [2] *Terpstra*, 65 *n*.

[3] Lists of sailings, in the Rijksarchief.

1607; there is nothing in the records to show why he left after only 15 months. In any case, his term expired while he was on the voyage home, and it may be taken as certain that when the ships reached Holland, neither he nor Floris was under any contractual obligation to the Dutch Company. The phrase used in Reynst's letter, "letting this person [Floris] leave their employment", seems to suggest that the services of Floris, at least, could have been retained by a suitable offer, but there is nothing to show whether or not any offer was made, either at Bantam or after his arrival in Holland.

From what has already been said, it will be obvious that there had been ample opportunities for the growth of the intimate association between Floris and Antheunis which was manifested in their dealings with the English Company. They had served together for more than a year on the Coromandel Coast, where the relations between the factories at Masulipatam and Petapoli were very close; and they must have travelled together from the Coast to Bantam, and on the long journey from Bantam to Holland. It is possible, too, that their acquaintance was of older standing, for Antheunis, as we have seen, had been posted to Achin in 1602, and he may well have been there in the two following years, when he would certainly have met Floris. The Journal contains no hint of any disagreement between the two partners during the Voyage of the *Globe*, and we are entitled to infer that they formed a well-matched team, a phenomenon by no means too common at this period in the East.

Lastly, we have to recount what is known of the remainder of the lives of the two Dutch merchants. Antheunis, as has been said in a previous section, returned to London from the East in September, 1618. Some difficulties regarding his private trade were eventually adjusted,[1] and in the following year it was proposed to re-employ him. A gap in the Court Minutes makes it impossible to say what was eventually decided, but at this point his name disappears from the English records, and probably he settled down as a merchant in his native city. Ijzerman's biographical notice, which has already been quoted, shows that in

[1] *Court Minutes*, 8th September, 1618; 25th June, 1619.

1621 a merchant named Lucas Antheunisz was living in Rotterdam, where during the next twenty years he filled various public offices; he was buried in the first week of February, 1640. There is no direct evidence to identify this merchant with Antheunis of the *Globe*, but the dates fit, the name is distinctive, the city is that from which our Antheunis appears to have come, and the identification is reasonably probable. The only difficulty in regard to it is that, as we shall see, Antheunis had broken the law of Holland by conducting a voyage for the English Company; but in the conditions of the time a man possessed of substantial means would probably have been able to avoid molestation on this ground.

Floris, as has been said already, died in 1615, less than two months after he reached England. All that we know regarding the nature of his illness is contained in the following extract from the Court Minutes of 31st August, 1615: "Mr Governor made knowne unto this Courte the daungerous sickness of Mr Peter Floris, beinge landed with an extraordinary paine and swellinge in his joyntes thorough extremitie of could as is reported". Arrangements were made for a horse litter to bring him to town, "his bodie being unable to endure the ratlinge of a coach", and for Mr John Woodall, the Company's surgeon, to attend him on the journey; and Sir Thomas Smythe received him into his house in Philpot Lane, where the Company's business was transacted. The end had come by 25th September, on which day the Governor informed the Directors that

> Mr Floris, drawinge on out of the world, was most willinge to departe to be with God, haveinge an espetiallie [*sic*] care to leave a good name behinde him, and to shewe his thankfulnes he made a voluntary confession that his desire was to have a lodginge in Mr Governor's howse, which proceeded from himselfe without any other bodies motion, esteemeinge it as a greate favour, and acknowlegd the same with thankfulnes, and in testimonie thereof did give unto him as a legacie the some of 300 *li* to be taken out of his goods in the house at such rate as himselfe shall thinke fitt, or out of his stocke which he hath in adventure, acknowledging his good usage since his comeinge as he testifies by his guiftes in the howse to the servaunts.

The implication of this 'confession', or rather declaration, is not on record, but it may be conjectured that some of Sir Thomas

Smythe's enemies had insinuated that he had got the dying Dutchman into his own hands in order to facilitate some underhand dealings with the adventurers' goods. The record goes on to explain that the Governor objected to the legacy as being too great, and asked for only a small remembrance, but Floris insisted, and caused his will to that effect to be read. The will, it may be added, has not been traced at Somerset House.

The Governor then announced

that Thursdaye in the afternoone is the time appointed for the funerall, where Mr Governor, Mr Deputy and Mr Threasurer are to have mourninge garments, and therefore it was concluded that John Grimston, there officer, should warne all the Companie to be here to accompanie the corse, the overseers[1] haveinge appointed the Dutch officer to invite 40 or 50 Dutchmen to come, and 100 of the children of the hospitall to attend, whoe shall have 3 or 4*li* bestowed amongst them with bred as is accustomed, Mr Stone beinge nowe entreated to speake for them; and resolved to have the Beedles keepe of[f] the poore people and appointe them to Leaden Hall to receive there dole 2*d* a peece soe far as 3*li* will goe.

The funeral took place at the church of St Dionis Backchurch, which stood at the corner of Fenchurch Street and Lime Street, opposite to the entrance to Philpot Lane, in which the Governor's house was situated. The church was destroyed in the Great Fire, and its successor was demolished in 1878, when the contents of the graveyard were removed to the City of London Cemetery at Manor Park; but in the vestry, which still exists, a register records[2] that "Mr Peter Florres, straungr" was buried on 28th September, 1615. The 'hospitall' mentioned in the foregoing extract is Christ's Hospital, which at this period regularly let out children to attend funerals; and an entry in the Annual

[1] In such a context, 'overseer' meant, according to the *OED*, a person appointed by a testator to supervise or assist the executors of the will. Their names are given in the *Court Minutes* as William Ebert, Daniell van Hastwell and Phillip Jacobson; Ebert has already been noticed, the others were presumably Dutchmen living in the City. The meaning of 'Dutch officer' is an unsolved problem; the most probable guess is that it denotes an elder, or deacon, of the Dutch Church in Austin Friars, who had visited Floris during his illness.

[2] The name is misspelt as 'Forres' in *The Registers of St Dionis Backchurch*, issued by the Harleian Society in 1878.

Accounts for 1614 to 1617, kindly communicated by the Clerk of the Hospital, shows that the sum of 3*l.* was duly credited on the occasion of "the buriall of a Dutchman at Sir Tho: Smithes".

§ 7. Peter Floris, the Man

An attempt must now be made to estimate the character and abilities of Peter Floris; and the most convenient course is to consider first the general question, and then turn to two special topics—his indulgence in private trade, and his loyalty to his employers. Regarding his service under the Dutch Company we possess no formal appreciation: we know only that, having been chosen for the mission to Golconda in 1606, he was shortly afterwards selected for a more delicate task as leader of the pioneer expedition to Arakan; and we are entitled to infer that his superiors chose him for his merits. For his service under the English Company his Journal is the most important document, and its study undoubtedly leaves the impression that as the leader of a commercial voyage he was in his proper place—an expert merchant, tactful and resourceful, ordinarily prudent and cautious, yet prompt to take momentous decisions, and ready on occasion to risk his life in his employers' interests.

It may perhaps be objected that since the Journal was intended for the eyes of the writer's employers, it probably exhibits his conduct in an unduly favourable light. To this objection it may be replied that the Journal presents to us a competent, but not a perfect, man; and attention may be directed in particular to an entry under 25th January, 1613, where Floris recorded a serious mistake which could have been concealed without difficulty. At Petapoli a large quantity of cloth was ordered of an unsuitable design: Floris and Antheunis should have known this, because a similar mistake had been made, and corrected, when they were in Dutch service; but they forgot the incident until too late. The fact could obviously have been concealed from the Company in London, for if Floris and Antheunis had said nothing about it, there was nobody else on the spot in a position to know what had happened inside the Dutch factory five years before; but Floris told the story and accepted the blame in a perfectly straightforward passage. The Journal is then reasonably good evidence.

Of appreciations from outside, we may refer first to the letter which has already been quoted from Gerard Reynst, the Dutch Governor-General, who thought very highly of Floris, and wished that he could be secured for the Dutch service. On the English side there is but little material. We might expect to find the worst that could be said in the letters of the factors, for there was a certain amount of envy and backbiting among the men who addressed each other as 'loving friends', and there was sufficient national feeling to induce resentment at the employment of foreigners in high positions. Nothing of the kind, however, has survived. We possess detailed accounts[1] of portions of the Voyage from Adam Denton and George Chauncey, two of the factors who took part in it, as well as from John Skinner, who was for some time master of the *Globe*, but there is no complaint of Floris, and on one occasion Denton records that his patience contributed largely to saving the enterprise from disaster.

The one formal appreciation we possess is that of John Jourdain, the head of the Company's business at Bantam, and it gains in importance from the circumstances in which his opinion was formed. When Floris came to Bantam, he was already prejudiced against Jourdain, who, he had been told, had interfered with the factor he had sent to Macassar in such a way as to risk the loss of a season. At Bantam there was a very definite clash of interest between Floris, eager to do the best he could for the adventurers (including himself and his partner) in the seventh Voyage, and Jourdain, working for a wider object, the success of the Company as a whole. The bitterness of some of the latest entries in the Journal shows how strongly Floris felt the obstacles which Jourdain put, as his duty doubtless required, in the way of the *Globe's* business. Jourdain's word "muste thus passe heere for currant payement"; "they playde with mee as the catte doth with the mouse"; "I muste thinke myselfe yett muche beholding for this aggreement and the greate discretion shewed unto mee. Well, looke to it better another tyme!" Floris then was no friend to Jourdain, but the latter's considered

[1] *Letters Received*, ii. 112, 293; iii. 130.

opinion, contained in a formal letter[1] to the Company, was that "Mr Floris is a good merchant and one that is indifferent [*i.e.*, impartial] for all voyages, not leaning to the one side or other; although he have more interest in the seventh Voyage than in the rest, yet he do more respect a general good than his own private voyage". In the circumstances that is high praise, and we may accept it as the truth.

A word may be added to draw attention to the note of unaffected piety which characterises the Journal, and which justifies us in accepting as something more than merely conventional the phrases, already quoted, which Sir Thomas Smythe addressed to the Directors: "Mr Governor acquainted them that Mr Floris, drawinge on out of the world, was most willinge to departe to be with God, haveinge an espetiallie care to leave a good name behinde him". In that spirit he died. He had finished the task he had undertaken. The fruits of his work were to be enjoyed by others.

We must now pass to the topic familiar in the records of the period under the name of private trade. Both English and Dutch Companies forbad their servants to engage in trade on their own account; and, if further evidence were needed to show that they were right, it will be found in the Journal, where Floris records how the markets for the goods belonging to the Voyage were spoiled by the competing offers of private merchandise brought on the same ship. The Dutch authorities in the East endeavoured, on the whole, to enforce the prohibition, while the English did not; and the Directors in London dealt with ordinary offenders so leniently as almost to justify the statement that permission to trade was an unwritten condition of their service, so long as the trading was kept within certain rather elastic bounds.

It appears to be probable that both Floris and Antheunis had engaged in private trade while in Dutch service. In the case of the latter, there is on record a formal charge[2] that when he reached Bantam from Petapoli in October, 1608, he sold to the English factors a large consignment of cotton goods suitable for the Banda markets, where they were re-sold at a profit, to the

[1] *Letters Received*, ii. 317. [2] *Terpstra*, 66.

injury of the Dutch factory there. No similar allegation against Floris has been traced, but his attitude in the matter can be inferred from an entry in the Journal under 25th October, 1612, where he complains that the Dutch allowed "Maleysians, Chinesians and other Moores of these contries" to share in the trade of the Spice Islands, but "forbidde it theyr owne servants, contryemen and bretheren uppon payne of death and losse of goods; surelye a token of a greate ignorance or envye, suffering Turckes and heathen to growe riche rather then their owne countryemen shoulde gette their living: surelye a greate ingratitude, and a token that Gods punishement is comming uppon theym". That is 'surelye' the language of a man who had either traded, or wanted to trade, in those regions for his own profit.

Account must also be taken of the fact that Floris and Antheunis between them invested the substantial sum of 1500*l.* in the Voyage of the *Globe*. It does not seem possible that they could have saved this sum out of their wages in Dutch service. We may reasonably presume that Antheunis was not a capitalist when he returned from his period of captivity, and Ijzerman tells us[1] that he was allowed no wages whatever for the time so spent. At most then he can have had only the wages of a factor for two years, a matter of perhaps 150*l.* in all, while Floris would have a junior factor's pittance, say from 30*l.* to 50*l.* a year, for a somewhat longer period, reduced in each case by whatever they might have drawn while still in service. Either then they obtained capital for the investment from friends and relatives in Holland, or they had resources other than their accumulated wages; and the most probable view seems to be that each of them had built up a stock of capital by private trade, that they found the business too dangerous, and that they decided to leave Dutch service, and put the bulk of their capital into an English venture, where it would be employed under their own control. This view, it must be emphasised, is not established by evidence: it is the most probable explanation of a series of actions the motives of which are not on record.

On entering the service of the English Company, Floris and

[1] *Ijzerman*, 166 ff.

Antheunis agreed to abstain from private trade under a clause which reads as follows:

Item That duringe the said voyadge they shall neither by themselves, nor any other for them or to their use directlie or indirectlie, use or exercise any private trade or marchandizeinge whatsoever But shall applie themselves and their whole endeavours for the good and advancement of the generall stocke, and the said Governor and Companie doe promise to use their best care and diligence to prevent the like private trade or marchandizinge to be made by the said Captaine, Englishe marchauntes or any other marriners whatsoever.[1]

That was the theory of the Voyage. We have no means of knowing whether Floris and Antheunis intended at the outset to conform to it, but, if they did, they were led by circumstances to disregard it. Before the *Globe* left Bantam in June, 1612, they had learned the English practice, and Floris could complain that "Truely the Company hath tyed us to[o] strictly, seinge the Englishemen trade so openly and grosly, as heere in Bantam wee have seene and bene informed, and fynde by Mr Browne". Representations were made to Captain Hippon to stop the sales of the crew's goods, as he was bound to do under clause 15 of the commission for the Voyage; but Hippon was personally interested in the sales, and naturally took no effective action against his subordinates. At Patani the crew had one of their number "who lyke a factor laye on land, and hath solde goods 50 per cento better cheape then I do"; and it is not matter for surprise that Floris and Antheunis, whatever their original intentions may have been, should have decided to follow the established practice.

Naturally no details of their private transactions are on record, but we know from the Court Minutes[2] that "Mr Floris brought goods to the valew of 1700*li* with the charges which came to a matter of 200*li*, and that Mr Antheunis tooke up goods here to the valew of 800*li*, besides 2000 dollers left in the countrye". The Directors expressed the usual dissatisfaction at such con-

[1] *First Letter Book*, 366.

[2] *Court Minutes*, 4th December, 1618. The expression 'tooke up', used in this passage, ordinarily meant 'borrowed'; but the context requires that it should be read here in the sense of taking the goods out of the ship, or the custom-house.

duct, but decided not to proceed "in extremitye": a gratuity of 150*l.* which had been promised to Antheunis was withdrawn, and apparently the goods were not brought to the account of the Voyage, but left in the hands of their owners, subject to the payment of all charges. The facts then are plain. Both Floris and Antheunis broke one of the conditions of their agreement, a condition which was ordinarily treated in the East as non-existent: the moral implication of the facts may be left to casuists.

Turning now to the question of loyalty, the evidence is conclusive that, except in this matter of private trade, Floris rendered perfectly loyal service to his English employers. As regards his loyalty to his own country, we must first examine the legal question involved. It appears to be certain that a factor remained under no formal obligation to the Dutch Company when once he had left its employment on the completion of his engagement. At this period there was nothing like a permanent Service. Engagements, as has been said already, were made for short periods, ordinarily two or three years, their renewal was matter for negotiation when the time came, and no suggestion has been found that any engagement contained any condition limiting the future freedom of either party. That question had, in fact, not yet arisen. By taking service under the English Company Floris and Antheunis established a new precedent, and in doing so they were not infringing any contractual obligation.

The question whether they were breaking the general law of their country must be distinguished. The *Octrooi*, or Charter,[1] of the Dutch Company was drawn in very wide terms. The preamble declared that the Company was established in the national interest, so as to regulate a trade the success of which was vital to the country as a whole; and the 34th clause prohibited the despatch of any independent trading voyage from Holland to the East, on pain of forfeiture of ship and goods. Standing by itself, this clause would not cover the action of Floris and Antheunis, but it must be read with the 46th clause, which applied to all that went before, and required all "subjects

[1] The text is given by J. A. van der Chijs on pp. 118 ff. of *De Stichtinge van de Vereenigde O.-I. Compagnie*, Leyden, 1857.

and residents" to observe the terms of the Charter; anyone who contravened, or caused to be contravened, any provision, in any manner, directly or indirectly, either within the country or outside it, was declared liable to punishment "as an enemy of the common weal, and a transgressor against [the] ordinances and commands" of the States-General. It is dangerous for a layman to offer an interpretation of the law of another country, and another century; but a prosecutor could have contended that Floris and Antheunis were in effect concerned, outside the country if not inside it, in setting out a trading voyage which infringed the monopoly of the Dutch Company, and that they were liable to punishment both as investors in, and as the servants of, the competing organisation in London.

These provisions of the Charter were re-enacted[1] by the Statute (*Placaet*) of 1st July, 1606, with the significant addition that the penalty recovered should be divided equally between the Company, the poor, and the prosecutor. A further Statute, made on 9th September of the same year, recited that attempts were being made to contravene the Charter in indirect ways, and enacted that no subject or resident should voyage or trade in any manner beyond the Cape of Good Hope, whether from Holland or from any other country, except in the service of the Company. Even then if Floris and Antheunis did not contravene the original Charter, they were certainly punishable under this Statute, for they voyaged and traded in the forbidden region on behalf of employers other than the Dutch Company.

There is no reason then to be surprised that they decided to change their names for the English venture, and apparently the change served its purpose in Europe. Up to the end of August, 1610, the Directors of the Dutch Company had heard[2] only that their English rivals, influenced by a profitable sale of Coromandel goods in the Banda Islands, were contemplating an entry into the Coromandel trade, and the terms of their Resolution allow us to infer that they were still ignorant that two of their former servants were at the moment completing

[1] *Groote Placaet-Boeck* (The Hague and Amsterdam, 1658–1797): the Statute of 1st July is ii. 1323; that of 9th September is i. 547.

[2] *Terpstra*, 66.

the arrangements for the Voyage. Four months later, the local Directors at Middelburg, that is, the Zeeland Chamber, having heard that Lucas Antheunis and another former employee (not named) of the Company had entered English service, proposed[1] to the Amsterdam Chamber that a proclamation should be made at their places of residence, forbidding them to voyage for a foreign nation in contravention of the Charter. The reply is not extant, but the next letter, written on 19th January, 1611, suggests that the proposal was carried out—too late, of course, to be of any use, for the *Globe* left Gravesend on 15th January (New Style). The Zeeland Chamber proposed further that the Governor-General should be instructed to endeavour to arrest the offenders, and secretly to spoil the markets for them. No such instructions have been traced, and the attitude of the Governor-General towards Floris, as shown in the letter which has already been quoted, indicates that, if he had in fact received such orders, he was ready to ignore them.

It must be admitted then that Floris and Antheunis were law-breakers, but at the same time it must be recognised that the law which they broke did not in fact operate to prevent other Dutchmen from actively supporting the English Company. Recurring gaps in the Court Minutes make it impossible to tell the full story, but in the year 1614 there are records of applications for employment by four Dutchmen, one of whom had served the Dutch Company for seven years as a factor, while at least two residents in Holland were allowed to invest in the Company's stock, the large sum of 6000*l.* being mentioned in one case. In the next year the Directors found it necessary to make a reply to "those who distasted that so many Dutchmen were admitted to buy adventures", so that at this period the practice must have been fairly common; and references to Dutch candidates for employment continue until, at the end of 1618, it was decided that in future no Dutchman should be engaged for the Company's business.[2] If, then, Floris and Antheunis were breakers of the

[1] Kamer Zeeland: *Copie-boeck van uitgaande Brieven*, MS in the Rijksarchief.

[2] *Cal. S.P.* ii. 287, 289, 311, 324, 332, 341, 435, 440; iii. 216. Readers of *The Life of Jón Ólafsson* (Hakluyt Society, 1932) will recall the prominent part played by Dutchmen in the Danish enterprise in the East.

law, they were by no means alone, and the law did not in fact operate effectively as a deterrent. This position will not come as a surprise to readers who have studied the early history of the Dutch Republic, and have realised the gap which existed between theory and practice in such matters as trading with the enemy, forbidden in the most stringent terms, but carried on openly with the connivance of the magistrates in the commercial centres.

There remains the moral question. Whether or not Floris and Antheunis had broken the law of their country, was their action regarded by their countrymen as discreditable? The facts given in the Journal appear to furnish a conclusive answer to this question. Where they encountered Dutch hostility, as at Pulicat, no personal question was raised. Jan van Wesick did not object to them as renegades: he objected to the English Company trading where the Dutch had a monopoly. Similarly, Floris was on friendly terms with Wemmer van Berchem, the head of the Dutch factories on the Coromandel Coast; when the latter "protested" against some of Floris' actions at Masulipatam, no personal issue was involved; and he esteemed Floris sufficiently to stand surety for his conduct on that occasion. When the *Globe* left Bantam for Patani, Floris and Antheunis were "conducted aboord" by Matheo Coteels, the Dutch president, and Pieter Segertsz, the Dutch senior factor, a compliment they would scarcely have gone out of their way to pay to men whom they regarded as discreditable. At Patani, Hendrick Janssen, the Dutch chief, and Floris were "great friends"; and from his letters Antheunis seems to have been on excellent terms with Maerten Houtman, the Dutch chief in Siam. On the Coromandel Coast again, Pieter Gilliesz van Ravesteyn was Floris' "special friend", and carried a private letter for him to Bantam. All of these were men holding responsible positions under the Dutch Company, and, taken together, they constitute a sample well above the average of integrity of the period. The only possible inference from their conduct is that they did not regard Floris and Antheunis as discreditable persons, with whom a decent Dutchman could not associate. The same inference follows from the letter of Gerard Reynst, the Dutch Governor-General, which has already been quoted more than once. He regarded

Floris as an exceptionally able merchant, regretted his loss to the Dutch service, wished it were possible to get him back, and asked for news of his safe arrival in Europe. There is here not the slightest suggestion of anything discreditable in his conduct; and it does not seem to be necessary at the present day to be more censorious than was the Dutch Governor-General, who knew all the facts.

§ 8. The MANUSCRIPT

The manuscript of the Journal is in the records of the India Office, where it is classed as Marine Logs, XIII. It was written on uniform sheets of paper, the watermark of which bears the date 1613, and was bound in a vellum cover with the inscription

PEETER WILLIAMSON FLORIS
his JOURNALL for the 7th VIAGE
translated out of Duitch.
who arived in England
Anno 1615
& died 2 monethes after
his said arivall in London.

Below this inscription there is a paper label of later date. The handwriting is of English rather than Dutch type, but there are occasional peculiarities, notably a contracted form of final *-en*, and a *t* with a very full loop, which might puzzle English transcribers, but are quite familiar in Dutch commercial manuscripts of the period.

The identity of the translator is unknown, but from internal evidence it is clear that he was a Dutchman with an imperfect knowledge of English idiom, that he was not personally familiar with the events of the Voyage or the details of eastern trade, and that he had occasional difficulty in reading Floris' handwriting. The first point is illustrated sufficiently by the somewhat numerous foot-notes in which the meaning is given of phrases which are literal reproductions of Dutch idioms; such expressions as "a mighty cake of wind", "to speak to the cargason", or "to do it him good", are not English, but they re-translate themselves directly into idiomatic Dutch.

As an instance of the translator's ignorance of the events of the Voyage, it may be noted that the surname of Symon Evans, the second factor on the *Globe*, appears first as Judis and then as Irens; no one who had been on the ship could have made such mistakes, but they are quite natural misreadings of the Dutch commercial script of the period. Similarly the appearance in a single entry of the forms 'benjamin', 'beniuni' and 'benivin' exhibits a man toiling at an unfamiliar handwriting, and ignorant of such a well-known staple as benzoin. Apparently Floris, like some other Dutch merchants, used distinctive digits, which the translator could not always read; this is the most probable explanation of the occasional blanks where a careful merchant would certainly have entered the figures as he wrote.

A characteristic feature of the manuscript is the presence of alternative phrases, which are written one over the other, as

off and on our mens
"wee wente to and off", or "thus was the peoples amazement sette aside". It may be explained that, for convenience in printing, the more suitable phrase has been retained, while the alternative is shown alongside it in parentheses.

In the absence of any information on the subject, we may guess that when Floris arrived in London, his original Journal was made over for translation to one of his compatriots on the spot, a simple matter, for we have seen that 40 or 50 Dutchmen were to be invited to his funeral. The translator did the best he could, and in cases of doubt left a blank, or wrote alternative phrases, hoping to revise his work in consultation with Floris; but when the death of the latter rendered such a revision impracticable, he handed his work over as it stood to the officials of the Company, who doubtless wanted it as soon as possible.

The question of the completeness of the manuscript is of some interest. The abruptness of the conclusion is obvious; and even if we should assume that Floris thought a record of the homeward voyage from Bantam to be unnecessary, he would certainly have recorded the date of sailing from that port, and wound up with pious expressions of thanksgiving and prayer such as characterise the Journal as a whole. If he wrote no more than we possess, we should have to assume that he was too ill to do so from the time the vessel left Bantam; but this assumption is contradicted by the attribution of his illness to "extremitie of could", an attribution which suggests that he must have been in health as far as the Cape of Good Hope, which was reached in May, that is, towards the end of autumn, and is the first point on the voyage where extreme cold could have been experienced. The manuscript closes in the middle of a line in the middle of a page, so that there is no question of the last sheets having been mislaid, or omitted by the binder; while the incomplete line is filled by certain marks which look like C×C×C×C×. Similar marks do not appear at the end of other paragraphs, and these were probably meant to indicate the conclusion of the translation. The most reasonable explanation seems to be that the officials of the Company, being in a hurry, as has been suggested above, told the translator to stop at Bantam, relying on the ship's log for the events of the homeward voyage.

On these questions we must be content with hypotheses, for the original Journal written by Floris has not been traced, and the other records of the Voyage are no longer accessible. One of these is the ship's log, which was kept by Nathaniel Marten, one of the master's mates. Purchas printed some extracts,[1] but he curtailed it greatly in order to pass to Floris' Journal, thinking that "these meere marine relations are (though to some profitable) to the rest tedious". It would certainly have been profitable to us, and possibly it would have given precise information as to Floris' illness; but it is not now among the India Office records, nor is it in the British Museum or the Bodleian, whither some of the early logs have found their way.

The other missing record is a book in which Floris had recorded various details of eastern commerce. A few apparent references to it occur in the Journal, as in a passage where, having mentioned his desire to have a factory in Bengal, he added "looke further of this in my description"; but our only precise knowledge of its existence is derived from an entry[2] in

[1] *Purchas*, I. iii. 314.

[2] *Court Minutes*, 25th September, 1615.

the Court Minutes, which relates that "Mr Governor understandinge that he [Floris] had dedicated a booke to the Companie, wrytten with his owne hand, which did concern the setlinge of some factoryes and many other materiall things observed in his voyage", took measures to ensure that the 'overseers' under the will should search for the book in the presence of representatives of the Company. The result of the search is not on record, and the book itself has not come to light: the Journal now printed thus stands as the sole surviving record of the Voyage.

It has not previously been printed as a whole, but Purchas had access to it, and gave lengthy extracts as Chapter xiv of Book III of the First Part of his *Pilgrimes*. Melchisedech Thévenot inserted in the first volume of his *Divers Voyages Curieux* (Paris, 1663) a version which, as his Table of Contents shows, was translated from Purchas; and it may be added that the translation is occasionally rather loose. That prolific publisher Pieter van der Aa of Leyden included the narratives of Hippon (or rather Marten) and Floris in vol. 24 of his collection, *Naauwkeurige Versameling der Gedenk-waardigste Reyzen na Oost- en West-Indiën*, published in 1707, and twenty years later he reproduced this version in the sixth part of his enlarged and improved edition of Johan Lodewyck Gottfried's Voyages, entitled *De Aanmerkens-Waardigste...Reyzen* (Leyden, 1727); both these editions are 'enriched' with illustrations, which, however, are obviously works of imagination, and not worth reproducing. It has occasionally been supposed that this Dutch version represents Floris' original Journal, but the separate title-pages state that it was "now first translated out of English", and comparison shows that it was condensed from Purchas, the difficulties of his text being more or less judiciously evaded by the Dutch translator. No other versions have come to light, with the exception of those which later compilers, such as Thomas Astley, borrowed from Purchas.

It is of some interest to compare the version made by Purchas with the original Journal, because it may help us to appreciate the historical value of those parts of the *Pilgrimes* of which the documents have not survived. The passages omitted are extensive, and many of them are interesting, but we cannot blame the compiler on this ground, because it was not his purpose to make a collection of documents; to use the language of his *Epistle Dedicatorie*, he "framed this Historicall World...out of a Chaos of confused intelligences"; and he was clearly within his rights in extracting only so much as served his purpose. As to what he took, his extracts are not in all cases verbatim, nor does he claim that they are: as he wrote, they are "for the most part in their owne words transcribed or translated"; and, if we may generalise from a single instance, his method of working was to follow the original document carefully, frequently copying word by word, but at other times condensing the language while preserving the sense. And this condensation was carefully done; foreign names and words were occasionally distorted, but no instance of serious distortion of the sense has come to light. An example will make his method clear:

The Journal

17th April, 1614. "Atmachan departed for Golconda to give upp his accounte, the yeare comming to an ende, as also to renew his gouvernment, which came very well to passe for him; for the King deposed the greate treasurer, and made Malick Tusar treasurer, who was a greate friende of this Atmachan, which caused greate joye in the Commonaltie, hoping for a better gouvernment. This also came well for mee, for by this Atmachan was assured of his gouvernment, whereof before he was in greate hasard, and thus my dette also was secured, for as long as they be gouvernours there is hope of payement, but being once putte out there is butt small appearance to recover anything. A desperate case, and needfull once to be purged with a sharpe purge."

Purchas' version

"In Aprill, 1614, Atmachan departed for Golanda [*sic*] to give up his accounts, the yeare comming to an end. It was well for him, the King having deposed the great Treasurer, and given his office to Malick Tusar, Atmachans friend: and well for us, these Governours Debts beeing good whiles they continue their place; otherwise doubtfull."

It will be seen that Purchas omitted one not very important fact, the popularity of the change of treasurer: he summarised the rest with substantial accuracy, in decidedly better English, and in less than half the number of words used in the original.

It was, however, inevitable that the method followed by Purchas should involve a certain loss of atmosphere and perspective; and a striking instance of this will be found in his account of that "desperate peece of service", the arrest of the son of the Governor of Masulipatam as a pledge for his father's overdue debt. In the condensed version that incident comes upon the reader rather suddenly, and with an inadequate explanation of the facts which led up to it, or of the motives which impelled Floris to act as he did; one feels that his action was high-handed, to say the least; and some readers might even be tempted to adopt the attitude of a recent popular writer who thanked his insular deities that the "outrage" was not the work of an Englishman. Reading the full text of the Journal, one realises how for four months past the question had been becoming more and more critical. The Governor clearly meant to put Floris in the dilemma of either giving up the debt or losing a year in the attempt to recover it; and by "the rules of the game", as played in Asia, Floris should have negotiated for a compromise, in which he must necessarily have had the worst of the deal.

Floris, however, was not prepared to do this. The debt was 5000 pagodas, or over 1800*l.*, too large a sum to be sacrificed or materially diminished, while the precedent of sacrificing it would have been ruinous to the prospects of future trade, and it is noteworthy that throughout the Voyage Floris was particularly anxious to create good precedents, not bad. He therefore took all possible means to recover the debt. He wrote three times to the Governor's official superiors, his second and third letters conveying distinct threats, and got only fair words in reply. He planned, in accordance with established precedent, to seize shipping as security, but, as he tells us, his plans were frustrated one by one; and at last, when the progress of the season rendered an immediate decision necessary, he decided to risk his life in the interests of his employers. He certainly knew what he was doing, for his experience of the administrative methods in vogue in Golconda must have taught him that, in the event of failure, he would inevitably have paid the penalty with his person. Following all the facts in the Journal, one is driven to the conclusion that the coup was justified by the antecedent conditions, as it was to be promptly justified by its success, for the debt was promptly paid, the local mercantile community was favourably impressed, and, when the *Solomon* arrived a year later, the permanent factory was established without any unusual difficulties.[1] It is in such ways as this that the full text of the Journal throws new light on the story of the years with which it deals.

[1] It may be added that the King of Golconda appears to have taken the view that the Governor was wholly in the wrong, for he was heavily fined, and dismissed from his office, in consequence of his conduct in the matter (*Letters Received*, iv. 6). Probably it was in the course of the settlement of accounts following his dismissal that he was bastinadoed to death, as recorded by William Methwold (*Golconda*, 11).

NOTE ON CURRENCY, WEIGHTS AND MEASURES

Some units which are mentioned rarely in the Journal will be explained in the foot-notes: those which occur more frequently are enumerated below.

CURRENCY

REAL OF EIGHT (real, rial, ryall, etc.; symbol in the text, R 8). A Spanish silver coin, imported into Asia by the Dutch and English, and current along the seaboard. The value depended partly on the weight and fineness of the individual coins, partly on the supply and demand in each market; it ranged about two Indian rupees, 4*s*. 6*d*. English money, or 2½ Dutch guilders.

PAGODA (symbols P[a] and Pa). The principal unit on the Coromandel Coast, a gold coin worth at this time from 7*s*. to 7*s*. 6*d*. A fuller description will be found in *Golconda*, 92 ff.

TAEL, MAS. The silver currency of Siam and Patani. The tael (symbol t[a]) was approximately 2¼ reals, or 6 guilders, that is, roughly 10*s*., but so large a coin was not current, the principal one being the tical, known in Siam as *bāt*, ¼ of a tael. The mas (symbols m[a] and ms) was ¼ of a tical, making 16 to the tael (*van Vliet*, 94). A smaller coin, the copan, which is not mentioned by van Vliet, was apparently ½ of a mas; it must be distinguished from the Japanese kobang, a gold coin, the name of which was sometimes written as coban or coupan. The Malay names 'mas' and 'copan' do not appear in Mr R. Le May's recent study, *The Coinage of Siam* (Bangkok, 1932); from the equivalents given by him (p. 51), the mas must be the Siamese *salu'ng*, while the copan would be the *song pai*.

WEIGHTS

POUND. The pound avoirdupois (lb.) had its present value. The Amsterdam pound used by the Dutch was 1·09 lb. There is some reason to suspect that the symbol lb. in the text occasionally denotes Dutch pounds.

CANDI, CANDY. In South India, candy denoted 20 maunds, a variable unit. In Masulipatam the maund was approximately 26 lb., and the candy therefore about 520 lb. (*Golconda*, 89).

BAHĀR. In India the bahār was equivalent to the candy: in Siam it was substantially less, being 3 picul, or under 400 lb.

PICUL. This unit varied slightly, but seems always to have been close to 130 lb. In Siam, *van Vliet* (*l.c.*) made it equivalent to 118 Dutch pounds, or 129 lb.
SACK. The sack of pepper at Bantam was about 62 lb. (*Purchas*, I. iii. 161).

MEASURES

LAST, TON. The shipping, or measurement, ton was the space, about 60 cubic feet, occupied by a tun of wine. The Dutch *last* was two of these tons.
LEAGUE, MILE. The Dutch *mijl* was approximately equal to three English miles, or one league; in the text 'mile' must be read as 'league', except where the phrase 'English mile' occurs.
HĀSTA. The cubit used on the Coromandel Coast, about 18·7 inches (*Golconda*, 88).

The VOYAGE of PETER FLORIS

[CHAPTER I

THE OUTWARD VOYAGE]

IN THE NAME OFF GOD, AMEN.

Anno Domini 1610, *Stilo Anglicano*

Havinge covenanted and aggreed with the right Wor^{ll} the Gouvernour and Deputies of the Company trading for the Easte Indies resident in London, uppon suche conditions as are mentioned in the contracte,[2] whereof one [part] is in custodye of the said Mr Gouvernour, and the other of Hans van Elbinck dwelling att Amsterdam, wee imbarked ourselves in the shippe called the *Globe*, which God preserve, and sette sayle att Gravesende uppon this sayd daye. God Almightye graunte us a safe and prosperous voyage, and defende us from all adversitie, to the glorye of His name and our safetie. Adi[1] 5 *Janu:*

Wee sette saile from the Downes with a N.W. wynde. 5 *Febru:*

Wee came oute of sight of the Lizard, setting oure course towards the sea S.W. 7 *ditto.*

We had a man fall overboord, but having a contrarye wynde, and the shippe making butt little waye, there was by the diligence of Capt. Hippon a brase[3] caste unto him, who caught hold of the same, to his good and our generall joye. 11 *ditto.*

Wee were in the heighte of $33\frac{1}{2}$ degrees, and sawe the Iland[4] of Porto S^{to} W. by S. aboute 7 leagues from us. 21 *ditto.*

[1] *Adi*, a common prefix to dates in Dutch documents of the period, is the contemporary Italian *a dì*, representing Latin *ad diem*, 'on day'. Along with some other Latinisms, it seems to have reached Holland through the practice of 'Italian' book-keeping; it is found in standard treatises in both languages such as Angelo Pietra's *Indrizzo de gli Economi*... (Mantua, 1586), and Nicolaus Petri's *Practique om te leeren Rekenen*... (Amsterdam, 1605–6). The year is 1611, New Style; writing for the English Company, Floris used what he called the 'Anglican', that is, the Old Style, which the Dutch and most other nations had already abandoned.

[2] The contract, or agreement, is printed in *First Letter Book*, 363. Hans van Elbinck, or Elbing, was Floris' brother.

[3] *I.e.*, brace, a rope used in trimming the sails.

[4] Porto Santo, one of the Madeira Islands.

24 ditto. Wee were in the heighte of 30 degrees and sawe lande before us, being an iland of the Canaries, called Lansarotte [Lanzarote]. Towards the evening wee turned to seaward, W.

25, 26, 27 *ditto.* Wee had variable wether and a rough sea: towards evening rayne, which rayne (broughte) caste read sande over all the shippe.[1]

28 ditto. Being mistye wether, and aboute 10 of the clock in the morning, wee sawe land hard by us, which was the Iland of the Great Canaries,[2] and cleering upp towards the evening, wee sawe verye perfectly the verye high *pico* [peak] of Teneriffe.

3 *Martii.*[3] Wee passed *Tropicum Cancri* with a good speedye waye. Being
16 *ditto.* att the heighte of 3 degrees by N. *de lynea* [*i.e.*, of the Equator], wee sawe a greate shippe, butt coulde not come to speake with hir.

25 ditto. Wee were aboute the height of the lyne, and sawe 2 shipps N. from us, and a sayle S. from us, but coulde not speake with theym.

27 ditto. Wee came by 2 Portugall carvells,[4] whereof the one came to speake with us, butt wee coulde not understande muche by him.

Adi primo *April.* Wee were in the heighte of 2 degrees 40 minutes by S. of the lyne, having spente aboute 15 dayes in great calmes and rayne; wee then gott the generall S.E. wynde, and had 4½ degrees variation, so that wee were well aboute the E.,[5] setting our course S.S.W. and S. by W. to passe the Abrollos.

4 ditto. Wee sawe 2 sayles, the one being a carvelle, crossing S. before

[1] This phenomenon is described (p. 215), and discussed (pp. 324 ff.), in D. A. Bannerman's *The Canary Islands* (London, 1922). The red sand is carried from Africa by an east-to-west current in the upper air.

[2] *I.e.*, Gran Canaria. Teneriffe lies west of this island.

[3] Martii, or sometimes Marti, was the book-keepers' form of the name; the Dutch form was Meert (now Maart).

[4] Carvels, or caravels, were light, fast-sailing vessels.

[5] Here, and in several subsequent passages, 'aboute' is used in the sense of 'towards', denoting direction. At this period, long before the invention of the chronometer, there was no satisfactory method of determining longitude. In *Boteler's Dialogues*, written soon after 1620, it is stated (pp. 212, 213) that "the longitude cannot be taken at all", on which the editor noted that "the variation of the compass was found to be of some use". From this and other passages in the text it will be seen that Hippon regularly used the variation for this purpose. The importance of being well over to the east lay in the fact that ships for the Cape could not sail directly into the "generall S.E. wynde", that is, the trade wind, but had to steer W. of S. close to Brazil, until they picked up a westerly wind to carry them across the South Atlantic. If they were too far to the west, they would be unable to clear the Abrolhos, a shoal lying off Brazil between Bahia and Rio; while if they were sufficiently to the east, they had a clear course southward.

us, the other a greate shippe being E.-ward from us, taking her course N.W., so that wee tooke her to bee a shipp of the Indies. Att the first shee made directly towards us, butt seing the Portingall barke and us, whome shee tooke to bee a Portingall, shee tooke hir former course; and att noone wee were in 5 degrees and 36 minutes, the wynde being E.S.E., making good waye.

Wee were in 18¾ degrees, so that in the night wee passed the Abrollos, the wynde for the mooste parte being S. and E. by S., also E. by N. with a good gale; heere wee had ii degrees[1] variation. 14 *ditto. Passing off the Abrollos.*

Wee were in the heighte of aboute 34 degrees, having a greate storme oute of the W. and W.S.W. lasting till the 17th, during which tyme of 36 oures wee hulled,[2] fearing to come to neare the shoare in the night with so strong a wynde, having no more then 3 degrees variation, notwithstanding that wee made accounte to bee further of; for wee sawe dyvers foules that keepe [*i.e.*, live] aboute the Cape, which wee had not seene att sea before, as *mangas de veludo*[3] and other sortes with blacke wings and a crosse over the backe, also greate quantitie of feysons, being a speckled foule as a pigeon. These followed us from the Ilands of Tristan d'a Chuna [da Cunha] to the Cape, whereof wee tooke some with byrde lyme. Adi 14 *May.*

Early in the morning wee sawe the land of the Capo de Bona Esperanza [Good Hope], having the Table [Mountain] from us N.E. by E. The wynde falling N.N.W., not being able to gette the baye that daye, wee wente (to and of) of and on till the 19th, and then wee had a greate storme from the N.W. continuing till the 20th att noone, and then, the wether clering agayne, wee were oute of sight of lande. 18 *ditto.*

[1] This figure may represent either two or eleven. It will be noticed that there is a gap of a month at this point of the Journal, and the change in course from W. of S. to E. is not recorded; the next entry indicates that the ship had passed near Tristan da Cunha.

[2] 'To hull' is to drift to the wind with sails furled.

[3] The authorities of the Natural History Museum write that *mangas de veludo* (Portuguese, 'sleeves of velvet') must be the Wandering Albatross (*Diomedia exulans*, Linné); and the *feysons* (Port. *feijões*) the Cape Pigeon (*Daption capensis*, Linné). The "other sortes with blacke wings and a crosse over the backe" may refer either to the Yellow-nosed Mollynauk (*Thalassarche chlororhynchus*, Gmelin) or to the Black-browed Mollynauk (*T. melanophris*, Temminck); but the description is somewhat vague, and might cover certain petrels of the genus *Prion*.

21 ditto. Wee sawe land agayne, and that evening came into the baye, Captayne Hippon being acquaynted with the place.[1] Att our comming in wee sawe 3 fyres under lande, which wee founde to bee 3 shipps; and having caste our anker, 2 boates came aboord of us, the one being the boate of Isaac le Mayre, and the other of the *Lyon with the arrowes* and the shipp *Gouda*, which was commanded by Henryck Brouweer,[2] butt [we] came not att roade by those shipps till in the morning.

The comming into the Table Baye off Cap: de Bo: Esperanz.

Being by Gods grace heere arryved, wee presently fell to the ordering of the shippe, and hooping of our caske to fill freshe water, for muche refreshing was not heere to bee had att this tyme of the yeare, by the greate quantitie of rayne, being nowe in the chiefeste of winter so that the mountaines laye covered with snowe: during which tyme wee used greate diligence in seeking of the roote Ningimm[3] according to our instruction, the aforesayde 2 Holland shippes being expressely come thether for the same purpose, being one of Japan that fyrst discovered the

Description off the roote Ningim.

[1] Hippon had been master of the *Dragon* on the third Voyage, and was at Table Bay in December, 1607 (*Purchas*, I. iii. 190; *Letters Received*, i. 13 ff.).

[2] Hendrik Brouwer's fleet left Holland in December, 1610; it included the *Gouda* and the pinnace *Leeuw met Pijlen*, or *Lion with Arrows* (*van Dijk* (J), 39; *MacLeod*, i. 105). Isaac Lemaire was a prominent Amsterdam merchant, and one of the original Directors of the Dutch Company, but he soon quarrelled with his colleagues. About this time he was sending out independent whaling expeditions to the Cape; and a few years later he despatched the ships which under the command of his son Jacob, mentioned below, discovered the passage round Cape Horn, known as Lemaire Strait (*Biographisch Woordenboek der Nederlanden*, *s.nn.*).

[3] From the facts given in the text and by other observers, especially Richard Cocks (*Letters Received*, v. 17, 18), it appears that a Japanese sailor had found near Table Bay a root which he supposed to be identical with the Korean ginseng, and to which he gave the corresponding Japanese name *nangin* or *ningin*. Ginseng "has an extraordinary reputation in China as a restorative" (*Hobson-Jobson*, *s.v.*), and at this period it was worth its weight in silver in Japan; consequently it was for a short time the practice to look for the root while ships were in Table Bay, but the results were unsatisfactory, and no trade was established. The identity of the root found at the Cape has been considered by Dr J. Burtt Davy, and by the authorities at the Imperial Institute and the Royal Botanic Gardens. From the descriptions quoted above it may have been *Lichtensteinia interrupta*, Meyer, a medicinal plant which is rather widely distributed in South Africa, but has not been recorded near Table Bay; in the alternative, it may have been some species of *Annesorhiza*, either *montana* or *macrocarpa*, though there is no record of any medicinal value being attributed to these. Probably the Japanese discoverer was misled by superficial resemblance.

secret; butt, being winter tyme, there was for this tyme no more to bee done but to go awaye as wyse as wee came, for the olde roote being decayed and rotten, the newe leafe began onely to come foorth, so that had it not bene by reason of some information which was gotten of one who heere shalbee nameles for dyvers considerations sake,[1] wee shoulde have bene fayne to have departed withoute any notice thereof, the right tyme of gathering the same being in December, January, and February, being called of these inhabitants Canna.

The aforesayd 2 shipps departed for Bantam the 26 of Maye, having layne heere 18 dayes, and butt indifferently refreshed theymselves; and wee, having filled our water and refreshed *6 off June.* ourselves with 80 sheepe and 20 neate [*i.e.*, cattle], sette sayle oute of the baye for the furthering of our voyage, leaving behynde us in the baye the boate of Isaac Le Mayre, wherein was his sone Jacob le Maire, who laye there to barter for hydes and skinnes and to make trane oyle, who was to continue there till in December. To him wee gave some letters both to the Company and particular [private] friends, declaring what there had happened unto us. Heere wee gott notice of Sir Henry Middletons shipps,[2] who was departed oute of the baye the 10 of August, and David Middleton homewards the 21 January.

Wee passed the Cape of Bona Esperanza with fayre wether, *7 ditto. Passing the Cape off Bona Esperanza.* and N.W. wynde, withoute seing the lande.

Wee passed Capo d'Aguillas [Cape Agulhas] with fayre wether, att $35\frac{2}{3}$ degrees. *8 ditto.*

Being att the heighte of $34\frac{1}{3}$ degrees, wee sawe land, having *11 ditto.* 5 degrees 55 min: variation northwesting, so that wee did guesse it to bee the W. corner of the Baia de Lagoa [Algoa Bay], which was 40 (miles) leagues[3] from our guessing, for by our accounte

[1] Presumably the information was obtained clandestinely from someone in the Dutch fleet.

[2] Sir Henry Middleton, on the *Trade's Increase* (sixth Voyage), was at Table Bay from 24th July to 10th or 12th August, 1610 (*Purchas*, I. iii. 247; *Lancaster's Voyages*, 145). David Middleton, on the *Expedition* (fifth Voyage), sailed from Bantam for England in November, 1610, reached Table Bay in January, and left 'with all despatch' (*Purchas*, I. iii. 246).

[3] The Dutch *mijl* was approximately an English league of three miles; here and elsewhere the translator gave both words, but 'leagues' is correct. 'Guessing' is Dutch *gissing*, 'estimate' or, at sea, 'reckoning'.

wee (were so) shoulde bee muche more easterly then wee founde us, which came by reason of the greate streame that runneth aboute [*i.e.*, towards] the west.

16 ditto. The wynde turned S.E. with rayne, being the afterspring[1] of the full moone.

17 ditto. The wynde yett S.E. with storme and rayne; in the night wee tooke in our sayles, for not blowing of.

18 ditto. Earlye in the morning wee sawe land, not being 3 (miles) leagues from it, the storm continuing very hard with rayne, thunder and lightning, a verye close ayre, so that wee coulde not see muche from us; not being able to gette any advantage by sayling, [we] were, with greate force of the waves, (putte) beate towards the shoare, so that in mans judgement wee were paste helpe and assistance, beginning to looke very moanefully one uppon an other; butt being in this greate perplexitie and seing no helpe of man to assiste us, it pleased the Almightye God to shewe Himselfe a true helper in the neede and to shewe His omnipotent power; for towards noone the foule wether ceased and it became cleare. Then did wee see the danger wee were in, butt God sending us a S. and S.S.W. wynde wee turned E. to seaward and sawe the highland of Terra de Natall, thanking God for His great mercies; and were att the height of 31 degrees.

They are in great danger by Terra de Natall.

26 ditto. Wee were att the heighte of 24 degrees and woulde fayne have had the sight of Capo das Corrientes,[2] butt coulde nott gette it, notwithstanding that wee made oure course for it W.N.W. untill night.

27 ditto. In the night wee passed the Baixos da Judea with fayre wether.

Adi primo *July.* Wee sawe the Iland of the Premeiros, having greene water and 48 faddem [*i.e.*, fathom], butt afterwards wee came att 5 faddem; this (shallownesse) shoale lyethe mooste N.E. and S.W. with the mooste easterlyeste iland. The nexte daye wee passed the Ilands of Angonas, being 4 in number.

[1] *I.e.*, 'offspring' or 'result'.

[2] The course taken was, as usual at this season, up the Mozambique Channel. At this stage of the S.W. monsoon ships usually did not venture to cross the Indian Ocean, but steered 'inside Madagascar', and then turned eastward. Cape Correntes ('the cape of currents'), 24° 6′ S., marks the entrance to the channel; Baixos da Judea is a shoal lying midway in the entrance; the Primeira Islands are off the African coast half-way up the channel; Angonas must be for the Angoche Islands, a little farther north; Mezinguale, or Moginkwal, is nearly 50 miles south of Mozambique.

Wee sawe the high lande of Mezinguale, being aboute 10 (miles) leagues from Mezambicke, and from hence tooke our course N. by E. and N.N.E. till att the heighte of 6 degrees. *3 ditto.*

Wee passed the Iland of Zanzibar, and the 9 the Iland of Pemba. *8 ditto.*

Wee passed the lyne the second tyme with a greate pace.[1] *12 ditto.*

Wee passed the Ilands of the Malcivas[2] att 8½ degrees withoute seing any land, notwithstanding that wee tooke in our sayles and hulled all night, for wee sawe a greate many little sea-crabbs, whereof wee tooke parte and ate theym. *26 & 27 ditto.*

In the evening wee caste the lead att 45 faddem, being the poynte of Capo de Commori [C. Comorin], butt coulde not see the Cape in the morning. *29 ditto. Capo de Commori.*

Aboute 9 of the clocke wee sawe the Iland of Ceylon, falling juste within the Punta de Galle.[3] From hence wee wente along the coaste making for the fyrste (droughthe) shallownesse,[4] being 5 months and 26 dayes that wee sette saile in the Downes. Adi primo *Auguste. See the Iland off Ceylon.*

[1] Again the change of course is not noted. After passing Zanzibar they must have borne considerably to the east of the former course in order to sail south of Ceylon

[2] The course was apparently through the Eight Degree Channel, north of the Maldives *Pyrard* (II ii 351) described various crabs in this region, and his editor noted that the islands are "a perfect paradise for crabs"

[3] *I e*, the south-west corner of the island

[4] Here and elsewhere 'droughthe' represents Dutch *droogte*, 'shoal'.

[CHAPTER II
THE COROMANDEL COAST]

[*August*] 6 *ditto*. Having runne along the coaste of Ceylon, wee fell before Negapatam,[1] being 28 myles or leagues from our guessing [*i.e.*, reckoning], so that in that place the mappe is very false, for the same hath happened also to the Hollands shipps; so that a man muste take good heede, especially in the night tyme, for hee woulde bee a shoare before hee bee aware. Neyther founde wee the Iland to bee so broad as it is in the mappe; the latitude wee founde to bee a the [*sic*] greate faulte of Mr Molinecx,[2] master of the *Hector*, who layeth Punto de Galle att 4 degrees, whereas it lyethe att 6 degrees. Towards the evening wee passed hard by the roade, and might see the towne and the howses very playnely. There laye a greate shippe att roade with dyvers masulls[3] and boates, butt according to our commission wee did not annoye theym.

7 *ditto*. In the night wee passed Tanagapatam[4] where the Hollanders keepe a factorye; but having notice of the sayde place, as lykewyse wee were informed afterwards, there is no greate matters to doe there, for the Hollanders are resolved to breake upp the sayd factorye or *cantoor*.[5]

[1] The seaport of Negapatam was in the territory of Vijayanagar, but at this time was *de facto* in the possession of the resident Portuguese community (*Golconda*, 2).

[2] Matthew Mullineux; the spelling of the surname varies rather widely (*Letters Received*, i *passim*).

[3] Surf boats; see *Hobson-Jobson* (*s.v.*), where the dubious etymology is discussed. The Royal Commission for the Voyage (*First Letter Book*, 361) prohibited any attack on the subjects of the King of Spain or other friendly nations, but authorised defensive measures in case of attack, as in the affair off S. Thomé mentioned just below.

[4] This name, which Purchas misread as Lanagapatam, represents Tegnapatam, now Fort S. David. The Dutch factory there was established in 1608 (*Terpstra*, 85 ff.).

[5] *Cantoor*, now written *kantoor*, was the regular Dutch equivalent of the English 'factory', *i.e.*, agency. At this period it was frequently written *comptoor*, *compthoir*, etc., indicating its relation to French *comptoir*.

Wee mette a masull comming from St. Thome,[1] and being desirous to heare some newes from the shoare wee manned our pinasse,[2] myselfe going in her. Comming towards theym, they began to shoote, and thoughe wee shewed theym all tokens of friendshippe, yet woulde not they beleeve us, butt shotte still att us, so that a muskett bullett flewe over my head; whereuppon I commanded to enter [*i.e.*, attack] and use theym in hostile manner, the which being done accordingly, they had enough to doe to save theyr lyves; butt I brought theym aboord, and, after consultation had, wee did release theym and all theyr goods; during which tyme wee came before St. Thome, whereas[3] roade a navette with some masulls and tselitones. So passing the evening, wee ankered in the night, having resolved to come in Paleacatte,[4] being informed by some Portingalls that the Hollanders had a factory in Paleacatte, to see whether any good was to bee had there for our voyage and Companye. *8 ditto. St. Thome.*

Wee came before Paleacatte att ancker, passing over the (droughthe) shallowe, not being in lengthe above a muskett shott, having butt 3 faddem water, which is very dangerous for greate shipps. Heere came 2 boates aboord of us, the one being sente from the Sabander,[5] the other from the Hollanders. Of these wee understoode all the particularities, praying the Sabanders men to doe oure commendations unto him, telling him that wee were Englishe marchants, desiring therefore to *9 ditto. Paleacatte.*

[1] S. Thomé, now a suburb of Madras, was, like Negapatam, *de facto* in the possession of the resident Portuguese community.

[2] 'Pinnace' at this time usually meant a small sea-going ship; "I know no difference between a ship and a pinnace but in the bulk and burthen" (*Boteler's Dialogues*, 197). Sometimes however, as here, a small pinnace was carried on a ship, thus approximating to the modern sense of the word.

[3] 'Whereas' is used frequently in the text in the sense of 'where' or 'whereat'. *Navette* is Portuguese *naveta*, a small sea-going vessel. *Tselitones* were harbour-boats. The name is discussed in *Golconda*, 69 *n.*; the form there is *celytones*, but Dutch writers frequently gave the Indian *s* as *ts*.

[4] The Dutch factory at Pulicat was quite new, having been established only in 1610 (*Terpstra*, 120 ff.).

[5] 'Sabander', Persian *shāhbandar*, properly denoted a consul, in the contemporary sense of the head of a community resident in a foreign seaport, but during the sixteenth century it came to be applied by the Portuguese to the official in charge of a port, and this erroneous use became general in the East (*vide* JRAS, 1920, p. 517).

sende us a *caule*[1] or conducte to lande some of our men and to make an aggreement to trade there; which they promised us, and so wente a land.

10 ditto. Came the Sabanders men aboorde agayne, bringing a *caull* or conducte from the Sabander that wee might come freely on shoare. Whereuppon it was resolved that I and Mr Browne[2] shoulde goe ashoare. Goinge ashoare wee were by the greate roughnesse of the sea turned over altogether, so that wee were in greate distresse, especially Mr Browne, in regard of his sicknesse; butt God bee praysed no man was drowned,[3] so that the greateste harme was in hurting of apparell and losse of weapons and such lyke. Comminge ashoare, the Sabander came to meete us and bringe us into the towne, bemoaning our mishappe; and having receyved us very friendly, wee wente in a boate upp the river towards the towne, and after wee had discoursed together of many things, hee appointed us a house according to the fasshion of the contrie, promising us to procure a letter from the King, [and] to wryte to the Gouvernesse Condamaa[4] of oure arrivall. Wherewithall wee were well contented.

11 ditto. Mr Lucas[5] came on shoare, and so wee wente together to the Sabander to conferre with him more att large; and having sitte there a little while, there came John van Weesick, being President of the Hollanders on the coaste of Choromandel; and having conferred a little together, hee shewed us a *caul* or safeconducte

What happened in Paleacatte.

[1] 'Caule', Arabic *qaul*, 'promise', was used widely by Europeans in India in the sense of a document guaranteeing a safe conduct, and sometimes in the vaguer sense of a written promise of any sort.

[2] Robert Browne was one of the three principal merchants on the *Globe* (*First Letter Book,* 380).

[3] In the text the words 'caste or' are written above the line and marked for insertion before 'drowned', but the pen has been run through them, and it is not clear whether or not they were meant to stand.

[4] *I.e.*, the lady appointed as Governor by the Queen, who held Pulicat for what may be described as her privy purse. The correct form of the name is Kondamma.

[5] 'Mr Lucas' is Antheunis; it is noteworthy that Floris never uses his surname. Jan van Wesick, misread Wersicke by Purchas, had been on the Coromandel Coast since 1608. At the end of 1610 he was appointed Director of all the Dutch factories on the Coast with headquarters at Pulicat (*Terpstra,* 156). The terms Director and President were in practice more or less interchangeable at this time, both denoting an officer in superior charge of a group of factories.

from the King of Narsinga,[1] Wencapati Raja, which hee had graunted to the Hollanders. Among other privileges this was one, that it shoulde not bee lawfull to trade there for any that came oute of Europe butt suche as broughte a patent from His Excellencie Prince Mauritius,[2] and, wee not having the same, the aforesayde Van Wesick desired our departure; butt wee made him answere that wee knewe not of his *caule* or safe-conducte, neyther did it touche us; yf the King had promised him, hee might looke to the performance; wee came with commission from His Majestie of England, and wee therefore woulde doe what wee coulde; hee might looke to that what hee had to doe; so that wee came to high woordes, till the Sabander tolde us that wee shoulde not bee offended, that hee had newes of the Gouvernesse that shee woulde come to the towne within 3 dayes, and what shee in that case shoulde judge bothe parties shoulde reste contented withall, for it was not the Kings pleasure that any stranger shoulde bee forbidde his countrie, muche lesse to us that were so mightye a nation; so that for that tyme nothing more coulde bee done butt to go home and expecte the comming of the olde Gouvernesse.

Came Conda Maa, the Gouvernesse, in Pleacatta [Pulicat], *17 ditto.* and, wee beinge ready to go to hir howse, Captain Hippon, in regard of Mr Brownes sicknes, being come on shoare to the ende that all might bee done with good counsell, there came to us a *recado*[3] from the Gouvernesse as that nowe it was no fitte tyme to speake with the Gouvernesse, and that wee shoulde tarry att home till the nexte daye, and then shee woulde call us; which seemed very strange unto us, so that wee began to suspecte that the Hollanders were in oure waye, having understoode the night

[1] Narsinga, representing Narasimha, the name of the King who ruled early in the sixteenth century, was commonly used by the Portuguese to denote the dynasty and kingdom of Vijayanagar. The ruling King is reckoned by some historians as Venkata I, and by others as Venkata II. His full name was Venkatādri, and various honorific additions were also made; that in the text probably stands for Venkatapati Rāja. His grant to the Dutch Company is printed in *De Jonge, Opkomst*, iii. 348; it did, in fact, give the Dutch the monopoly which they asserted.

[2] *I.e.*, Prince Maurice of Nassau, at this time Stadholder of the Netherlands.

[3] *Recado* is Portuguese for 'message'.

before that they had corrupted the Gouvernesse to forbidde us the trade there.

18 *ditto.* The nexte daye drawing towards noone and no *recado* comming to us, neyther from the Sabander nor the Gouvernesse, wee sente to the Sabander to knowe the reason why wee coulde not come to the speeche of the Gouvernesse, seing others coulde speake with hir. Hee sente us answere shee had nothing to saye to us, in regarde that place was by patent of the King graunted to the Hollanders, and that it was not in hir power to breake the same; butt yf wee woulde goe to the King ourselves shee woulde bee contented: which made us not a little amazed. Yett notwithstandinge, consulting together what to answere to so suddayne a denyall, to go to the King[1] ourselves wee founde not fitting, for besydes the greate charges, it woulde bee 6 weekes or 2 months before wee shoulde come to the ende of our embassage, and thereby hazard our voyage of our monson[2] for Bantam, and furthermore to loose our voyage for Petanie, especially seing the Hollanders had 2 elephants a sayling,[3] woorthe a greate deale of money, which they made readye to sende to the King. Wherefore, to loose neyther longer tyme nor bee att needelesse expenses, it was resolved to prosecute our voyage for Petapoli and Musilpatam, where wee were acquaynted, not doubting butt there wee shoulde bee welcome; and therefore sente answer to the Sabander to looke wel to it howe hee delte with us, for that wee were come on shoare uppon his *caul* or safeconducte; and seing they were not desirous of any marchants in theyr countrye, wee woulde not tarry there agaynst there wills, desiring leave to departe, sending him 3 yardes of cl[o]ath and a looking glasse for a present. And shortely after that came his answere and leave to departe, the Sabander muche excusing himselfe, onely

[1] At this period the King frequently resided at Vellore, about 90 miles inland from Pulicat; his other residences were more distant.

[2] This phrase is unintelligible as it stands; perhaps the translator accidentally reproduced the original *of*, which in Dutch means 'or', instead of translating it. 'Monson' or 'monsoon', from Arabic *mausim*, means 'season', and the phrases 'to lose one's voyage' or 'one's monsoon' were interchangeable. Patani, on the east coast of the Malay Peninsula, was one of the main objectives of the Voyage.

[3] Presumably this means that the elephants were being brought by sea from Ceylon, the usual source of supply for this region. In the conditions of the time, a present of such value would probably have been decisive at Court.

that hee coulde not helpe it as being the doing of the Gouvernesse; but yf wee woulde take residence in [blank in MS], being a place scituated betweene Paleacatte and St. Thome,[1] hee woulde procure that the same place shoulde bee given to us, with privilege that nobody shoulde trade there butt wee. Butt wee seing the place not muche frequented, and havinge no convenience to settle or place any factory there, as also that Musilpatan and Petapoli can furnish more apparrell and other goods then the Company is able to imploye or to vente [*i.e.*, sell], wee resolved to departe and to advertise the Company of all what had happened. And so wee departed from Paleacatte, to the greate griefe of the common people, not once beinge able to come to the speeche of that olde whore,[2] what meanes soever wee used for itt; butt comming aboorde in the evening, wee sette sayle att night.

Wee arryved before Petapoli;[3] whereas presently there came some aboorde of us from the *sangerims*,[4] with whome wee sente a *recado* to the Gouvernour, desiring a *caull* or safeconducte, which hee sente us. And so wente ashoare the nexte daye, whereas wee were well receyved, and aggreed aboute the custome or toll for $3\frac{3}{4}$ per cent, resolving that Mr Lucas with Mr Browne shoulde staye in Petapoli and that I shoulde departe with the shipp for Musilpatam, in regarde the shippe had a better roade there then att Petapoli; so that heere was brought on shoare a cheste with 8000 ryalls, one (case) bale of clothes and $\frac{1}{2}$ (case) bale of carseyes,[5] and 188 piggs of lead, [resolving] that Mr Browne, being very sicke and not being able to go ashoare by reason of the greate roughnesse and falling of the sea, shoulde tarry a boorde, and being a little amended hee shoulde travell **20 *ditto*.** ***Petapoli.***

[1] Contemporary records disclose no place of any commercial importance on this section of the Coast; conceivably it was the village of Madraspatam, where Fort S. George was to be built about 30 years later.

[2] This need not be read as a specific imputation; similar phrases occur in other Dutch documents of the period, where they are obviously nothing but general expressions of dissatisfaction.

[3] Petapoli, more accurately Peddapalle, situated near the mouth of the Kistna, was the second seaport of the kingdom of Golconda, Masulipatam being the first; it was also called Nizāmpatam.

[4] *I.e.*, *jangadas* or *jangars*, rafts made on double canoes (*Hobson-Jobson*, *s.v.*); Dutch writers commonly represented initial *j* by *s*.

[5] Reals of eight, shown in the text below as R8, were Spanish silver coins worth about 4*s*. 6*d*. 'Clothes' here denotes broadcloth; carseys, or kerseys, were also woollen, but lighter and cheaper than broadcloth.

thether by lande, ordering our matters in suche sorte as that wee sette sayle in the night the 28.

31 *Auguste.* Wee came on the roade of Musilpatam, where wee founde the shipp of Hadsie Baba of Arracam,[1] and a *pagell* going for Tenesserin. Here presently came aboord of mee Zalelchor Chan[2] with a *caull* or conducte, uppon which I, Mr Essington[3] and Simon Judis went a shoare, where wee were wel receyved and muche viseted of my olde acquainted friendes; and seeking *Muslipatam.* presently to aggree aboute the toll and custome, the Gouvernoure woulde not yeelde to it, sayinge hee was sente for by the greate Gouvernoure, Mir Sumela,[4] not knowing whether hee or another shoulde come backe agayne, desiring us to have patience till then, which was very hard for me to endure. Heereuppon I sente presently for Mr Lucas from Potapoli [*sic*] to consulte together what were beste to bee done.

5 *September.* Came Mr Lucas from Petapoli, and having consulted together what wee woulde doe touching the toll or custome, wee wente to the Gouvernour, Mir Sadardi,[5] who, after long debating, woulde not graunte us any abatement but that wee shoulde paye as other strangers did, which is 5 per cent of import and 5 per cent for exporte, besides the *t'siappa* and *dalelli*,[6] which

[1] Presumably Hājī Bābā of Arakan. 'Pagell' must represent the 'buggalow' of *Hobson-Jobson*, a name for vessels of the local build; Pinto wrote the word *paguel*, and do Couto and other writers used the corresponding plural *pagueis* (*Dalgado, s.v.* Paguel).

[2] Zalelchor, misread by Purchas as Zaldchar, might represent either Jalālkhūr or Zalālkhūr, but neither of these names is known, and the formation is unnatural; probably the translator misread what Floris wrote.

[3] Thomas Essington was senior of the four factors named in the commission for the Voyage. There is no name like Judis in the commission, and the reference must be to Symon Evans, the second factor. A subsequent entry shows that Floris probably wrote the surname 'Ivens', which in the Dutch script could easily be misread as Judis.

[4] *I.e.*, Mīr Jumla, the designation of the Chief Minister of Golconda. The incumbent at this time was Mirza Muhammad Amīn.

[5] Probably Mīr Sadar-ud-dīn.

[6] A local impost, known as *chhāpa-dalālī*, 'stamping-brokerage'. Expressions like "6 in 7 per cent" recur below, and leave no room for doubting that the original of 'in' is *a*, a particle which was ordinarily used by Dutch merchants in giving approximate figures, and is best translated 'or': Mr G. P. Ambrose informs me that this use of 'in' occurs frequently in letters written by English factors in the Levant in the seventeenth and eighteenth centuries, but it has not been found in printed books of the period. The tax in question was, how-

amounteth to 6 in 7 per cent. Whereon wee woulde not condiscend, but tolde him yf hee woulde not graunte unto us as wee had aggreed att Petapoli, that then wee woulde departe; by reason whereof hee, fearing wee woulde doe as wee sayde, did graunte to our shipp to paye no more then 4 per cent inwards and 4 per cent outwards,[1] withoute naming any further charges; and taking a wryting of the same, wee began to bring some money on shoare for a beginning for our buysinesse.

Wee did assemble the Counsell,[2] shewing unto theym what *caul* wee had gott of the Gouvernoure for our shipp, as also that in regard of the knaverye, deceyte and change of the Gouvernours, who are butt little or nothing att all to bee trusted, which is very dangerous for shippes that might come after, especially for suche persons as never have bene there before, to whome the knaveries and inconstancies of the Gouvernours is unknowen, which might tende to the great hinderance of the Company; to the preventing whereof wee did moove the Counsell, yf so they thoughte it good, to give a present to the greate Gouvernoure, Mir Sumela, att the generall charges of the Company,—hee being a person of verye greate credit with the King and one that dothe farme oute all the Kings lands and domeynes[3] and taketh accounte of the same, payeth the souldiers and hath other greate offices besides,—for to obtayne of him a confirmation of our foresayde *caule* for all shipps that shoulde come heereafter with a patent of his Majestie and commission from the Company in London, that no greater charges shoulde bee layde on theym then us, in regard wee were all subjects to one King and servants 6 *ditto.*

ever, higher: in 1606 it was reckoned as 12 per cent. (*Terpstra*, 42), and in 1614 as about 11 per cent. (*Golconda*, 65). Floris, who must have known this, speaks of it as two taxes, not one, and possibly in this passage the original word was not *a* but *en* (and), which the translator carelessly rendered 'in'; the claim would then be for 13 per cent. for the two taxes together, which would agree with the other authorities, allowing 1 or 2 per cent. for bargaining.

[1] These were the rates which the Dutch paid under their agreement of 1606 (*Terpstra*, 42).

[2] Article 13 of the commission for the Voyage constituted the captain, merchants and factors as a Council to deal with "all difficult matters" (*First Letter Book*, 384).

[3] The kingdom was administered almost entirely on the farming system (*Golconda*, 11, and *passim*); and apparently the Chief Minister at this time had taken a superior farm of the entire administration.

to one master, wee not douting butt to obtayne the same. The which being heard and well considered by the Counsell, they thoughte it very fitte and convenient, resolving to putte it in practise, the sooner the better, as more att large appeareth by theyr resolution heerein taken.

7 ditto. Mr Brouns decease. Aboute 9 of the clock att night deceased Mr Robt. Browne aboord of the shipp, having bene sick the space of 6 weekes. The nexte daye in the morning hee was buryed on shoare, and, for a remembrance to suche as maye come after, wee erected a tombe[1] for him. Wee have a greate losse of him, butt yett wee muste take patience, seing it is Gods will and pleasure, who graunte him a happye and joyfull resurrection, and us all when wee shall followe. Amen. Hee was the fyrst that wee loste in this voyage; hee dyed very godly, and made a large will. But besides his will hee hath had 1765 reals, whereof hee made no mention in his will, butt requested us to take the sayde money into our handes and to imploye it to his greateste profitte, upon certayne conditions, for our provision.[2] Butt being contrary to the Commission, wee founde ourselves aggrieved therein, and woulde not accepte of it; butt according to his will, wee contented everyone, deducting the charges of his buryall, putting upp the reste and given [giving] it in custodye of Capt. Hippon, that comminge att Bantam it might bee used according to the occasion of the tyme. The cause that wee woulde not give the money to the company of the shipp, who were verye desirous thereof, was that, the moneye being in theyr handes, the markett and pryses of the callicoe lanes [*i.e.*, lawns] woulde bee spoyled for us, being, withoute that, hard enough for us to prevent.

[1] The tomb was close to the shore (*Letters Received*, iii. 131). It is not recorded in the Madras volume of *Indian Monumental Inscriptions* (1905), and may have been destroyed by a tidal wave, such as that of 1864, "which practically wiped much of the town off the face of the earth" (*Imperial Gazetteer*, xvii. 217).

[2] It may be inferred that the will did not dispose of the residuary estate, but was confined to specific bequests. The words "for our provision" indicate that Browne wished the residue to be employed as part of the capital for the Voyage; but Article 7 of the commission required that everything belonging to a deceased factor should be "safelie reserved and brought home for England". It is not apparent why the crew should have claimed the residue, but probably they wanted only the use of it for the Voyage, in order to employ it in private trade.

Wee dispatched the great *Lingua*[1] with the orderered [*sic*] presents for Condapeli, according to the resolution formerly taken. *10 ditto.*

Departed the Gouvernours, Sabander and mooste all persons of any office towards Condapoli, to the greate Gouvernour Mir Sumela. *15 ditto.*

Wee gotte a letter from the foresayde *Lingua*, putting us in good hope for the obtayning of that which hee was sente for. *27 ditto.*

Returned the Gouvernour Mir Sadardi, the Sabander and *Lingua*, having effected nothing, to our greate admiration [*i.e.*, surprise]. Howbeit, hee gave us good reason and contentment, the principall occasion being that this Gouvernour hathe anewe farmed the countrie for 3 yeares nexte ensuing; and hee, understanding what wee requyred of the greate Gouvernour, hathe obtayned so muche as a denyall,[2] hoping to gette some profitte from suche shipps as might come heereafter, or else att leaste thinking to make suche shipps beholding to him for the abatement of the custome, or else that it shalbee in his power to doe as shall seeme good unto him. Butt yett wee are well assured that before hee will suffer any shipp to departe hee will give abatement in the custom, so that the next shipps that come, if they stand stifly in it, shall have leave to trade to their contentment. Howbeit, wee are hartely sory that our good intent hath had no better successe. *4 October.*

Besides this, no matters of importance happened to us, butt wee putte our trade in practize with good successe, selling our goods to reasonnable profitt, as appeareth by the bookes thereof kepte more att larg, till the 30 December, whenas it was resolved that the shipp shoulde departe for Petapoli, to hasten forward the weavers there for the deliverye of their goods, as also the paynters[3] att Musilpatam to make an ende of the paynted lawnes which were in their hands. And this daye the shipp departed,

[1] *I.e.*, chief interpreter; *lingua* is Portuguese. Kondapalli is a famous fortress on the north bank of the Kistna; at this time it was also an administrative centre.

[2] Perhaps this means that it was a denial *pro forma*, not a final refusal, but 'a move in the game', leaving the Governor free to bargain with the merchants of each ship as it arrived.

[3] *I.e.*, the craftsmen who 'painted' the plain cloth ('lawnes'), to produce the goods demanded throughout the markets from Java eastward.

having in hir 68 packes of lawnes, the reste of the capitall to bee imployed with all possible speede for to bee readye to goe for Bantam by the fyrst of February.

[1612 *N.S.*] *20 January. The King off Musilpatams decease.* Deceased Cotobaxa,[1] King of Baddaga or Lollongana, being lykewyse King of Musilpatam, (in regard whereof) whereby it was thought a great tumulte woulde have bene; butt it was prevented by the wisedome of Mir Masunim, who presently electing [*read* elected] Mahumad Unim Cotobaxa,[2] being sone to the brother of the deceased King who lefte no childeren behynde him, to the kingdome, being a younge man of greate hope of aboute 21 yeares, to the greate joye of the common people, who did hope for a better gouvernment then had bene in his uncles tyme, who had putt all in the handes of the Persians,[3] butt this shewethe himselfe wholly to the contrarye, and an ennemye to Mir Sumela, the fountayne of all tirannie. What will come of it tyme will shewe; in the meane tyme wee were in no small perplexitie, fearing the woorste, I having in Musilpatam very neere readye 40 packes, which, notwithstanding, I gott licenced[4] with little laboure, and were sente in 2 boates for Petapoli, where they arryved in safetye.

26 ditto. My buysinesse being almooste done and cleared, thinking

[1] Muhammad Qulī Qutbshāh; the last word is the formal title of the dynasty, the *x*, misread by Purchas as *r*, having the sound of *sh* in Portuguese. Baddaga represents *vadagar*, 'northerner', a name used in Vijayanagar to denote the Telugu-speaking peoples to the north; quotations in *Hobson-Jobson* (*s.v.* Badega) show that this name was familiar to the Portuguese on the East Coast, who usually furnished the interpreters. Lollongana is probably the translator's misreading of Tellengana, *i.e.*, Telingāna, the older local name of this part of the country.

[2] The name of the new King was Muhammad, son of Muhammad Amīn, and in popular speech he would have appeared as Muhammad-i Amīn. The correct name of the 'king-maker' as given in the chronicles is Mu'min Khān, who held the post of *Pīshwā*. In a later entry the name appears as Mahumim, which is more nearly correct; this is one of several instances where the translator misread *h* as *s*. The interchange of *m* and *n* in the two names may be either an interpreter's metathesis or, more probably, the translator's misreading; in the Dutch script of the time *-min* would be represented by six practically uniform up-and-down strokes, and the position of the dot over the *i* (sometimes omitted) would be the only guide to the reader.

[3] Golconda politics were dominated by the feuds of three parties, the Deccanis or local men, the Habshis or Africans, and the Persian immigrants; the Mīr Jumla of the moment was Persian, and Floris here doubtless reproduced the aspirations of the Opposition as he heard them in Masulipatam.

[4] *I.e.*, for export.

onely to go reckon with the Gouvernour aboute his custome, but comming thether I founde another crowe to pull; for having solde to him some cl[o]ath and lead, bespeaking for theym some sortes of lawnes with him, whereof the mooste parte was delivered unto mee, some fewe onely excepted, which I thoughte to shorten him in the custome, hee woulde heare of no reconing, saying hee had bargayned or contracted with mee for the somme of 4000 pagades,[1] which I shoulde fyrste take of him and then hee woulde recken with mee. Uppon which false speeches I coulde not tell almooste what to answere, as being the greateste lyes that ever were spoken of mee in my presence. Att laste I asked him howe, where, when, by whome, in whose presence, what broker, what sortes of lawnes, att what pryce and other circumstances I had contracted and aggreed with him, where his or my wryting of any suche contracte was to bee seene, or who were witnesses to suche a contracte. Butt all these weyghtye reasons were not suffecient to bring this villaine to any reason, butt answered that, seing I had not kepte promise with him, hee woulde also breake his, thinking to recken the custome att 12 per cent, which wee had aggreed att 4 per cent, all his reasons being that hee was a Mir and sayde hee was borne of Mahomet posteritie, and that his woords were of more strengthe then myne, being a Christian.[2] In this difference wee were, I seing no meanes howe to come to an ende with suche a knave, for all my money was imployed, and in Petapoli were butt aboute 500 R[eal]s, which coulde stande butt in little steede; thus not knowing at laste howe to come to an ende, some meanes or other muste bee used, the tyme not suffering to write to Golconda to the newe King, and seing I had no meanes to ende with friendshipp, I resolved to begin with enmitye, and caused all my goods, being 10 packs of lawnes, my cheste and other luggage, to bee broughte att the custome howse, and so wente to the Gouver-

Difference with the Gouvernour off Musilpatam.

[1] The pagoda, the principal gold coin current in Golconda, was worth at this time about 7*s*. or 7*s*. 6*d*.; the unit is discussed in *Golconda*, 91 ff.

[2] Professor H. A. R. Gibb informs me that in strict Islamic law the evidence of a Christian can in no circumstances be accepted against that of a Moslem. The Governor thus had the law on his side; the additional claim to superiority as a Mīr, or Saiyyid, that is, a descendant of Muhammad, is a matter of usage, not law.

noure, telling him that my intent was to leave all the aforesayde goods with him in his custodie till the next yeare, hoping as then to aske accounte of him for theym and the interest according to the tyme; and in regard that att present I had no tyme to wryte to the Company for to complayne of his villanye, I tooke all the Moores [*i.e.*, Moslems] to witnesse of what had passed, for in future tyme to certifye and affirme the King and his Counsell of my innocencye; and yf anye unquyetnesse did followe, to ascribe the same unto him and not to us, not owing one penny to any body nor having wronged any one, butt any body doing to us to the contrary, wee had wherewith to revenge us. But notwithstanding all these threatnings hee sette little by theym. The Moores, doing their beste to take upp the matter, att laste broughte it so farre that I shoulde take of him a percell of *poupenys*,[1] which were naughte [*i.e.*, worthless], and yett woulde sell theym very deare, whereunto I coulde not condiscend, till att the verye laste, when I sawe there was no other remedye, taking the same, as God knoweth, muche agaynst my will, as not being woorth halfe the money. The knave having had his will, all things wente smoothly before the wynde, and wee reconed together; but, when it came to paying, I had enough to scrape and gather oute of all corners for to paye him. Being contented, hee shewed mee the beste countenance hee coulde possibly, and so wee parted in good friendshippe as it seemeth.

Aggreement with the Gouvernour.

Adi primo *February*. *Departing from Musilpatam.*

Wee departed from Musilpatam overland for Petapoli, whereas lykewyse was a little brabbling [*i.e.*, contention], butt all wente of well.

7 ditto.

Having imbarqued ourselves withoute having made any penny in badde dettes, or leaving any remnants behynde us on shoare, having gayned so muche by our marchandizes as to cleare all charges of giftes, customes and otherwyse, besydes the imploying[2] of 644 R 8, so that wee were wholy to our owne wisshing, having

[1] Poupenys, or popenys, appear in a list of goods sent for sale in the north of Siam (*Letters Received*, iii. 156). They were some kind of 'painted' goods, but their exact nature has not been determined; a later entry suggests that they were shawls or wraps of a particular type.

[2] 'Besydes' means 'apart from'. The reference is to the fact that a chest of reals, which was ear-marked for Bantam (*First Letter Book*, 386), had to be drawn on in order to pay the customs at Masulipatam; its recoupment is recorded below under 28th April.

yett a good monson to perfourme our voyage, our estate is att this present in verye good being, thankes bee to Almightie God, who hencefoorthe prosper the same to the glorye of His Holy Name and our comforts. Amen.

Before our departure from Petapoli wee had newes of the arryvall of the shipp called *der Goes* in Musilpatam, comming from Bantam, which had taken 2 or 3 small pryses, so that it seemeth there is warres agayne,[1] but in regarde of the shortenesse of the tyme wee woulde [? could] learne butt little newes. *The shipp* der Goose *arriveth in Musilpatam.*

In the month of October wee had newes by the waye of Dabul, where 2 shipps of Mocha[2] were arryved, saying that in June laste there had bene 4 English shipps att Mocha, who living att fyrste in good friendshipp, att laste brabblings arose, so that the English wente awaye muche discontented; some saye that att [*i.e.*, on] both sydes some have beene slayne, and althoughe it bee diversly reported, yett I do confidently beleeve that some suche thing there is, and that it muste bee Sir Henry Middleton; and so muche the rather, because that even nowe att our departure there came flying newes that 2 shipps shoulde bee in Suratta, but are not assured of it, for att our arryvall wee dispatched letters overland to the Englishe residing att Suratte,[3] butt have nott heard anything backe agayne. This is all woorthye the noting that wee have learned during our aboade uppon those coastes.

[1] The allusion is to the truce for twelve years between Spain and Holland, which came into force in the East in October, 1610, but had little or no effect in practice as between Dutch and Portuguese. The *der Goes* was a Dutch ship employed at this time in the Company's Asiatic trade.

[2] See *Letters Received*, i. pp. xxxiii ff., for a concise account of Sir Henry Middleton's voyage to the Red Sea in 1610–11. Dabul, or Dabhol, was a port on the west coast of India, which at this time had a regular trade with Arabia.

[3] One letter is printed in *Letters Received*, i. 136. It was addressed to "Will. Finch or other merchants they suppose to be resident in Surat". Finch had left Surat for Agra more than a year before, and there was no regular factory there at this time; the letter was handed to Sir Henry Middleton on 27th December, 1611 (*Purchas*, I. iii. 271).

[CHAPTER III

BANTAM]

Being come aboorde wee have bene hindered by calmes and contrary wyndes to gette from the lande till wee founde ourselves 40 leagues in [*i.e.*, at] sea; then, getting E. and N.E. wyndes, wee sette oure course towards the lyne, S.S.E.

17 Marche. Wee were att the height of 6 degrees, and passed between Ceilon and Atchin with fayre wether and many calmes.

Anno 1612. *27 Marche. The passing of the lyne.* Wee were even passed the lyne, having somtymes calmes and hard showres of rayne. Wee founde by the variation that wee were driven muche aboute [*i.e.*, towards] the west.

7 Aprill. Wee came by 3 ilands, and shortely after wee sawe the land of Sumatra, and were att 4 degrees, having 4 degrees variation, which differed 100 (miles) leagues from our guessing [*i.e.*, reckoning], being driven so muche more aboute [*i.e.*, towards] the W. then our guessing was.

11 ditto. Wee passed the Iland of Engana,[1] lying aboute 19 lèagues withoute the land of Sumatra.

12 ditto. Being Easterdaye, wee entered the Straite of Sunda, and came aboute 2 (myles) leagues neere the Salte Iland, whereas wee mette with a mightye streame which putte us backe agayne oute of the Strayte, not being able to gette the lande either att one or other syde, dryving in that fasshion till the 22, and then wee came att an ancker att the mooste westerlieste corner or pointe of Java. There wee tooke in some freshe water, and sett sayle agayne the 24th in the morning, keeping along the coaste of Java till wee came to discover the passage betweene Java and the ilands, being a very fayre place to enter, having good grounde for anchorage att the syde of Java, with which wee did stoppe it

[1] The course taken was 'outside Sumatra', not through the Straits of Malacca. Engano is the most easterly of the islands lying off Sumatra, and on this course was the regular sea-mark for the Sunda Strait leading to Bantam. The 'Salte Iland', mentioned just below, denotes the Krakatoa group inside the Strait.

that night till the 26 of Aprill, whenas wee arryved in the roade of Bantam, our men being in good and healthfull disposition. God Almightie bee thanked for all His mercies shewed unto us. ***The arrivall att Bantam.***

Being arryved in the roade of Bantam there came presently aboorde of us Mr Augustine Spalding,[1] who declared unto us the state of Bantam, and that since the departure of David Middleton there had bene no Englishe shipps heere, neyther had they heerd any newes of Sir Henry Middletons shipps, which makethe us to presume that the newes of Mecha [*i.e.*, Mocha] is true. Moreover, hee sayde there were arryved 3 Holland and Sealands [*i.e.*, Zeeland] shipps, whereof the shipps called *der Veer* and *Banda* were gone for the Moluccas, together with the pinnas called the *Halfe Moone*, and that the shipp *Bantam*, beinge arryved a whole month after the others, not being able to come to the Moluccas, laye att present att Jacatra,[2] to go for Joor [*i.e.*, Johore] and Patanie; which foresayd shipps brought newes that the *Hector*, the *Clove* and the Irishe shipp[3] were not come foorth in Maye laste. Whereatt wee marvayled very muche, not being able to guesse what might bee the cause thereof, seing wee ever feared to come to late to Bantam. God Almightie preserve theym, granting theym a prosperous voyage to the good contentment of their masters. 26 *Aprill.*

After that wee had discoursed together, wee have consulted what were beste to be done (for) by us to aggree with the Gouvernour in the matter touching the custome, in regard both the English and the Dutche had payde no custome before this tyme; but this Gouvernour had broughte in the matter per force, setting the custome att 5 per cent. Whereunto the Dutche not

[1] Spalding appears to have gone out to the East on the first Voyage. He was in the Moluccas with David Middleton, and in 1609 was appointed to the charge of the factory at Bantam (*First Letter Book*, 95 *n.*; *Letters Received*, i. 5).

[2] Jakatra, the port east of Bantam, where the Dutch subsequently established their capital, Batavia.

[3] The *Clove, Hector*, and *Thomas*, constituting the eighth Voyage, sailed from the Downs on 18th April, 1611 (*Purchas*, I. iv. 337). Writing to Surat, Antheunis and Floris said they were to be followed by "the *Hector*, the *Clove* and a ship built in Ireland" (*Letters Received*, i. 137); apparently when they started they had not heard that the third ship was to be named *Thomas*.

willing to condiscende, lade and discharge all their goods att Jacatra, thinking to breake upp their lodging[1] att Bantam. The which being well considered by us, wee coulde not tell well what to resolve, fearing to have the name of bringing in an evill custome; yett in regard the Company had neyther howse nor men att Jacatra, and that wee were compelled to bring some goods on shoare, wee thoughte it fitting to speake with the Gouvernour to see whereunto hee coulde bee broughte.

27 ditto. Thus this daye Mr Spalding and I went ashoare, taking with us a present of lawne, comminge to speake with him the same night, and after dyvers complements fell to our purpose, asking him leave to lande our goods (to) in the manner formerly used. Hee, understanding our meaning, sayde it might not bee so, alledging dyvers purposes which were not altogether withoute reason; yett wee propounding unto him that our shipp was the fyrste that was come from Choromandell, and had bene att great charges, which wee desired him to consider, hee putt us in good hope, suffering us to departe homewards that night, with promise to call us againe the nexte daye and, having consulted with his [blank in MS] to give us a good answere; whereuppon wee departed.

28 ditto. In the morning very early the Pangaran[2] caused us to bee called, and, after many friendly woordes and excuses, hee tolde us that it might not bee that the custome or toll shoulde bee given altogether free to us, in regard the King was att greate charges and his revenewes butt little, and yf hee shoulde receyve nothing of suche shipps, who then woulde bee able to doe it? Yett to shewe us honoure and give us contentment, hee was contented to give us some abatement, and that wee shoulde offer ourselves what wee were willing to give. Whereuppon, after long consultation had, seing it impossible to come of otherwyse, wee offered him 2½ per cent. Whereuppon hee was contented to lette it att 3 per cent, the which wee accepted, referring the reformation of this to the shipps that maye come hereafter, which may beare it oute with a fitter opportunitie, though wee, who[3] had

The aggreement aboute the toll or custome at Bantam.

[1] Contemporary Dutch *logie*, 'residence'. [2] Malay *Pangĕran*, Governor.

[3] The grammar is defective; some such words as "were helpless in the matter" should be supplied after "might bee loste".

no laysure and were but in a manner readye for a flight, either for one place or another, leaste any monson might bee loste. Thus being aggreed with him, wee ordayned a cargasoon,[1] something of every sorte, to bee landed, to see howe the pryses woulde fall oute, causing to that effecte a shoppe to bee made for to sell as well by the small or retayle as in grosse.

Heere Mr Spalding shewed us the accounte of Mr Heamsorte,[2] and the letter of Sir Henry Middleton, being writte from the baye of Saldana,[3] wherein hee expresly charged the liegers[4] att Bantam to buye as muche pepper as was possible for the lading of his shipp or shipps, and yf in case they had no money nor stock, then to use their credit, bothe att Bantam, Priaman,[5] as also in the Moluccos, and that att his comming hee woulde give good contentment to everybody. Whereuppon the sayd Heamsorte tooke of one Nachoda Tingall[6] 6000 R8 att $3\frac{1}{2}$ and 4 per cent per month, more then a yeare agoe, buying as then the pepper att $1\frac{3}{4}$ and 2 R8 the sack, which att this present is woorthe 12 in [*i.e.*, or] 13 R8 the 10 sacks, and apparant to come to 1 R8 the sack with this newe growthe aboute.[7] Some 14 dayes before our arryvall deceased the sayde Nachoda Tingall, making his sisters sone his heyre, who to his good fortune gott this recognition [*i.e.*, acknowledgment] of Heamsorte closely[8] into his handes; whereas the Gouvernour of Bantam did crosse [*i.e.*, oppose] the will, desiring that Nachoda Tingalls brothers sone shoulde bee chiefest heyre. Whereuppon the cousins entered theyr sute att

The historie off Nachoda Tingall & th borrowing off 6000 R8 by Mr Heamsorte.

[1] The Spanish word *cargazon* was at this time used in both English and Dutch. The dictionaries give only the meaning of 'the cargo of a ship', but in the East the word was occasionally used, as here, in the narrower sense of a portion of a cargo, or 'consignment'.

[2] Thomas Emmesworth sailed with David Middleton on the fifth Voyage, and was left at Bantam, where he died shortly afterwards (*First Letter Book*, 302; *Purchas*, I. iii. 238, 245).

[3] 'Saldana' is Table Bay, not the bay farther north now called Saldanha.

[4] This word was used in various senses; here it may be taken as 'representatives or residents abroad' (*OED*, seventh meaning).

[5] One of the pepper ports on the west coast of Sumatra.

[6] 'Nachoda' is *nākhudā*, Persian for the captain of a ship; the correct form of Tingall is matter for conjecture.

[7] Presumably the new crop of pepper coming forward.

[8] *I.e.*, 'secretly'.

lawe, not being come to an ende att our departure; and nobody knowing of this money butt onely the aforesayde sisters sone, who had the recognition, hee requested that it might bee kepte secret, for else the Gouvernoure woulde gette a hande in it; which was promised him by Mr Spalding and performed by us. For wee, seing so chargeable an intereste running on att the charge of the Company, offered him payement of the whole somme in apparell according to the markett pryse; butt hee, fearing that thereby the matter might come to light, durste nott accepte of it, but woulde rather staye till the nexte shipps that shoulde come to receyve his payement then in money. Whereuppon wee tolde him that that woulde not so come us to pass,[1] seing wee offered to give him contentment, or else hee shoulde desiste from asking henceforward any interest. But hee alledging his reasons agayne, wee fynally aggreed that hee shoulde not have any interest for the next 3 months ensewing; and yf hee were not payd by that tyme, then to have interest as before. Wherewithall hee was contented, and a wryting being made of it, it was delivered in handes of Mr Spalding. And this is all that according to reason wee coulde doe in this matter.

Succadama. By order of David Middleton there was sette a factory in Succadama,[2] and is continued by Mr Spalding; but our witts are not able to conceyve to whose profite this is done, for the dyamonds are bought there att 16 R8 the carratt, good and bad, one with another; and, besides, there coulde not bee imployed in that place passing 2[000] or 3000 R8 yearely; uppon which stock 5 Englishemen att the leaste muste bee mayntayned and as many Moores [*i.e.*, Moslems]. The charges of setting foorth the junckes, the presents in Succadama, and other charges woulde stande att leaste in 2000 R8 yearely. Nowe, everyone maye make a reconing what a stone of 1 carratt will come to stande in; butt I do firmely beleeve that the same is sette upp and continued for the dryving of a private trade, David Middleton having sente thether for his owne selfe 400 R8, besides that what others

[1] Dutch *komen te pas* means 'to suit'.

[2] Sukadana on the west coast of Borneo. David Middleton ordered Spalding to send a vessel there to buy diamonds; his journal does not say that he ordered the establishment of a factory (*Purchas*, I. iii. 246).

doe; so that it is easie to bee thought what becommeth of the beste stones, and who beareth the charges. Truely the Company hath tyed us to strictly,[1] seinge the Englishemen trade so openly and grosly, as heere in Bantam wee have seene and bene informed, and fynde by Mr Browne, so that wee have good reason to complayne; butt nowe wee muste go thorough, for our complainte cometh to late.

They take Mr Brounes money for the accounte off the Globe.

Mr Brownes money, in regard wee founde no shipps heere wherewith to make it over, was founde good to bee kepte for the accounte of the *Globe*, for dyvers reasons, whereof wee shall wryte to the Company more att large.[2]

Heere wee founde 4 China junckes, which had brought very little goods of any importance, as rawe silkes, velvetts, damasks or taphaties [*i.e.*, taffetas], and suche bad and filthy geare as ever came in Bantam, the beste whereof was boughte upp by the Dutche, and the reste by some of China and other strangers, to bee transported for Atchin and Priaman, so that there was butt little lefte to bee boughte by us. And in regard of the scarcitie of the R8 in Bantam, which for the mooste parte were boughte upp by the Chinesians, the lawnes were in small requeste, onely to barter agaynst pepper, to which wee woulde not harken, hoping that towards the newe growth the lawnes wilbee better requested and the pepper better cheape. And seing that for this tyme heere was nothing else to bee done, wee resolved to departe hence for Patanie towards the fyrste of June nexte comming, and so for Siam, and to leave heere suche lawnes as wee hope maye bee beste requested; and according to this resolution wee have ordayned to leave heere all our *tapés kitchill*[3] and *tapé*

[1] The question of private trade is discussed in the Introduction, § 7.

[2] See the entry of 7th September, 1611, regarding Browne's estate. Some explanation of the action now taken was required, because it was contrary to the provisions of the commission for the Voyage; the letter, if one was written, is not extant.

[3] *Tapé* represents Javanese *tapih*, which at the present day means a woman's skirt; but the word seems to have been used by Dutch and English merchants in a wider sense, equivalent to the Malay *sarong*, the nether garment worn by both sexes, and the most important single item in the trade of this region; they were usually of 'painted' cloth, made on the Coromandel Coast. *Kitchill* is Malay *kĕchil*, 'small'. *Tapé* girdles may mean sashes made of the cloth used for *tapés*, but the exact nature of these goods is uncertain.

girdles for the making upp[1] of the 4000 R8, the reste to remayne to bee imployed for the accounte of the shipp the *Globe*, as appearethe more att large by the instruction lefte with Augustin Spalding and George Chancey,[2] according to which they are to rule theymselves, as also an instruction for the nexte shippes that were to come and to go for the coaste of Choromandell.

The lawnes[3] which fyrste wee had ordayned for the account of the 4000 R8 wee have kepte for the accounte of the shipp, seing that att this tyme they were nott heere requested, and especially because wee woulde fayne have of all sortes in the shipp, to trye what sorte woulde yeelde beste profitt, for a direction agaynst the second tyme, and lefte the *tapé sarassas*[4] att Bantam, as before is mentioned, seing those are mooste requested there and yeelde mooste profite.

George Chanci lefte on land.

Mr Browne and Simon Irens[5] being deceased, and being tyed by order of the Company to leave a man att Bantam, which fell very harde to us, wherefore wee woulde fayne have taken Augustin Spalding into oure service agayne,[6] offering him 10*li.* sterling, butt coulde not perswade him, whereof I thinke Succadama to bee the cause, wee have bene faynte [*i.e.*, fain] to helpe

[1] See the entry of 7th February, above; the chest of reals ear-marked for Bantam had been drawn on to pay the customs at Masulipatam, and was now recouped in goods.

[2] George Chauncey was one of the four factors on the *Globe*, and, as mentioned below, was left at Bantam under clause 19 of the commission (*First Letter Book*, 386).

[3] 'Lawnes' denotes here the plain calico or piece-goods bought in India, as distinct from the 'painted' goods.

[4] Malay *sĕrasah* denoted a particular kind of 'painted' cloth used for skirts; it follows from this entry that the 'small skirts' mentioned above were made of *sĕrasah*.

[5] This must be Symon Evans, one of the factors named in the commission; Floris probably wrote the name 'Ivens,' and in some forms of Dutch script *r* and *v* are almost identical.

[6] The word 'again', which is used twice in this sentence, does not mean that the men concerned had left the service of the Voyage and now returned to it; the Dutch equivalent *wederom* was often used to indicate a second or consequential act in a series, and the meaning appears to be that, requiring somebody to replace Chauncey, they first offered the position to Spalding, and, on his refusal, appointed Persons (or Parsons, as in *Letters Received*, i. 312). The commission authorised the employment as factors, in case of need, of the purser and his mate; the purser was Robert Littlewood, so it may be inferred that Persons was purser's mate.

ourselves with suche as wee founde, ordayning that George Chancy shoulde tarry heere on land to followe the order of the Company, taking on againe in his place John Persons, promising him 50ss. per month, giving him the name or tittle of merchant, for, having a good reporte, wee have putte so muche uppon him the better to incourage him to do us further service. *John Persons taken on.*

Thus, seing that there was no more to bee done heere, wee have followed our resolution, and having writte our successe [*i.e.*, results] att large, with the coppies of our bookes and other remembrances, wee sealed those papers in a booke, leaving the same with Augustin Spalding to bee sente for England with the fyrste shepps [*i.e.*, ships, Dutch *schepeu*], to Sir Thomas Smith and [the] Company. Wee embarked ourselves from Bantam the laste of May, having buryed a man att Bantam, being the 7th person that dyed in our whole voyage, and lefte another to Augustin Spalding, whome hee sente for Succadama.

[CHAPTER IV

PATANI]

Primo *June*. In the night wee sette sayle, being conducted aboord by Sr. [*i.e.*, Signor] Cuteles, Pr. Segers and others.[1] And being the halfe waye of Sumatra wee gott a mightye cake[2] oute of the E. of rayne, wynd and foule wether, so that wee ran behynde certayne ilands under the coaste of Java, till towards the evening the wether growing more tractable, and then wee sette sayle agayne.

3 *ditto*. Wee came under the coaste of Sumatra, and having passed a greate breache, by reason of a shole, in passing from Java to Sumatra. Heere wee tooke oure course N.N.E.; butt eschewing dyvers sholes, wee wente somtymes E. and sometymes W.

4 *ditto*. Wee passed the sholes of Sumatra, and the 5 wee came by the lowe Iland,[3] which lyeth hard [*i.e.*, close] under Sumatra, so that it can hardly bee discerned to bee an iland. Heere wee loste a man by the flixe [*i.e.*, flux, dysentery].

6 *ditto*. Wee passed betweene the iland of Lusapara [Lucipara] and the land of Sumatra, and before wee came neere the iland wee had scarce 4 faddem depthe and muddy ground aboute some 2 (miles) leagues from the shoare. But having gott the iland southerly as [well as] easte, wee presently gott deeper water of 11 and 12 faddem, sandy grounde.

[1] Matheo Coteels succeeded Jacques l'Hermite as President for the Dutch Company at Bantam in 1611, and held that post till his death in 1613 (*van Dijk*, 11, 17, 20, 44). Pieter Segertsz had been in the East since 1607, and at this time was senior factor at Bantam (*De Jonge*, *Opkomst*, iii. 74, 397; iv. 5).

[2] 'The halfe waye of Sumatra' means half-way across the mouth of the Sunda Strait. 'Cake' is Dutch *kaak*, which has many meanings besides 'cake'; at sea, as here, it means 'squall'.

[3] From the map, this must be Boom Island. The islands, etc. mentioned below are shown on the map, so far as they can be identified; most of them are sea-marks, important only in navigation, and they are referred to in footnotes only when necessary.

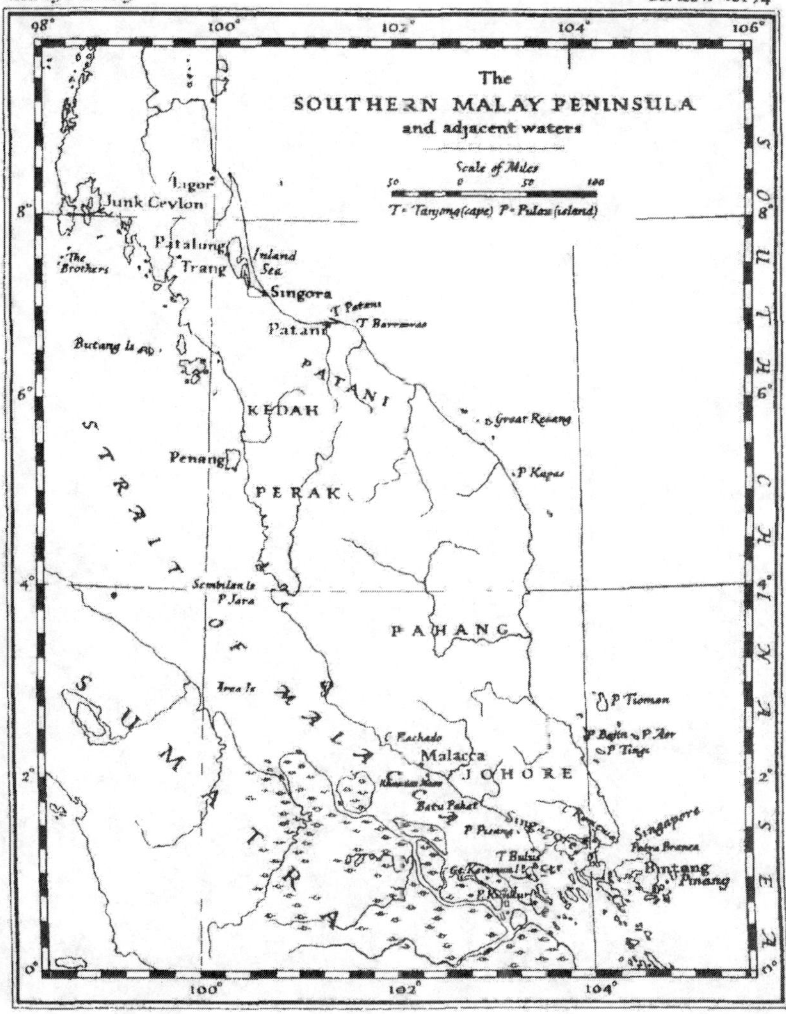

The
SOUTHERN MALAY PENINSULA
and adjacent waters
Scale of Miles
50 0 50 100
T = Tanjong (cape) P = Pulau (island)
98°
100°
102°
104°
106°
8°
6°
4°
2°
0°
Ligor
Junk Ceylon
The Brothers
Patalung
Trang
Inland Sea
Singora
T Patani
T Barramas
Patani
Butang Is
PATANI
KEDAH
Great Redang
Penang
P Kapas
PERAK
Sembilan Is
P Jara
PAHANG
Arua Is
P Tioman
C Rachado
P Aor
P Tinggi
Malacca
JOHORE
Batu Pahat
P Pisang
T Bulus
Singapore
Pedra Branca
Bintang
Pinang
STRAIT OF MALACCA
SUMATRA
SOUTH CHINA SEA

Wee came in the Strayte of Palimbam,[1] betweene Banca and Sumatra. *7 ditto.*

In the night wee came by the river of Palimbam, called *Arbocas de Palimbam.* Heere wee were forced to come to an ancker by reason of the greate streame which came against us, having very read water on the coaste of Sumatra, a league or more from the shoare att 8 or 9 faddem. This daye wee loste 2 men with the flixe, to witte John Hunte and Chareboute, having dyvers other sicke of the flixe; yett wee hadd every daye fayre wether and a wholesome ayre, butt it was the corruption of Bantam which nowe brake foorth dailye. *8 ditto.*

Wee passed the mounte Manupin [*i.e.*, Manoembing], being the N.W. corner of the iland of Banca and att the ende of the Straite of Palimbam, beginning heere to bee very broad. This daye wee came mooste oute of sight of the mounte, and in the evening wee sawe the Ilands of Pulo Tayo,[2] or the Seaven Ilands; taking our course N. and N. by E., wee had 15, 16 and 17 faddem, sandy grounde. *9 ditto.*

In the morning wee had Pulo Pon juste att our stearne, and towards evening sawe the Iland of Linga sticking oute with his hares eares.[3] This morning dyed Arthur Smith of the flixe. *10 ditto.*

Aboute noone wee sawe Pulo Panying [*i.e.*, Pinang], and shortly after the Iland of Bintam [*i.e.*, Bintang]. *11 ditto.*

In the morning wee were by Pedra Branca[4] and sawe him, butt were not knowen. Att noone wee sawe N. from us 2 high ilands, whereof the W. is called Pulo Tingi, with a high tipp, *12 ditto.*

[1] *I.e.*, Palembang, now usually called Banka Strait. *Arbocas*, just below, represents Portuguese *as bocas*, 'the mouths'; the map shows several rivers flowing into the Strait from the direction of Palembang town.

[2] Malay *pulau*, 'island'. The Seven Islands are now marked as Tuju, or, on Dutch maps, Toedjoe.

[3] Like several subsequent passages, this is a reference to Linschoten's *Reys-Gheschrift*, which Floris quotes more than once as his guide to these waters. In ch. xxvii Linschoten refers to a hill on Linga which has two summits like the ears of a hare, forming a conspicuous sea-mark.

[4] Pedra Branca, 'White Rock', is the sea-mark on the north for the eastern entrance to the Strait of Singapore. Below, under 3rd November, 1613, Floris, following Linschoten, says it is "butt a rocke full of fowle and bedungd, which causeth the toppe to bee white, whereof it beareth the name". The words "were not knowen" seem to be a mistranslation, perhaps for "did not recognise him"; the rock was uninhabited.

and the E., being aboute 7 (miles) leagues seawards, is called Pulo Laor.[1] In the evening wee sawe Pulo Pisan, taking our course withoute aboute the ilands.

13 *ditto.* In the morning wee were E. from the Ile Pulo Timon [*i.e.*, Tiomar], being a great and high iland with 3 little iles att the north syde; lyethe under 2¾ degrees.

14 *ditto.* Att noone wee sawe the firme land,[2] making our course N.W. towards it.

15 *ditto.* Wee came by 3 or 4 ilands lying not passing [*i.e.*, more than] 1½ (miles) leagues from the land, called Pulo Capas; and this daye wee loste a man called Hugho Moore, a Scottsman.

16 *ditto.* Wee came by a greate many ilands lying att aboute 6 degrees, and are from Patanie aboute 26 (miles) leagues, and are called Redange.

19 *ditto.* Wee were by a great oute-poynting corner, having had butt little speede during these 3 dayes. When this corner is paste, those of Patanie beginne to see the shipps over the lowe land called Sabrangh,[3] being as then yett att the leaste 6 (miles) leagues from the roade; for one muste passe a lowe poynte, being sandye, with some fewe trees, and then to go on S. by W. and S.S.W. towards the roade, to shunne a shole of sande which is lefte lying att the lefte hande; all the reste is muddye grounde. From this corner seawards, about a (mile) league from the lande, lyeth a little rock above water, aboute which the depthe is 7, 10 and 12 faddem.

22 *ditto.* *Thei arrive in the roade off Petanie.* Wee came in the roade of Petanie, where wee found a Hollands shipp of Enckhusen[4] called *Bantam*, which was arryved there 10 dayes before us. The marchant, Wm. Jansen Neblet, with Matchys de Maire and Lambert Jacobsen, came aboord of us,

[1] Laor represents the Aor Islands. Pisan must be Bajin.

[2] Up to this point the course had lain outside the coastal islands; now they drew near to the mainland of the Malay Peninsula.

[3] The map shows a peninsula, Tanjong Patani, projecting sharply towards the north-west and sheltering the Bay of Patani. The town lies some little way up the river, and 'the Sabrangh' would thus denote the lowland between the town and the coast. The name is Malay *sabĕrang*, meaning 'across the river', but apparently it was used in Patani as a proper name.

[4] Enkhuizen, north of Amsterdam, on the Zuider Zee, was the seat of one of the 'chambers' in which the Dutch Company was organised. Each chamber sent out its own ships in conformity with the policy laid down by the central organisation.

of whome wee learned the manners and custome of the countrie; and att noone wee came to an ancker hard by the shipp *Bantam*, uppon 3 faddem depthe, att the heighte of 7 degrees, [blank] min. In the evening wee sente John Persons and Nasarchan[1] on shoare, to give notice that wee were Englishmen, and that wee had a letter[2] from His Majestie to the Queene of Patanie.

Heere arryved a Hollands pinasse called the *Greyhound* [*Hazewind*] of Enckhuysen, whereof was master Evert Janse[n], and Foulon Dragon merchant. They came from Benjarmasingh,[3] where in company of 3 pinasses they had burned and pilled the towne, in revenge of certayne wrongs done to theyr men heretofore. This pinas had order to go for Japon. In the afternoone our men came aboord agayne, bringing some officers of the countrie along with theym, who tolde us that wee shoulde staye with our letter till next Thursdaye, being the 26, for they muste fyrste make theymselves readye too receyve it honorably. And after wee had bestowed some presents uppon theym, they wente on shoare agayne. 23 *ditto.*

Some came aboorde agayne, among other the Chattis,[4] for to translate the Kings letter into the Malusian tongue; and after some questioning touching the opening of the letter, it was aggreed that hee [they] shoulde open it, and, having translated it and receyved some presents, they wente on shoare agayne. 25 *ditto.*

Wee wente on shoare in verye greate state, taking with us a present of aboute 600 R8 to accompanie the Kings letter, which 26 *ditto.*

[1] Probably the Nāsir Khān who is mentioned in Methwold's Relation as going with the party sent from Ayuthia to Chiengmai (*Golconda*, 45).

[2] No letter addressed to the Queen of Patani is given in the *First Letter Book*; presumably it was one copy of the general letter printed on p. 421.

[3] In the year 1607 the King of Banjarmassin, on the south coast of Borneo, caused a Dutch trading party to be massacred for the sake, it was supposed, of the goods they had brought (*Begin ende Voortgangh*, Matelieff's Voyage, p. 62). The failure to punish this outrage had an increasingly injurious effect on Dutch prestige, and eventually the authorities at Bantam decided to send this punitive expedition, which early in May of this year surprised, sacked and burned the town. The factor on the *Hazewind* was named Hans, not Foulon, Dragon (L. C. D. van Dijk, *Neerland's Vroegste Betrekkingen met Borneo*..., Amsterdam, 1862, pp. 1–6).

[4] *I.e.*, Chetties, merchants from the South Coromandel Coast; quotations in *Hobson-Jobson* (*s.v.*) show that the word was sometimes written 'Chattis' by the Portuguese. 'Malusian' must be the translator's misreading of Maleisian, *i.e.*, Malay.

otherwyse woulde butt little bee esteemed. Comming on shoare wee were reasonnably well receyved according to the manner of the countrye; the letter, being layde in a bason of golde, was carryed uppon an elephant, with minstrells and a good many lances and little flaggs. The Queenes Courte being sumptuously prepared, whereas the letter was redde; and understanding that it was for to have a free trade, shee did graunte it unto us, paying the dueties of the countrie as the Hollanders did. Againste which wee had little to replye for that tyme, but did accepte of the Queenes offer till wee shoulde bee infourmed of the lawes and dueties of the countrie; and so departed from the Courte withoute having seene the Queene. From thence wee were broughte to Dato Laxmanna,[1] the Sabander and chieftayne of the strangers. There a banckett of fruites was sette before us. From thence wee muste go to the Oran Caya Sirnora[2] in company of the Hollanders, who lykewyse were called thether. And after wee had eaten something there and some speeches had, and intreaties of Hendrick Janse[n][3] to lodge in his house that night, wee as yett not being provided of a howse, the which wee accepted, wee rid uppon elephants homewards.

They go a shore in Patanie, with his Majesties letter.

27 ditto. In the morning came Dator Besar[4] and Dator Laxmanna downe in the Ballaia, where wee had dyvers speeches, among the reste that wee had a letter to the King of Siam; and in regard the mounson was farre spente, wee desired leave of theym to builde a packhouse of brick, as the Hollanders have, to bring some of our goods on land, and to leave some of our men with

[1] Malay *dato'* has various honorific senses, but from the examples given below it was used in Patani as a prefix to the designations of the various Ministers, and it may be compared to the English 'Lord' in Lord Treasurer, Lord Justice, etc. Malay *Laksamana* is defined by Dr C. Otto Blagden as "a title roughly equivalent to Admiral, to which certain administrative and court duties on shore were also attached".

[2] Malay *Orangkaya* is a general title for persons of high position. 'Sirnora' may represent Sĕri Nara, *sĕri* being the Malay form of the Indian honorific prefix *srī*.

[3] The head of the Dutch factory at Patani.

[4] 'Dator' is probably the translator's misreading of Datoe, which appears in several later passages, and is Malay *dato'*. Malay *bĕsar* means 'great'; from the text, this officer was probably higher in rank than the Laksamana, and in Patani the term may have denoted the Chief Minister. *Balai* means a hall of audience, or court of an official.

theym till the shippe came backe from Siam, and that for wante of suche a howse wee shoulde bee in greate danger and hazard of our goods by fyre and other mischances. And notwithstanding that they suffered us to sette a factory there, according to our owne desire, yett they refused us to builde a packhouse which shoulde not bee subject to fyre, alledging that the Hollanders had traded there full 10 yeares before without it, butt having suffered fyre 2 severall tymes to theyr great dammage, it had bene graunted unto theym to builde the same howse, of which wee coulde not complayne as yett. Butt when wee answered that it woulde bee to late to builde suche a howse when the goods were burned, and that therefore wee muste looke to it before that come to passe, att laste, having longe buysied ourselves with these blockheads a great while, they harkened to our reasons a little better, and woulde certifye the Queene of it. And so wee parted from theym and wente aboord. Towards the evening the Queene sente us a refresshing aboord of some meate and fruites.

29 *till* primo *July.*

Wee ran dayly upp and downe to have licence for the building of a howse, and to knowe the customes of the countrie, because wee understood they were extreame high heere and more then wee had founde in any place before, butt coulde attayne to neyther of bothe, for nowe they woulde not consent to it, saying the Kings letter made no mention of it; and then they woulde builde a howse for us theymselves; and anon agayne that they woulde consider of it; so that suche people woulde have stinted a madde brayne.[1]

3 *July. The pinnas, the* Grey-hounde, *departeth for Japan, and send the Companys letters to Mr Wm. Adam.*

Departed the pinasse the *Greyhounde* for Japan, having in her 33 cases of silke and silke wares and a parcell of waxe. With which sayde pinasse wee sente the letters of the Company and other particular persons to Mr Wm. Adam,[2] which came as fitt

[1] No Dutch phrase has been found which could be mistranslated so as to give this curious expression. The context suggests that, in the original, 'madde' was used as predicate, not attribute; while 'stinted' may be an example of the occasional confusion recorded in the *OED* between 'stint' and the obsolete 'stent', meaning 'to stretch', as on the rack. The phrase may thus mean 'such people would have stretched, or racked, a brain to the point of madness', or more concisely, 'driven a man mad'.

[2] William Adams, a Kentish man, reached Japan in the year 1600 on the Dutch ship *de Liefde*, settled in the country, became a person of some

for us as ever anything could happen. Mr Skinner made acquayntance with the masters mate of the pinasse, and [*read* who] was even the verye same man which had broughte the letter from Mr Adam to Bantam to the Englishmen there, whereof himselfe was verye glad, as having an occasion to do a kyndnesse to Mr Adam, to whom hee was beholding, promising to deliver the letter to his owne hands; wee making no doute of the deliverie thereof, for otherwyse wee shoulde have had no meanes to do it, tor those of Japon are att enimitie with this place, and have burned Patanie twyce within these 5 or 6 yeares.[1] As yett wee cannot learne what is to bee done att Japon, butt att the returne of the aforesayde pinas wee hope to have better information, for as yett wee thinkethe that the trade for Japon is butt of small importance.

After muche running, toyling and giving of gifts, wee gott leave to builde a packhowse, they ordayning us a place hard by the Dutche howse, 30 faddem in lengthe and 20 in bredth. The howse shoulde bee 8 faddem long, 4 faddem broad and 10 *hastas*[2] highe, with the which wee were not well contented, because the Dutche howse was a great deale longer and higher; but in regard it coulde serve our turne, the tyme being shorte and the charges verye great as woulde not well beare the building of another

importance, and rendered substantial services to the first Dutch and English merchants in the country. The literature regarding his career is somewhat extensive; reference may be made to C. J. Purnell, *The Log-Book of William Adams*, London, 1916, and vol. iii of *De Reis van Mahu en de Cordes*, Linschoten Society, 1925. The letter from Adams mentioned in the text is presumably that which is printed in *Letters Received*, i. 142; it was written in October, 1611, and should have reached Bantam shortly before Floris' arrival there in April, 1612. John Skinner was one of the master's mates on the *Globe*, and became master in the following November, as related below.

[1] Japan, as a State, was not at enmity with Patani or Siam, and the reference must be to individual Japanese, whether temporary residents or crews of merchant or pirate vessels. About this time merchants and pirates from the Japanese seaports were active in the Gulf of Siam (*Satow*, 139, 193); they had an exceedingly bad reputation, and Sir Edward Michelborne recorded that "the Japons are not suffered to land at any port in India [in the wide sense] with weapons: being accounted a people so desperate and daring that they are feared in all places where they come" (*Purchas*, I. iii. 137). *Anderson* (44) mentions that the first Dutch factory in Patani was burnt by Japanese about the year 1605.

[2] *Hāsta* denotes the cubit used on the Coromandel Coast, where it was very slightly over 18 inches.

howse, wee did accepte of it. But when wee herde the great and excessive customes and giftes which they demanded of us, whereof they shewed us good and certayne proofe that the Hollanders did yearelye paye so muche, then wee coulde nott tell what to do; for fyrstely they asked 72 t.ª 5 mª 2 copon for a gifte,[1] which muste be done in 4 severall tymes, to witte, the fyrste is wee muste *sombah datang*,[2] that is to saye, give notice of our arryvall; the second is *sombah benaga*, or aske leave to lande your goods and to have free trade; the third is *somba datching* or licence to have the waights; the fourth is *sombah muson*, that is leave to shippe your goods and to departe; which 4 *sombahs* amounte to the somme afore mentioned. Besides this, to paye 5 per cent. for all goods comming in and going oute, and the waying [*i.e.*, weighing] money besides, the pepper paying 5 ms. per *barre* [*i.e.*, bahār] for the buyer, and 6 coupons for the seller,[3] and all other wares accordingly; so that wee were even amazed with these great charges, and wee alledging that wee had alreadye bene att greate charges for the present which was given att the deliverye of the letter, they made us answere, what Kings gave one to the other was another manner of reconing, butt this belonged to the gentilitie and certayne officers, whereof the Queene onelye hath a parte. Wee, seing they woulde not listen to anye abatement, sayde that wee coulde not yeelde unto it, butt woulde go home and consider of the matter.

Being come home wee pondered the matter together what was beste to bee done, for what [*read* while] by one meanes and another wee guessed [*i.e.*, calculated] the expenses woulde come to 4000 R8, being $\frac{1}{6}$ of our whole stocke or capitall, and to the contrarye wee had a greate deale of Maleysian apparell[4] which

[1] See the Note on Currency, Weights and Measures. The abbreviations in the text denote tael and mas (16 to the tael); the tael was worth about $2\frac{1}{2}$ reals of eight, or, say, about 10*s*., so the 'gifte' would be from 35 to 40*l*.

[2] Malay *sĕmbah*, 'to reverence'; but derivatives of the word express the giving of presents by an inferior to a superior. *Datang*, 'to arrive'; *benaga*, now written *berniaga*, 'to trade'; *daching*, 'a steelyard'. *Muson* is perhaps for *musim*, the Malay form of the Arabic *mausim*, 'season' or 'monsoon'.

[3] *Ms*. must be the same as *m*.ª above, *i.e.*, mas, containing 4 copans. The bahār varied with the locality, and sometimes with the goods; in Patani it was about 400 lb.

[4] *I.e.*, the dress-goods made in India specially for the Malay market.

Resolution. wee had expresly caused to bee made for this place, which woulde nott bee requested in other places. Secondly, that wee perceyved that in future tyme heere was something to bee done. Wee therefore resolved, seing wee had spente so muche alreadye, to taste of a soure apple, and for this tyme to make a triall, to have the more experience agaynste the tyme to come. Wherefore, according to our resolution, wee wente the nexte daye before the Ballee [*i.e.*, *balai*], aggreing in manner as aforesayde. Whereuppon wee presently fell to the building of the howse, so that[1] the tyme for the going to Siam drewe on verye faste, which did importe us very muche, making therefore all the hast that possibly wee coulde.

Meane while wee had hired 2 howses, the one for us, the other for the sicke men, which were in great number, seeming as yf the plague had bene in the shippe; and among all the reste Captayne Hippon, who had complayned of the flixe ever since his comming from Bantam, having bene some 9 or 10 dayes on shoare, dyed the 9th of July in the night aboute 11 of the clocke, by which man wee had toto [*sic*] greate a losse, as well in the gouverment of the shippe as in matters touching the seas; butt wee muste take patience and committe it to God, who is able to helpe and comforte us. Wee gave him a stately buriall according as the tyme woulde suffer. God Almightye graunte him a joyfull resurrection, and the lyke to us all. Amen.

Death of Capt. Hippon.

13 *ditto.* Wee al together wente aboord, whereas wee found our men in greate perplexitie, but, having called theym together, wee caused the article to bee read (before) unto theym, and then opening the boxe[2] No. 1, wee founde that Robert Browne was to succeede, butt hee being deceased wee opened the boxe No. 2, wherein wee founde Thomas Essington to succeede, hee being present. Whereuppon wee prayde God sende him joye, and delivered the commission and other wrytings unto him in presence of all the folkes, authorizing him as captaine and marchant. The which being done, wee departed asyde and con-

Thomas Essington made captaine.

[1] We should perhaps read, "because the time...which was very important for us...".

[2] The practice of the time was to place conditional appointments in sealed boxes, numbered serially, to be opened only in case of need. 'The article' is clause 17 of the commission (*First Letter Book*, 385).

sulted together, that seing Anthonie Hippon had bene captain and marchant, and that nowe Thomas Essington was captain and marchant, who in matters belonging to the seas was not sufficiently experimented, besides that wee had dayly great neede of him on shoare, to chuse a master under him, who in his absence might take the regard [*i.e.*, control] and charge; the which was founde fitting, and so John Johnson was chosen, as being the eldeste masters mate and bore the fyrste place. Therefore, calling all the men together, wee declared our resolution unto theym, who were well contented with it, having nothing to saye agaynste it. Wherefore, assembling agayne the company of the shippe, wee authorized the foresayde John Johnson as master of the shipp called the *Globe*, who was joyfully receyved of the whole company. Thus with this was (the peoples) our mens amazement [*i.e.*, anxiety] not a little sette asyde; and having thus instituted the newe gouvernment, wee required the newe captain, Thomas Essington, to take accounte of all the officers[1] of the shippe, eache in his calling, to see what was spente and what was yett remayning both of victualls and other furniture [*i.e.*, supplies], for the keeping of a good ordre in everything; and not to bee dismayde, butt to seeke our owne credits and our masters profitt as long as wee had a good shippe and God shoulde give us health, and to do our uttermooste endevoures to deliver to our masters both the shipp, the goods, and a true accounte, according to oure duetye.

John Johnson made master off the shipp.

Deceased Mr Thomas Smith, masters mate, an excellent astronomer and seaman, whereby wee had a greate losse, for the reste, God Hee knoweth, are butt so and so. Butt seing it is Gods will, wee muste take patience, for what mans judgement cannot doe muste bee committed to God, who bee mercifull unto us and graunte us that which is tending to our good. Amen.

14 ditto. The death off Thomas Smith, masters mate.

In the night wee had theeves in the howse, and was the strangest robberye as the lyke hath not much bene heard of; for being in our hyred howses, which were onelye made of reeds, and buysied in building of our owne, being all of us in the howse

17 ditto. Theeves in our house and are indammaged.

[1] At this period the term 'officers' comprised everybody above the rank of ordinary seaman. *Boteler* (11–31) enumerates the officers of a ship from the captain down to the 'swabber', whose mates were the lowest on the list.

above 15 persons sleeping, Mr Lucas and I in a bedde aparte lyinge close together, having a great black dogge lying under my cabine, my truncke standing att my feete (hard) close to the boording,[1] being no greater space betweene the bedde and coffer butt that onely the lidde might shutte and open; yett notwithstanding the theeves, clyming upp att the outesyde, cutting of an ende of the boording which onely was bounde with rotan, passing over my trunke, kreeping under my bedd by the dogg, and there by force wronge of [*i.e.*, wrung off] a pattlock, taking oute of my cheste 283 R8 and dyvers other prety things as also apparell linnen, and my rapier, which had att leaste 25 R8 in silver uppon it, standing att my beds syde, leaving Mr Lucas his rapier which was not passing 3 foote from it; and it is to bee wondered that neyther I nor nobody else in the house did see or heare anything, a burning lampe hanging in the howse, and watche kepte in the yarde, nor the dogge once for to barke. Wee have indeede had dyvers opinions and guessings of our owne howse servants and some other persons, butt coulde never gette any certayntie notwithstanding all the meanes wee used. Doutlesse they were resolute villaines.

Adi primo *August.* Oure howse being nowe readye, wee have thoughte it good to discharge suche lawnes as wee thought woulde bee beste requested heere, and to lette Pr. Floris staye by theym, to bring the trade in a trayne and to establishe the factorye, leaving with him John Persons and sixe men more. And thus having ended all our matters, the shippe was readye to sette sayle in the night

4 *ditto.* *The shipp the* Globe *departeth for Siam.* for Siam. God graunte theym a prosperous voyage. Since wee came from Bantam wee have loste 12 men of the flixe and some other yett sicke, so that in all wee have loste 19 persons, besides one which was lefte over att Bantam going for Succadama, which makethe 20 persons lesse then wee had att our comming foorth. God preserve the reste.

[1] 'Boording', substituted in the text for 'seeling', must refer to the side of the house, which was of reeds, fastened with rattan canes. The meaning of 'under my cabine' is not obvious; presumably the sea-term *kajuit* (cabin) was used to denote part of the house partitioned off for the chief merchants, but the text shows that the dog was under the bed, not under the house. Dutch *onder* is treated in the *Woordenboek* as two separate prepositions, one meaning 'under', the other 'among', and possibly Floris may have used the latter in the sense of 'inside'.

There wente awaye from hence a juncke for Buncasey,[1] with whome I wrote a letter to Siam, wherein I wrote the state I was in, and the small trade and vente that was in the lawnes which I had heere, as appearethe by the copye thereof. *20 ditto.*

The aforesayd juncke arryved hether backe agayne, not being able to perfourme her journey, and the letter was delivered mee backe agayne, to my greate griefe. I soughte all meanes possible for the conveyance thereof, either by sea or land, althoughe I shoulde have spente 100 R8, but it was not possible, for by water it was not feaseble, and by land no lesse then 4 persons woulde go together for feare of the tygers and upperwaters,[2] for they muste passe many rivers, asking 3t.[a] a man and the money beforehand, which I durste not doe, so it remayned undone to my greate griefe, and the reste muste do as it maye. *6 September*

This monthe the King of Joor overrunne the suburbes of Pasan, burning upp all, and lykewyse Campon China, which happened for a small occasion.[3] It seemed that those of Patania woulde come to aide theym of Pasan, butt they never mente it, whereby the Joorists keepe Pasan hard besieged, so that there beginneth to come a greate dearth in Pasan. What wilbee the ende tyme will shewe. *Jorists besiege Pasan.*

Thus being heere with the lawnes, having no vente att all, which is greatly to bee wondered, especially for mee who 4 yeares agoe sawe suche a vente in theym that it seemed the worlde hadde not clothings enough to provyde this place as was needfull, muche lesse to overfill itt; and that nowe it was so overcloyed that it is hardly possible that in a greate many yeares they can bee muche requested. Heere it might bee asked howe and from whence commeth this suddayne change, whereas before it was suche a continuall and proffitable trade, yea, the greateste of all

[1] From the details given in Linschoten's *Reys-Gheschrift*, ch. xxi, it appears that Buncasey or Bancosea was a port in the north-west corner of the Bight of Bangkok; it has not been found on modern maps.

[2] Dutch *opperwater*, 'floods coming from higher ground'.

[3] 'Joor' is Johore, the State at the extreme south of the Malay Peninsula. 'Pasan' is for Pahang, the State adjoining it on the north; this is one of several instances where the translator misread Floris' *h* as *s*. 'Campon' is Malay *kampong*, 'quarter'; and 'Campon China' must indicate a Chinese settlement outside the town. It will be noticed that Floris frequently dropped the final *-g* in eastern names.

The cause why the lawnes are so little requested.

the Indies. Butt the cause why the same lyethe nowe so under foote is this: that the Portingalls bring the same quantitye of clothing in Malacca as heeretofore they have done; heereuppon followed the Hollanders, who have not onely filled Bantam and Javan butt also all the Ilands of Molucca, so that they have no utterance att Malacca;[1] besides this there bee some shippes of the Moores [*i.e.*, Moslems] which trade for Tanasserin and provyde Siam; besides this 2 Portingall and a Moores shipp have founde oute a newe haven this laste yeare called Tarangh,[2] is a place hard by Keda; and this yeare arryved a Gusarat [*i.e.*, Gujarātī] and another from Nagapatam att Keda, bringing the lawnes overland, and so over filled it that no man ever sawe the lyke; and to all these wee come with 200 packes, the rumour whereof being sufficient to cause the pryse not to ryse these 10 yeares, and whereas I myselfe have made 3 and 4 of one, cannot att this present make 5 per cento; the woorste of all being that there is no vente, so that I am muche in doute that, yf it bee lykewyse so in Siam, from whence wee shall gather a stocke or capitall for to go agayne towards the coasts,[3] whereuppon the whole benefitte of the voyage dependeth; but yett wee cannott helpe it, for it lyethe not in mans wisedome, butt patience is the beste herbe which wee can use att this tyme. Yett, notwithstanding, nott to bee utterly dismayed, both for my owne credit and my masters proffit, I have resolved to sende a cargason for Maccasar,[4] an occasion presenting itselfe to make a tryall of what maye bee done there, that the Worshipful Company maye

[1] The meaning of this somewhat involved sentence is that formerly the Portuguese supplied the demand of various eastern markets from Malacca; now the Dutch were supplying most of these markets from Java, and Malacca was trying to sell its surplus stocks in Patani and Siam.

[2] In the later Portuguese period, when the transit dues charged at Malacca were very high, the practice of carrying the trade between India and Siam across the Malay Peninsula developed largely, though it had been in existence for an indefinite period. Tenasserim, or rather Mergui at the mouth of the Tenasserim river, was the most usual port for this traffic, but the text indicates that other routes also were used. Tarangh, or Trang, is scarcely 'hard by' Kedah, being more than 100 miles north.

[3] *I.e.*, the Coromandel Coast. The project for the Voyage indicates (*First Letter Book*, 424) that the goods bought in Siam were to be sold principally in those markets.

[4] Macassar, the chief market in Celebes.

have a good information of all what is to bee had and done in one and other place.

Being thus resolved, I ordayned for this buysinesse John Persons as marchant and Thomas Brett boson [*i.e.*, boatswain], with a Chodsie,[1] Ibrahim Geisart, to embarque theymselves in the juncke of Empan, with suche a capitall and instructions as appeareth by the coppye, with order to come backe agayne hether with the same juncke, and to give account of whatt hee shall have seene and learned. Whereuppon they have sette sayle this daye, having in theyr company the [Dutch] shipp *Bantam* and a small pinnas, built heere, called *Enchusen*. They were fyrste to go for Joor, and then the juncke and the pinnas shoulde go for Maccasar and so to the Moluccos. I had aggreed for 5 per cento for fraight. The greate shippe was to go for Bantam and so homewards; by which shippe I sente 2 letters directed to my brother; the one wherein was inclosed the letter to Sir Thomas Smith I gave to Mr Jansen Noblet, the other, being a copye of my letter to my brother, I gave to Mr Frauncys Barber, wherein I have written att large what hetherto hathe happened unto us, as more att large appeareth by the coppyes thereof [*not extant*]. God sende theym all a prosperous voyage.

8 October. *The shipp Bantam departeth.* *John Persons sente to Maccasar.*

Heere arryved 2 junckes from Siam, with whome came Cornelis Van Nieuvenroode,[2] who broughte mee a letter from Mr Lucas and Mr Essington, wherein they make a greate complaynte of the great trouble, payne and miserye which there they muste endure, and especially of the small lykelyhoode of fynding of any good markett, in regard of the greate quantitie of lawnes that were come from Tenesserin and Tarangh, and the countrye filled with warres besides, those of Cambois, Laniam and Jagoman[3] makeing theymselves readye joyntlye to

9 ditto.

[1] *I.e.*, Khoja, for Khwāja, a Persian title of respect, given to, or assumed by, merchants among other classes. 'Geisart' must be the translator's misreading of 'Gusarite', *i.e.*, Gujarātī, which appears below under 18th September, 1613.

[2] Cornelis van Neijenrode had been for some time in Siam, representing the Dutch Company along with Maerten Houtman (*van Dijk*, 33). He subsequently served for some years in Japan (*MacLeod*, i. 503 ff.).

[3] Cambodia, Lanshan or Luang Prabang, and Chiengmai. The relations of these countries with Siam are sketched in the Introduction; the 'warres' were mainly anticipations, as is explained further on.

fall uppon Siam; which wee muste committe to the Almightye God, who can prevente it yf it bee His godly will, who graunte us what is for our good. Wee cannot helpe it yf it will go thus of all sydes againste us.

14 *ditto.* Wee gotte newes of the arryvall of a small Portingalls shipp in Tarangh; butt yf there come no more there nor att Keda, the lawnes might happen to stiffen a little, which tyme will shewe.

25 *ditto.* Departed hence almooste all the juncks which pretended [*i.e.*, intended] for E. or S., to witte for Bornea, Jambi, Java, Macassar, Jortan and other places;[1] among whome was the juncke of Orancaya Raia Indra Mouda,[2] who in person embarcked himselfe, being fyrste to go for Bantam, from thence to Jortan, and so forwarde for Amboina and Banda, and comming backe agayne to putte to Macassar, and so hether agayne; with whome I sente a letter to Mr Spalding to Bantam, as appeareth by the coppyebooke. This is a prettye passing voyage,[3] and, happening well, oughte doutelesse to yeelde some profitte. I cannot imagine what the Hollanders meane, to suffer these Maleysians, Chinesians and other Moores[4] of these contries, and to assiste theym in theyr free trade thorough all the Indies, and forbidde it theyr owne servants, contryemen and bretheren uppon payne of death[5] and losse of goods; surelye a token of a greate ignorance or envye, suffering Turckes and heathen to growe riche rather then their owne countryemen shoulde gette their living: surelye a greate ingratitude and a token that Gods punishement is comming uppon theym.

[1] Jambi lies on the river of the same name, near the east coast of Sumatra; Jortan is Surabaya in East Java.

[2] The correct form of this name would be Orangkaya Raja Indĕra Muda.

[3] The meaning of 'passing' is not clear. Possibly it is used in the obsolete sense, recorded in the *OED*, of 'surpassing', *i.e.*, 'remarkable'; or it may be intended to denote a round voyage calling at many ports, though this meaning has not been found elsewhere.

[4] 'Other' is inaccurate, for the Chinese were of course not all Moslems. Purchas added in the margin: "A Dutch-mans testimony of Dutch iniquitie in his owne words, as they are in the translated copie". The "iniquitie" was not destined to be of long duration, for in 1616 some Dutchmen were allowed to leave the Company's service and trade in the Spice Islands on their own account (*MacLeod*, i. 159).

[5] It is not clear that the capital sentence was imposed for such trading. The Dutch phrase *lijf en goed* denotes 'person and property', and probably this phrase, or some variant of it, was in the original.

[CHAPTER V

SIAM]

Heere arryved by the grace of God the shipp the *Globe*, comming from Siam, having bene 8 dayes in the waye; and in regard of the greate change happened in this shorte tyme I will relate this voyage more att large. *In Siam. 11 November. Come on the roade off Siam.*

After they were departed hence the 4th of Auguste, they arryved on the roade of Siam the 15 ditto, casting ancker in the evening att 3 faddem, being high water; butt the nexte daye, the water ebbing 13 houres, there was butt 7 foote depth, butt being a muddye grounde and verye fayre wether the shippe endured no greate hurte. The nexte daye, the water growing, they wente a little further of the shoare, setting att 3 faddem att a lowe water, being some 4 (miles) leagues from the bare [bar]. The 17 ditto Adam Denton, Nasar Chan and the Sinnar[1] were sente from hence to the river to carrye the newes of our arryvall, who, in regard the towne[2] lyethe some 30 leagues upp along the river, came not backe agayne till the 23 ditto, bringing along with theym the Sabander and the Gouvernour of Mancock [*i.e.*, Bangkok], being a place scituated by the river, to receyve His Majesties letters, butt chiefely for the presents they thought they shoulde receyve, so that it is as badde there for presents as in any other place of the Indies. Thus Mr Lucas and Mr Essington wente with theym to the towne, and comming there had no wante of trouble, whereof I referre myselfe to the letter [*not extant*] from Mr Lucas, who wrote att large of all what passed there, especially in seeking to builde a howse of bricke, which att laste by the Kings gifte was graunted unto theym, being as is

[1] 'Sinnar' is apparently the translator's misreading of Siam-er, referring to some native of Siam who had been taken on board at Patani to serve as interpreter.

[2] Ayuthia, then the capital of Siam, is about 65 miles from the coast in a direct line; the windings of the Menam river would bring the voyage to near 30 leagues.

reported the beste that is in Siam, standing hard by the Hollands howse, to whome [? which] it seemed unpossible for us to obtayne. The 17th of September they came before the King and had audience, who in shorte termes asked the disposition of His Majestie, and howe long wee had bene from home, and after that bidde us welcome and promised us free trade; and, after that hee had given every one a little golden cuppe and a little peece of clothing, they departed agayne.

Have audience with the King.

Obtaine a house off bricke.

After muche solliciting, running and trouble, by reason of the knaverie of the Mandorins,[1] wee obtayned that fayre howse given by the King, being a bricke howse butt something olde, which with a little reparation maye yett serve many yeares, and by reporte there is no better in Siam nor better scituated, standing hard by the Dutche howse.

Thus having bene with the King and gotten a howse of bricke, they tooke order to bring the goodes on shoare, hiring a juncke for the same purpose for 96 R8; and seing the shippe beganne to bee eaten by the wormes, and that it woulde bee 20 dayes before the juncke woulde bee able to gette upp the river, it was thoughte fitting to seeke a convenient place to have the shippe dubbled,[2] having broughte plankes from Bantam expresly for that purpose. The juncke beinge laden wente upp the river towards the towne, being some 30 leagues of, and nowe being in the tyme of raigning, the countrye being covered with water, the tyde came very fiercely downewards, so that the juncke did not come before the towne till the 25 of October. Whereas arose no small heavynesse[3] by their greate (force) violence and knaveryes, whereof the King was ignorant; for the Mandoryns sending aboord of the juncke to wryte upp and seale all the goods, and so to carrye theym into the Kings howse or fetorye,[4]

Variaunce between Mr Lucas and the Mandorins aboute the custome.

[1] A generic term for the high officials in these countries. For its derivation and history see *Hobson-Jobson*, *s.v.* Mandarin; *Dalgado* (*s.v.*) agrees that the original is the Indian word *mantrī*, a minister or councillor.

[2] Dutch *dubbelen*, 'to sheathe'. The English word 'double' was used in this sense, but the earliest example given in the *OED* is dated 1703.

[3] Cf. "Heaviness may endure for a night, but joy cometh in the morning" (Psalm xxx. 5 in the Prayer-book version).

[4] Portuguese *feitoria*, 'factory'. The King was the principal merchant in the country (*van Vliet*, 88), and his factors claimed the first choice of imports.

whereas they open all the packes and take oute what pleaseth theym beste, [ap]praysing the same as it seemeth good unto theym, and before any payement can bee had one muste give halfe as muche for bribes: truely a verye greate knaverye, the lyke whereof is not used in all the Indies, although there bee no wante of violence in all the Indies. But Mr Lucas, seing with whome hee had to doe, and that it was withoute the Kings knowledge, gave theym a resolute answere that hee woulde not yeelde himselfe to suche a bondage, and that hee had perfourmed his charge, which was to deliver His Majesties letters to the King, who had promised him a free trade, and yf hee might not have the same then hee woulde departe agayne, for hee was butt sente to one King alone and not to as many as hee founde theym.

In the meane while Mr Lucas had sente to Oya Phismachan,[1] being one of the chiefeste mandorins, to desire leave to depart in friendshippe, in regard that hee coulde not tarry because of the abuses offered unto him, and, being come in friendly manner, so hee was desirous to departe with friendshippe; the whiche the sayd Oya Phismachan understanding, wente presently to complayne to the King, who presently gave other ordre, charging theym to moleste our folkes no manner of waye, but that they might carry theyr goods to their howse and sell it to theyr pleasure, without making any mention of any custome. Uppon which the packes were carryed home without any molestation; and the 27th October Mr Lucas wente aboord to carry those men aboorde that were come upp with the juncke, and to dispatche the shippe, hoping to fynde some easement for his troubles on the shoare; but came juste from the smoake into the fyre, for the 26 of October in the afternoone aboute 4 of the clocke arose suche a suddayne storme and running[2] rayne that olde folkes had never seene the lyke in that countrye; the trees

Obtaine libertie off free trading and custome.

A fearefull storme in Siam.

[1] According to *van Vliet* (55), the mandarins in Siam were divided into six grades, the highest of which bore the title Oya. Dr H. G. Quaritch Wales informs me that this word may be transliterated Okyā, but the *k* is clipped in pronunciation, and might not be noticed by foreigners. 'Phismachan' appears below as 'Schismachan', and is clearly corrupt The correct title of the mandarin who would ordinarily handle such business was Phra Klang, which appears as Berkelangh in Dutch accounts, and as Barcalon in French; either Floris misread Antheunis, or the translator misread Floris, or both.

[2] Dutch *loopende*, 'running', in such a context is equivalent to 'pouring'.

were blowne oute of the grounde, and the King having made a fayre toombe for a monument to his father, [it] was also blowne downe. The shippe being in a thowsand dangers with 2 anckers oute, wente awaye, and by the manly courage of Mr Skinner and Samuell Huyts they gott a cable to the third anker and lette that fall, by which shee was stayde and so was saved, for it was alreadye gotte from 6 faddem to 4 and not passing an English myle from the land, whereas were very sharpe rockes. Mr Skinner was beaten from the anker (tree) stocke, but by a greate (chaunce) miracle hee gotte above, catching a rope in his hande and so helde himselfe, nobody knowing what had happened to him, for the sea was so rough and so beate over the shippe that it was not possible to go along the shipp, and under the halfe deck of the shippe was driftie water.

The shippe is in greate danger.

The boate with 8 men being gone a shoare and butt newly putte from aboorde, the storme arose, and before they coulde gette aboorde they sawe the shipp go awaye, so that they verely thoughte the shipp woulde have bene stranded; therefore, not willing to come in the shippe, they hunge att the shipps stearne by the falling ladder, whenas the shippe comming up or staying with the ancker, the boate was beate to the grounde and 4 men drowned, hard by the shippe; the boason, George Ponder [*or* Pender], being sone in lawe to Mr Johnson, present master of the shippe, was drowned a good while after, or else devoured of a whale,[1] having yett bene seene a little before, butt a little while after they sawe a greate whale there aboutes, and since was seene no more. The other three were caste on shoare in sundry places, as also the skiff and the boate, which lykewyse was suncke, the cable breaking, dryving some 6 (miles) leagues along the shoare with little harme, dryving juste past the rockes and on the other syde of the baye paste a river; and there they were bothe founde not verye farre asunder, and so broughte aboord agayne. This storme lasted not passing 4 or 5 houres, and then began to grow lesse, so that the nexte morning the sea was as smooth as yf there had bene no wynde att all; and it is to bee wondered howe the

5 men drouned.

Storme ceaseth.

[1] The Deputy Keeper of Zoology in the Natural History Museum writes that it is highly probable that whales of various species enter the Gulf of Siam from time to time, but no actual record of the occurrence has been traced.

sea can bee so rough in this baye, seing the corners poynte oute so farre, having some ilands,[1] and being by reporte one of the beste bayes that can bee wished, being butt [*i.e.*, only] this wynde comming from the S.S.W. or thereabowtes that can doe harme, for that maketh [*i.e.*, blows through] the opening betweene the land and the ilands. To conclude, the Almightye God, that in all this voyage hathe kepte us with suche a fatherly care, hath not withdrawen att this tyme, causing this storme as an instrument to make us more thankefull heereafter, to deliver us from a greater evill; and hathe bene a meane whereby greate treacherye and treason hath bene revealed, as it appeareth withoute any doute that it woulde have broughte foorthe, as manifestely appearethe by the action of these persons following.

The newe captayne, Mr Essington, commanding the boatson to doe a certayne matter, hee, relying uppon his father in lawe, Mr Johnson, refused to do it, and thereuppon falling oute with him, gave very injurious speeches to the captayne, which hee for feare of greater inconveniences suffered to passe withoute punishement; and Mr Johnson, who oughte to have assisted the captain agaynst his disobedient sone, to the contrary rejoyced att it, instigating him more and more; all which happened in the beginning of his mastershipp, and after that Mr Johnson ever sought for occasions of stryfe and contentions; as when any deceased mans goods shoulde bee solde before the maste, then Mr Johnson, being in his cabyne, refused to come foorth, whereuppon Mr Essington falling to the selling thereof, the other seeking occasion came running oute of his cabine, keeping a greate sturre, beginning to contemne the captayne, commanding everyone to give backe the goods they had boughte, for it shoulde bee of no force, nor entered into the pursers booke, because hee had not bene by att the sale thereof, using many other suchelyke woords, a matter which touched him nothing att all, and for that tyme was taken upp or pacifyed.[2]

[1] The map shows various islands in the eastern half of the Bight of Bangkok but the western half is open to the S.S.W.

[2] It is mentioned in *Boteler's Dialogues* (31) that since some masters had been given the command of merchant vessels, they were, as a class, setting up a claim to independence, and were sometimes unwilling to submit to the captain, when one existed. Presumably Johnson was acting in this spirit, but

After that, the shippe arryving by the grace of God att Siam, which happened not by his [*i.e.*, Johnson's] wisedome butt muche to the contrary, as all the men of the shippe do witnesse, hee not gouverning otherwyse then as yf hee had expressely soughte the ruine of the shippe, and Mr Lucas and Mr Essington going upp the river with His Majesties letter, leaving ordre and charge with the aforesayd Johnson for some things to bee done in theyr absence; the sayde Captayne Essington returning backe agayne founde all done wholly contrarye to his order; whereuppon, chiding with Mr Johnson, hee receyved for an answere that before a yeare shoulde come to an ende hee woulde make him sing another song. All which Captayne Essington did beare, not knowing which waye to right himselfe, and so lykewyse another injurye att the boatsons hand, so that hee was not to sure of his lyfe, yett overpassing all was fayne to have patience, as having no meanes to punishe suche mutinous persons. After this happened another opposition, for 5 men being ordayned to remayne on shoare in Siam, there was one of theym not very willing to tarry there, and being instigated by others, the captayne, according to his commission, beginning to use his authoritie, then came the sayd Janson [*i.e.*, Johnson] falling oute very harde with the sayd captayne, and woulde not suffer this man named Idan Stego by any means to tarry on shoare, saying they used him violently, which hee woulde prevente, and other greate threatning woords besydes, which caused no small uproare in the shipp, seing they had suche leaders which so did backe theym; which seemed that it woulde have come to a greater disorder, if the aforesayde Stego, considering his case a little better with himselfe, had not come to present his service and to staye on shoare, which was an occasion that this tumulte then ceased, albeit not the ill will, as appeared after the ceasing of this grievous storme.

In the morning the Captayne willed the men to bee called together to give thankes to God for His so mercifull deliverye. Mr Johnson, agayne opposing himselfe against this, sayde it

there was nothing in the commission for the Voyage to justify his attitude. Later entries in the Journal show, however, that Floris subsequently became doubtful whether Johnson was really to blame for the trouble in the ship.

was sufficient that every one gave thankes to God by himselfe; and aboute halfe an howre after, the Captayne comming uppon the halfe decke founde there Mr Johnson so drunke that hee coulde not well stande; whereuppon the Captayne reproching him that hee oughte to bee ashamed, and whether this were a tyme of suche drincking, which the other tooke upp very ill, answering the Captayne very scornefull and injuriously, calling him rogue, rascall, dogge, and other suchelyke vile woords, and rysing att laste, stroke att him, and so were wrastling together till some came to parte theym; whereuppon the Captayne caused him to bee nayled upp in his owne cabine, whereuppon Johnson, cursing and banning, wishing himselfe and the shippe with the divell, used many suchelyke blasphemous woords. The Captayne afterwards going to his cabine was warned by the gunner to take heede to himselfe, for the sayd Johnson was broke oute of his cabine, and had a naked dagger in his codpisse.[1] Whereuppon the Captayne caused the men to bee called together, and there asked theym whether they did acknowledge him for theyr captayne or no; whereuppon it was answered Yea. Then hee made his complaynte of the greate mutinie and disobedience of Mr Johnson, and [commanded] for to take the dagger from him and keepe him prisoner, which being heard of Mr Johnson hee fledde into the gunner roome, to what intent God knoweth. There hee called to the gunner and others for to take his parte, crying and bawling whether there were not one honeste man in the shipp who woulde take his parte; butt fynding nobody on his syde, yea to the contrary the men and officers of the shippe comming to take his weapons from him, hee att the fyrste did refuse to deliver theym, butt att the laste, seing no other remedy, delivered his weapons, calling to all the men that hee was a prisoner. Yf hee had done suche things in other shipps hee had bene hanged, butt all came intreating the Captayne nowe to keepe him sure, for yf hee should come to his rule agayne they woulde all go awaye; and some other things more happened, which Mr Essington can proove by attestation.

Wherefore hee putte the forenamed Mr Johnson from his

[1] *I.e.*, cod-piece, defined in the *OED* as a bagged appendage to the close-fitting hose or breeches worn at the period.

office, Mr Skinner gouverning in his place by provision till other order shalbee taken; so that nowe the company in the shipp was brought to some better order, and to their good happ that it had pleased God to call the boatson oute of this world the daye before, for doutlesse yf hee had bene alyve more evill woulde have inseuwed. God bee praysed. In this case Mr Lucas founde the shipp, and so, in regard of the shortenesse of the tyme and fewe men being in the howse,[1] nothing else hath bene done in this matter, butt all hath bene referred till the shippe shoulde come to Patania, taking his leave of the shipp the fyrste of November; and the shippe sette sayle from thence for Patania the 3 ditto, whereas it arryved the 11 ditto in the morning.

Nowe touching the estate of the trade in Siam, God Hee knoweth it hathe bene this yeare so lowe and under foote as the lyke hath not bene since Siam hath bene knowen; so that it seemeth that it is Gods will to crosse us in this voyage, as being the third chiefe place of all the Indies; and so farre distant as is Bantam, Patania and Siam, whereas wee fynde the trade so under foote; butt having partly touched the occasion thereof in Bantam and Patania, wee will also recite the occasion thereof in Siam.

Description off Siam. Siam is an auncient kingdome and hath alwayes bene very mightye,[2] butt afterwards it hath bene subdued by the King of Pegu, becomming tributaries unto him. Butt it continued not long in that estate, for this King,[3] dying, lefte issue 2 sonnes, which were brought upp in the Kings courte of Pegu; who flying[4] from thence to Siam, whereas the eldeste, called Raja

[1] That is to say, the staff of the factory was too small to decide a question of such importance, which required to be dealt with by the council of the ship.

[2] The story here related is re-told in the Introduction, § 4. Pegu was the capital of Burma in the second half of the sixteenth century.

[3] 'This King' denotes the King of Siam, but the text is not quite accurate. The two boys, Naresuen and Ekathotsarot, were not sons of the independent King of Siam, but of a prominent man, Maha Thammaraja, and after the fall of Ayuthia in 1564 were taken to Pegu as hostages for their father's conduct. A few years later Maha Thammaraja was made vassal King of Ayuthia (*Wood*, 117, 125, 128).

[4] The grammar is bad; read 'fled' for 'flying'. Naresuen was allowed to return to Ayuthia in 1571, being then 16 years of age, and during the next ten years he earned a great military reputation in the wars between Siam and

Api, in the Maleys language the Fyery King, butt by the Portingalls and other nations the Blacke King, setting upp himselfe as a King,[1] assembled a greate power; againste whome the King of Pegu sente the Prince his sone, who was slayne in these warres,[2] and hath bene an occasion of the destruction of the whole kingdome, and hath coste the lyves of many millions of Peguers; for the King, being sore grieved for the death of his sone, caused all his chiefeste lords and soldiers that were Peguers[3] to bee slayne, himselfe being of the kinred of the Bramaas. Which caused a great perturbation in his owne kingdome,[4] dyvers other kings, being his vassalls, whereof hee had 20 under him, falling dayly from him; which att the laste incouraged this Blacke King to make warre agaynste him, going to the cittie of Unxa[5] or Pegu, before which hee laye some 2 months withoute doinge anything; butt breaking upp his siege wente to Siam, where not long after, because of the greate dearth and mortalitie, hee

The occasion off the destruction off Pegu.

The King off Pegu thorough necessitie giveth himselfe into the handes off the King off Tangu.

Cambodia. In 1581 he was ordered by Nandabayin, the new King of Burma, to suppress a revolt in the Shan States; he accomplished this task successfully, but quarrelled with the Burmese Crown Prince, and returned to Siam. Some accounts state that his return was really a flight, as the text says (*Wood*, 128–31). Owing to a marked difference in complexion Naresuen was known as the 'Black Prince', while his brother was the 'White Prince'. *Api* is Malay for 'fire'; the soubriquet is sufficiently explained by Naresuen's record of extraordinary personal courage.

[1] Naresuen did not set himself up as king, but in 1584, on learning that Nandabayin had arranged to have him murdered, he renounced allegiance to Burma on behalf of his father, Maha Thammaraja, who thus became independent King of Siam; he succeeded to the throne on his father's death in 1590 (*Wood*, 131, 132, 139).

[2] This refers to the fifth invasion of Siam (1593), the last of the series. The Crown Prince of Burma, who was in command, was killed in single combat with Naresuen (*Wood*, 142; *Harvey*, 182). The expression 'many millions' must be taken as exaggerated, but the loss of life was in any case appalling (*Harvey*, 183).

[3] 'Peguers' denotes the Talaing, or Mon, inhabitants of the south of Burma, 'Bramaas', the Burmese living further north. Nandabayin belonged to the Toungoo dynasty, which was Burmese, as stated in the text. The slaughter of the Peguan lords is not mentioned in modern histories, but is probable enough.

[4] As explained in the Introduction, the resources of Burma had been exhausted in the successive invasions of Siam, and the kingdom inevitably fell to pieces.

[5] Unxa (the *x* pronounced *sh* in Portuguese fashion) probably represents Ussa, the old local name of the Pegu country, usually known as Hanthawaddy. The date of this siege is given by *Harvey* (182) as 1595.

willingly gave over himselfe[1] and all his treasures into the hands of the King of Tangu, least hee shoulde have fallen into the handes of the King of Arracan, who was comming on with a greate power. Butt the King of Arracan, comming before the towne, founde it almooste emptye, whereby hee made himselfe master of the towne and countrye, thinking to have gone into Tangu.[2] Butt the King of Tangu, fearing the power of the King of Arracan, sente ambassadors unto him, aggreing with him uppon certayne conditions that hee shoulde deliver to the King of Arracan certaine portions of the treasure of Pegu, the white elephant and the Kings daughter of Pegu, both which I have seene in Arracam[3] *anno* 1608, as also the King of Pegu, or else that himselfe shoulde kill him, as afterwards it happened that the King of Tangu slewe him with a pilon[4] wherewithall they stampe the ryce, as being free agaynst any stubbing. In this manner came this mightye empyre to ruyne and destruction, so that att this daye there is no remembraunce of itt.[5]

The King off Arracan taketh Pegu.

[1] The translation must be defective; as the marginal note shows, it was the King of Burma, not Siam, who surrendered. 'Tangu' is Toungoo, the country lying between Pegu and Ava; it was not a kingdom, but a province of Burma, ruled by a Viceroy, who, however, was at this time in rebellion. The surrender was in the year 1599; Arakan and Toungoo were acting in concert, and Siam was on the way to join them, but arrived too late (*Wood*, 150–2; *Harvey*, 182–3; there are a few discrepancies in details between these accounts).

[2] Modern authorities do not mention this difference between Toungoo and Arakan; according to them the spoil was amicably shared (*Harvey*, 183; *Wood*, 152). The Jesuit Andrew Boves, however, who was on the spot, wrote that Arakan was aggrieved, and was about to invade Toungoo (*Purchas*, II. x. 1748).

[3] As related in the Introduction, Floris had visited Arakan in 1608, while in Dutch service.

[4] The King was "hurriedly murdered" (*Harvey*, 183) by order of the Viceroy, to whom he had surrendered on a promise of good treatment. 'Pilon' is Portuguese *pilão*, 'pestle' (Lacerda, followed by various smaller Portuguese-English dictionaries, made the word mean 'mortar', but gave it as the equivalent of 'pestle' in his English-Portuguese section). In Burma, as in some other Buddhist countries, there was a theoretical objection to bloodshed, and this method of execution would be preferable to 'stubbing', *i.e.*, stabbing. Boves, however, wrote that the King's head was cut off (*Purchas*, II. x. 1748).

[5] At this time Anaukpetlun, who emerged as King of Burma in 1605, was restoring the power of the kingdom, but apparently his importance was not yet realised in Patani. Floris alludes to his activities in a later passage (23rd February, 1614).

The King of Arracan gave the towne or forte of Siriangh [*i.e.*, Syriam], lying uppon the same river of Pegu, in keeping to the Portingalls, especially to Philippe de Britte de Nicote, to whome hee gave the name of Xenga, which is honeste;[1] which honour Xenga did afterwards requite very well, taking his sone prisoner some 3 or 4 yeares after, and ransomed him [for] 110,000 tangans and 10 galeas of ryce,[2] so that the sayd Xenga is att this present yett dominering, not caring for any body.

The rising off Philip de Britte alias Xenga.

This in briefe is the destruction of Pegu, whereby Siam is come upp agayne, which, because of the domination of Pegu, was somewhat decayed, bringing under his subjection the kingdomes of Camboja, Laniangh, Jagomai, Lugor, Patania, Tenesserin, and dyvers other places and kingdomes,[3] till *anno* 1605, whenas the Blacke King deceased withoute any issue. Hee was a man of greate understanding; and lefte his kingdome to his brother who was called the White King,[4] who was a verye coveteous man butt injoyed his kingdomes in peace, doing no other thing woorthy of remembraunce. Hee dyed *anno* 1610, leaving dyvers childeren behynde him.

The rising againe off the Kingdome off Siam.

[1] Syriam, close to what is now the city of Rangoon, was the chief seaport of the kingdom. Philip de Brito y Nicote was a Portuguese adventurer in the service of Arakan (*Harvey*, 143, 183 ff.; *Journal*, Burma Research Society, 1926, pp. 101 ff.). Xenga is not a Burmese title, and appears to represent a "nick-name Nga Zinga, meaning in the patois of the seaports 'good man'" (*Harvey*, 189). The fate of de Brito is recorded in later entries.

[2] Arakan soon found reason to distrust de Brito, and sent a flotilla against him under the command of the Crown Prince; de Brito destroyed the flotilla, and captured the Prince (*Harvey*, 185). 'Tangan' is here presumably the Arakan *tanga*, a silver coin which, according to Manrique, was equal to the Indian rupee, being four Spanish reals, or half a real of eight (*Travels of Sebastian Manrique*, Hakluyt Society, i. 45, 124). In 1635 Bocarro (quoted in *Dalgado*, ii. 356) equated the *tanga* to 250 Portuguese *reis*, a unit which periodically depreciated in value; about the year 1600 it had been worth 0·16*d.* (*Hobson-Jobson*, 675), but if both Manrique and Bocarro are right, it must have fallen to 0·11*d.* by 1635. 'Galeas' probably denotes galley-loads, referring to the large rice-boats used in Burmese inland waters.

[3] *I.e.*, Cambodia, Lanshan (Luang Prabang), Chiengmai, Ligor, Patani, and Tenasserim; Purchas misread the first name as Cambaya. The credibility of the account which follows is discussed in the Introduction, § 4.

[4] King Ekathotsarot. The Black King was pre-eminently a fighter, while his successor devoted himself mainly to finance, and, perhaps unfairly, earned the reputation of being a miser. The dates given in the text, which were questioned by *Satow* (181 ff.), were accepted by Wood; Naresuen died on 16th May, 1605, his successor about the end of 1610 (*Wood*, 156, 158, 160).

His death hath caused a greate alteration, for hee, lying in his death-bedde, caused his eldeste sone to bee slayne, a yong man of very greate hope, att the instigation of one Jockcrommewaye,[1] being one of the principall lords of Siam, who, having a greate many slaves, thoughte to make himself King. This White King deceasing, this present King,[2] being his second sone, succeeded in the kingdome; who foorthwith was instigated to dispatche the foresayde Jockrommewaye oute of the waye, as afterwards it happened. This foresayd Jockrommewaye, among other his slaves,[3] had aboute 280 Japanders; these, after their master's death, thinking to revenge theyr master's death, and to do some valiant Romane facte,[4] ranne joyntly together to the courte of this yonge King, who was withoute any suche suspition. They tooke the courte and gotte the King into theyr handes, whome they compelled to deliver into theyre hands 4 of his principall nobles for to bee slayne, as being the causers of theyr masters deathe; and having some tyme used him even as they listed, att the laste they made an aggreement with him, which hee was compelled to subscribe with his owne blood, compelling him also to give theym some of the cheefe *palapos*[5] or priests into theyr hands for ostages or pledges; and so they departed with a greate

280 Japan slaves take the courte and King of Siam into their power.

[1] The name 'Jockcrommewaye' was read by *Satow* (182) as Okyā Krom Naiwai, the designation Okyā denoting a mandarin of the highest grade. In *Wood* (159) the name is given as Phya Naiwai, Phya being the modern equivalent of the older Okyā. As a designation, Krom denotes an officer in charge of a department, or of a troop of forced labourers. According to the Siamese authorities, the Crown Prince poisoned himself; *Wood* (160) accepted the statement that he was executed.

[2] Intharaja, usually known by the title of Songtham, 'the Just King'. According to *Wood* (160), he was son to Ekathotsarot by a wife of inferior rank.

[3] The description of the Japanese as slaves was questioned by *Satow* (182), and *Wood* (160) speaks of them merely as adherents. It is not possible to determine the precise nature of the tie which bound them to Phya Naiwai, but probably they formed his body-guard. About this time Japanese adventurers came to Siam in considerable numbers, and were employed in this way by the nobles.

[4] Dutch *romeinsche stuk*, 'a deed worthy of a Roman', hence 'a remarkable exploit'.

[5] Read *talapois*, a word which denotes monks rather than priests. Its derivation is discussed inconclusively in *Hobson-Jobson* (*s.v.* Talapoin) and in *Dalgado*.

treasure,[1] using muche violence att theyr departure. To which things they of Siam knew no other remedy then to sitte still and looke on.

Uppon the newes of this mischaunce happened to this young King, the kingdomes of Camboja[2] and Laniangh rebelled, as also one Bangade Laa,[3] a Peguer; and the King of Laniangh came the laste yeare into Siam within 3 dayes journey of the towne of Ondya,[4] hoping to fynde the countrye yett entangled with the troubles of those slaves of Japan; butt they being departed, the King of Siam came foorth to meete him, butt the King of Laniangh, being afrayde to abyde him, retyred backe againe.[5] Yett neverthelesse bothe the other Kings do not reste, butt, as it is spread abroad, have made a league bothe of theym joyntly to come together in Aprill uppon the King of Siam, so that by mayne force they thinke to putte this young King, being aboute the age of 22 yeares, from his throne; and although there is butt small lykelyhoode thereof, for as long as there is no treason in Siam nor other inlandishe[6] revolte or uprores, hee shalbee able wel enough to keep theym oute of his countrye. Butt wee are

Cause off the warre in Siam.

[1] *Wood* (161) states that the Japanese sacked Ayuthia, and then went to the town of Phetchaburi, about 50 miles south-west of Bangkok, where their leader set himself up almost as an independent king. They were driven out of that stronghold by King Songtham early in 1612.

[2] There is no other evidence that the King of Cambodia rebelled at this time; *Wood* (166) says he remained loyal to Siam until his death in 1618. Popular anxiety in Ayuthia would naturally multiply the number of enemies, and was doubtless reflected in the letters from Antheunis on which Floris relied.

[3] Here as elsewhere we should read *y* for *g*, the two letters being nearly identical in the Dutch script. The Burmese name is Binnya Dala, the first word being an honorific designation equivalent to 'lord', while the second is the name of the country opposite Rangoon; the Siamese form of the name is Phya Dala. King Naresuen had appointed him to be Governor of Martaban and the other provinces wrested from Burma; he was not, however, loyal to his master, but was playing for his own hand, and in 1613 he submitted to the King of Burma (*Wood*, 163–4; *Harvey*, 188–9).

[4] Read Oudya, *i.e.*, Ayuthia.

[5] In the Siamese version of this affair King Songtham defeated Lanshan on 5th April, 1612, and the rebel army fled in disorder (*Wood*, 161). It is curious that Antheunis should not have told Floris of this signal victory, gained only a few months before he wrote, and there is room for suspicion that the Siamese version may be exaggerated.

[6] Dutch *inlandsch*, 'domestic', 'native'. The anticipated invasion did not occur.

juste those that hitte on this badd tyme, the mooste or greateste halfe of our cargason imployed in goods serving for that place, as being the moost famous place of all the Indies; for wheras the mooste India cloth and red threed [*i.e.*, yarn] were wonte to bee vented in Camboja, Lanjangh Lau,[1] Jagoma, and those places, I lette others judge what there is to bee looked for att this tyme in trading. Butt seing the will of God to bee suche, wee muste submitt oure will unto His, expecting a better ende when it shalbee His godly will and pleasure.

What causeth the deadnesse off the trade.

[1] That is to say, the Laos country of Lanshan. The word Lao, or Laos, was used in a wide sense of the country north of Siam; see, *e.g.*, *Purchas*, III. i. 168.

[CHAPTER VI

PATANI (*continued*)]

This hath bene the occasion, as also the shortenes of the tyme, the foule wether, and the long waye from the shipp to the towne, that Mr Lucas hath not bene able to sende mee over any capitall for the increase of myne; for not having a sufficient capitall to perfourme the voyage along the coaste,[1] the shippe arryving to late, and the foresayde questions and mutinies arysing in the shippe, it hath bene an occasion of this following resolution. The shippe being safely arryved heere the 11 of November, and having maturely deliberated together uppon that which had passed in Siam, and nowe considering and waying [*i.e.*, weighing] the one and the other, wee have resolved together to keepe the shippe lying and wintering (to lye and winter) heere, and that chiefely for 3 principall reasons following, to witte: That the shippe arryved to late in this roade, being the very beginning and hardeste of the winter, having hard N.E. and N.N.E. wyndes, so that it was not possible to dobble the poynte of Redangh,[2] lying from us E.S.E. some 25 leagues, as dyvers Hollands shipps have striven to do, butt are returned backe with greate danger, and so to tarry all winter. Secondly, Mr Essington shoulde have bene fayne to tarry heere and I to departe with the shipp; butt seing the great tumulte and disorder in the shipp, by reason of the afore-recited occasions, I woulde not take it uppon mee to go with the shippe alone, for it was to bee feared that all woulde runne to naughts or bordello;[3] for I shoulde have

The occasion off the wintering off the shipp in Petania.

[1] From the context this must mean 'to the Coromandel Coast'. The original intention had been to make two trips between India and Siam, but the circumstances explained in the text involved the loss of a season.

[2] *I.e.*, the island of Great Redang, the most easterly land on the course southward to Bantam or the Straits.

[3] 'Naughts' is recorded in the *OED* as a rare variant of the more usual 'naught'. *Bordello* is Italian for 'brothel', and was also used in English in this sense, which, however, is inapplicable here. The word 'runne' (*loopen*)

bene fayne to bee alwayes on shoare, and the shippe lying withoute a head, drincking theymselves druncke, fighting, knocking, dycing and suche lyke good poyntes used among theym, which have gotten suche upperhand in this shippe as ever I sawe in any shippe; and all this happened mooste because of the milde gouvernment of the former deceased captaine, so that this is one of the principall reasons that the shipp muste tarry heere to greate charges and losse of tyme; howebeit wee hope, seing howe it goeth forwards, that all things yett maye come to the beste, partly because I gathered butt a small capitall, which att this present tyme, for wante of China and other commodities,[1] cannot bee imployed to proffite. Secondly, that Mr Lucas hathe not bene able to sende mee any supply, which nowe maye better bee done; also in the meane tyme John Persons maye returne, and, the junckes of China arryving, the capitall maye profitably bee imployed and a greate capitall bee gathered, which

Resolution. will yeelde more profite then to imploye it nowe uppon some apparrellings, the tyme and trade being nowe wholly dead, according as further appeareth by the resolution.

Butt yett notwithstanding all the forenamed matters, the beste order is not yett kepte in the shippe, for [*i.e.*, owing to] Mr Skinner being to muche inclyned to druncke drincking,[2] playing, dycing and other suche lyke good partes; yea, when anybody in the shippe wanted any racke [*i.e.*, spirits] hee woulde lende theym whole bottles, to paye him agayne when they shoulde receyve any from shoare; and himselfe playing with other

indicates that Floris must have used a variant of the Dutch phrase *in bordel loopen*, 'to go to ruin'; the *Woordenboek* refers this phrase to the colloquial Italian use of *bordello* in imprecations, giving *mandare in bordello* as equivalent to 'to send to the devil'. Floris obviously meant that everything would go to rack and ruin. A close parallel to his language occurs in a letter written by Jan Pietersz Coen in 1614 (*MacLeod*, i. 133): "*soo sal de geheele negotie in bordel ende te nyet gaen*" ("then the whole trade will be utterly ruined").

[1] 'China commodities' was the regular term for goods exported from China; and one of the objects of the visit to Patani was to procure silk, porcelain, and other Chinese specialities. 'Secondly', just below, should be 'thirdly'; there were three principal reasons for the change of plans, (1) the season, (2) the state of the ship, (3) the want of capital. A portion of this resolution is printed in *Letters Received*, i. 198.

[2] The *OED* records an obsolete intransitive verb 'to drink drunk' in the sense of to drink to excess: the corresponding Dutch phrase was *droncken drincken*.

officers, and that not for small summes, for some had loste 14 and 10 *li*. sterling; butt as soone as it came to our eares it was forbidden, and promise made that it shoulde bee done no more. Butt it is hard for a leopard to alter his spotts, for Mr Martins[1] wrote mee a letter repeating or rehearsing suche matters as it were a shame to lette go unpunished, for I am ashamed to repeate suche things here, butt referre me to the letter lying in my counting howse; surely it is a pitifull case when one muste make suche a change as is olde copper for rusty iron, and I am of the mynde that olde Johnson hath bene accused [out] of envye,[2] albeit hee doutlesse hath committed greate faultes, butt having not as yett sitte in justice uppon him, the tyme will shewe that: in the meane tyme patience muste bee had, and as good care taken as possibly can bee done.

Disorder in the shippe.

Also there is a greate disorder among the men in the private trade,[3] not onely att Bantam, where wee were offered for our *tapés* [*i.e.*, skirts] 15 R8, and hath bene solde by our men for 10, 11 and 12 R8, whereby wee coulde not come to sell any; and although wee gott intelligence thereof, and made complaynte to Captain Hippon, butt as afterwards wee founde oute by a letter that Captain Hippon with some of his consortes, and especially Mr Smith, were partners, which letter Mr Essington hath in his keeping, whereby it is easily to bee perceyved that when suche men go before and bee in company with suche as they shoulde forbidde it, what order maye bee looked for. And so wee, seing att laste that there was no remedye for it, and being resolved to departe, wee gave every one leave to sell his goods att Bantam, because [*i.e.*, in order that] they shoulde not spoyle oure marketts in other places, this seeming to us the beste that

A shorte memorandum touching the private trade off the men.

[1] Nathaniel Marten was one of the master's mates on the *Globe*, and wrote the ship's log, portions of which were printed by *Purchas* (I. iii. 314).

[2] Adam Denton, the factor on the *Globe*, who thought very highly of Johnson, attributed the whole trouble to a conspiracy between Essington, the captain, and Skinner to get Johnson out of the ship (*Letters Received*, ii. 115). The question was not investigated at the time, because, as is recorded below, Johnson refused to put his case before a jury chosen from the ship's company, and the truth cannot now be ascertained.

[3] This topic is discussed in the Introduction, § 7. 'Mr Smith' is presumably Thomas Smith, master's mate, whose death is recorded above under 14th July.

was to bee done; yett notwithstanding it fell oute to the contrarye, for yett att this dead markett they sufficiently helpe all under foote, according as thereof I have bene fayne to heare dyvers complaynts of my usuall customers in presence of Mr Essington and Adam Denton, and also is to bee seene by the bookes and papers of John Downes after his death, who lyke a factor laye on land, and hath solde goods 50 per cento better cheape then I do; and although sometymes there is made a great shewe for the searching oute of this matter, yett neither heeretofore nor as yett anything hath bene done against it, butt for this voyage muste go his olde course. God sending me home in safetye, I shall knowe to infourme the Company of dyvers other things, putting this onely heere by the waye of a remembrance.

[November] 21 ditto. Heere dyed John Downes, the servaunt of Anthony Hippon, who dyed a very suddayne death, sitting att dinner att noone, was dead att night. I had reasonnable good service of him, howebeit hee hath troubled himselfe to muche in selling of the shipps companies goods withoute any knowledge of myne; oute of which proceeded a greate disorder in respecte of his suddayne death, having dyvers dettes extant among those of China, so that some will come to shorte by him.[1]

31 December. The Queene goeth forthe on hunting. The Queene, being accompanyed with a greate traine of prauwes,[2] above 600 in number, wente to sporte hirselfe, going att the fyrste to lye att Sabraugh,[3] where they assembled theymselves; where wee wente to salute hir, having both sight and speech of hir in company of the Hollanders, being a comely olde woman, nowe aboute the age of [blank] yeares;[4] shee was tall of person and full of majestie, having in all the Indies not seene many lyke unto hir. Shee was accompanied by hir sister, being hir nexte heyre, and hir yonger sisters little daughter,

[1] That is, the Chinese merchants living in Patani. 'To shorte' represents Dutch *te kort*.

[2] Malay *pĕrahu*, ship or boat.

[3] Read Sabrangh, the lowland towards the coast, mentioned above under 19th June.

[4] Purchas has "threescore years of age"; probably he took the figure from the later entry of 18th March, 1613.

which hath bene marryed to Raja Siack,[1] brother to the King of Joor. This hir sister, being commonly called the Young Queene, was yett an unmaried mayden aboute 46 yeares of age. After wee had had some conference with hir, shee lette fall the curtaine, which signifyed as muche as that wee muste departe. Afterwards shee lette us knowe that wee shoulde come agayne the nexte daye, for not being ready as yett; which wee were fayne to promise unto hir. *Wee have sighte and speeche off the Queene.*

In the morning wee came thether agayne, where they intertayned us reasonnably well. There were 12 women and childeren to daunce, which did effecte it so well that I have not seene better in all the Indies. That being done, all the gentilitie were commanded to daunce, from the greatest to the smalleste, or att leaste make a shewe or demonstration thereof, which caused no small laughter; which both wee and the Hollanders muste do lykewyse, wherewith the olde Queene was muche rejoyced. And so wee departed agayne and came home att night. Shee had not bene foorth oute of hir howse in 7 yeares, and nowe shee woulde go on hunting of wilde buffes [*i.e.*, buffaloes] and bulls, whereof there is greate abundance there. [1613 *N.S.*] Primo *January.*

Shee with all hir trayne passed along by the cittie, and comming betweene our howse and the shippe, wee did salute hir with shooting of some peeces from the shippe and some muskett shott ashoare. Shee wente to Quala Buca.[2] *3 ditto.*

In this winter of November and December the water, by reason of the continuall rayne, was so high heere that no mans remembraunce can speake of the lyke, so that many beasts dyed, many howses driven[3] awaye, and muche other harme done. *High waters in Patania do harme.*

Aboute this tyme there was not yett had any newes from the

[1] The description of Johore given in *Begin ende Voortgangh*, Matelieff's Voyage, p. 11, states that the reigning Raja had three brothers. The eldest, who had married a Princess of Patani, held the country of Siaka, and was called Raja Siakai; he lived quietly at his home, and was a simpleton, "adorned with no kingly qualities". The second, Raja Bonsu, or Bongsu, mentioned below as Raja Boungson, was a capable man, and the real administrator of the country; the third was a vicious nonentity.

[2] *Kwala* in Malay means 'river-mouth'. The Admiralty chart marks the river on which Patani stands as Sungi [river] Kwala Bukka; but no place of the name has been found on the maps, and it is uncertain whether the text refers to some small village, or generally to the country at the mouth of the river.

[3] Dutch *drijven*, 'to float'.

The Hollands shipps forgotte to come from Japan. Hollands shipps, both the pinasse called the *Greyhounde*, as the shipp called the *Lion with the Arrowes*, which were ordayned to go from Bantam to Japan, notwithstanding they were looked for heere by the ende of October and November, as alwayes *15 January.* heeretofore they have done; and nowe, halfe January being paste, some mischance is to bee feared, for they have expresse order to come from Japan hether and to discharge the silver,[1] for the factory is but homelie provided. What and howe the matter is tyme will shewe.

Marchandizes requested in Japan. Touching the commodities which I understand to bee requested and vented att Japan, whereof the shipp the *Lion and Arrowes* shoulde have carryed good quantitie, is dyeper,[2] dyvers Nurimbergher wares, crimson or stammell clothes and carseyes [*i.e.*, kerseys], dyvers looking glasses, muskett, ordinaunce, and suche lyke Europa wares. Butt from hence and Siam are carryed all manner of China wares, rawe silke of the courseste called lincange,[3] all manner of silkewares, as taphyties [*i.e.*, taffeta], satyns, damasts, tuffetaphaties, velvetts, all sortes of porseleyn, also all sortes of spices, especially pepper, also waxe and deare skinnes from Siam, and the skinnes or scales of a certayne fishe called in Maleys tongue[4] [blank in MS]. The waighte of Japan

[1] At this period Japan was one of the few countries from which silver could be freely exported; this fact constituted the principal attraction of the trade for merchants like the Dutch, who required silver in large quantities. The objection raised in *Anderson* (64), that about this time silver was being sent from Siam to Japan, was based on a misleading abstract in the *Calendar of State Papers*. The text of the document in question (*Letters Received*, iv. 87) shows, not that silver was being shipped, but that a small quantity was lent to a Japanese in Siam, to be repaid on his arrival in Japan.

[2] Diaper is cloth woven in a diamond pattern: Nuremberg was famed for fancy goods made of metal and carved wood: stammell was a woollen cloth, usually dyed red.

[3] 'Lincange' probably represents Lancing, *i.e.*, Nanking, whence much silk was exported. Taffeta, satin, 'damast' or damask, and velvet are European trade-names, applied to Chinese products of the same types. 'Tuffetaphaties' has not been found elsewhere, and no confident explanation of the term can be offered; the most probable guess is that the translator misread *tapehas tuffe*, and that the goods were taffeta skirts, the name thus falling into line with tapeserasas, tapechindos, etc., designations of various types of cotton skirts which are mentioned elsewhere in the Journal.

[4] *Satow* (147, 155, 177, 210) mentions shark-skins and ray-skins being brought as presents from Siam to Japan, to be used to make shagreen for sword-hilts.

and China are all one; from Japan is brought nothing butt silver, whereof they have there 3 sortes, the one yeelding more profet then the other, butt the certaintie of the gaynes, as also of comming and going, I have not bene able to learne as yett, because, as before I have sayde, there comes none of Japan hether nor in Siam; wee maye trye what tyme will shewe.

18 ditto. *Examination.* Wee did sitte together[1] to see what should bee done with Mr Johnson; and having caused him to bee called before us, some matters were layde to his charge to have bene done by him, to make answere thereunto. The which hee for the mooste parte denyed, construing theym quite otherwyse then they were understood. Whereuppon wee found it good to sette a jury of 12 persons to consider of his matters, and according to the same I, beinge ordayned thereunto, named 16 persons, being all in offices,[2] for him for to chuse 12 oute of theym whom hee shoulde beste lyke. The which hee refused to do, saying they were disable and unfitte, partely because for the mooste parte they were his enemyes and butt a number of cavillers and suche as mooste had accused him, therefore not fitting to judge of his matters. Secondly that they had never sitte on any juries and [were] altogether ignorant of the lawes of the lande, so that they coulde nott tell what to judge. Butt wee, not being therewith contented, desired him to accepte of theym as being the Kings subjects, and thought woorthy of the Companies service. Butt *Mr Johnsons appeale.* hee refusing itt did appeale to the King and his Majesties Counsell, and there to answere for himselfe, which seemed very strange to mee, that a man should appeale in a thing whereof hee is not yett condemned, so that I knowe not what to thinke; either hee muste knowe himselfe to bee very fowle, or else hee muste have to greate enemyes whome hee fearethe that they might wreste his cause, as partely I perceyve, and those of the principall officers of the shippe. Howbeit tyme will shewe it, and thus the matter for this tyme was stayed, to see what order maye bee taken heerein; the greateste parte woulde fayne have him oute of the shipp; some others woulde fayne see him hanged,

[1] The record of this Consultation is printed in *Letters Received,* i. 198.

[2] *I.e.,* officers, a term which, as explained in a previous note, covered all ranks above ordinary seamen.

to bee the more assured of theyr places; and this is the course of the world.

25 *January*. Heere came letters overland from Siam from Martin Houtman to Sr.[1] Hendrick Jansen, dated the 28 November, wherein hee wryteth that Sr. Lucas had solde more then the halfe of his goods, and that the King had boughte a greate percell thereof, naming dyvers sortes but withoute pryces, and that the goods were reasonnably good, saving 2 sortes which were to shorte and to narrowe—I thinke that it is the *dupetis*, *popenis* and *misardarens*[2]—moreover that wee had no more white tulbands [*i.e.*, turbans], which are muche requested there—I thinke hee meaneth bleached *betilles* and white *cassas*[3]—and prayseth Mr Lucas very muche to have broughte upp there many good customes; for whereas other strangers muste bring theyr goods into the Kings customehowse, letting it lye there a long tyme, and then att laste they take the greateste parte, if not altogether, for the King, and so is rated and prysed by the Kings fectors according to their owne will and pleasure, against which the strangers maye saye nothing, and then yett muste give ⅓ awaye for to gette his money. Butt Mr Lucas to the contrarie hath brought his goods into his owne howse, and when they came in the Kings name he fyrst aggreed uppon the prises, and afterwards not to departe from [*i.e.*, part with] the goods till they brought testimonye from the King that it was for him. Whereuppon Oya Schismachan[4] came into the howse, remayning as suretye that it was for the King, and so the goods were lette go. Wherefore Houtman writeth that hee is not much beloved, and that hee is excused in regard hee was butt fyrste come thether.

[1] *I.e.*, Signor, frequently used at this period as a prefix, irrespective of nationality. Maerten Houtman was now the Dutch Chief in Siam (*van Dijk*, 33).

[2] Dupetis (Hind. *dopatta*) were cotton sheets, either plain or printed, worn as wraps. Popenis were some kind of print; no other reference has been found to misardarens, but from the wording of this passage it looks as if popenis and misardarens denoted two kinds of printed *dopatta*.

[3] *Betilles* (Portuguese *beatilha*, 'veiling') was the trade name for the muslins of Golconda, and *cassas* (Persian *khāsa*, 'special') for the high-grade muslins of Bengal; both were suitable for turbans.

[4] See *ante* under 11th November, where the designation appears as Phismachan.

Hee also writeth that Mr Lucas was mynded to sende a percell of red yarne to Jangnna an[d] Lamangh,[1] where the same was well requested; butt touching the warres hee maketh no mention. All which in trueth was very joyfull newes to mee, wishing that I might have understood as muche by his owne wryting. Tyme will shewe the truethe thereof. *Good newes from Siam.*

There came hether a small *caffula*[2] overland with Moores [*i.e.*, Moslems] from Keda, bringing newes that att Keda were arryved 2 small shepps from Negapatam and one from Musilpatam, muche contrarye to all our opinions, being butt 10 dayes journey from hence, have bene there 3 months without having any newes thereof, the reason being the high upperwaters [*i.e.*, floods] which this yeare have bene over all the land. With this *caffula* Hendrick Jansen receyved a letter from Keda written by John de Labistraete,[3] whome wee lefte as cape merchant att Musilpatam, dated the 31 December, wherein hee writeth howe that aboute some 1500 persons were come from St. Thome in Paleacatte and have taken the Hollands howse,[4] which they had builte there with greate charges, slayne the men, taken the goods along with theym, and raysed the howse to the grounde, and so departed homewards agayne with a greate bootie; for the principall capitall of that coaste was in Paleacatte, as being a place of their greatest confidence. Butt howe it was done hee doth not wryte, whether it bee done with the wincking (att) of the inhabitants, as partly I beleeve; a more particular relation maye bee knowen with the nexte. Moreover hee wryteth that the Portingalls take greate paynes to have the Hollanders oute of Lanagapatam [*i.e.*, Tegnapatam], eyther for money or by force, *ditto. Newes from Keda. The Hollanders howse in Paleacatte destroyed by the Portingalls off St. Thome.*

[1] Chiengmai and Luang Prabang.

[2] Arabic *qāfila*, caravan, frequently used at this time in India for consignments of goods sent by land, as well as for fleets of coasting boats.

[3] Jan, or Joan, de Labestrate was chosen to succeed Jan van Wesick as senior factor at Masulipatam at the close of 1610, when van Wesick was promoted to be Director of the Coast factories (*van Dijk*, 10, 18; *Terpstra*, 155); the year, 1613, given by van Dijk for Labestrate's departure for Achin, must be a slip for 1612. 'Cape merchant' meant chief merchant; the term was generally used for the chief merchant on a ship, but sometimes, as here, it was applied to a senior factor on land.

[4] For the Portuguese attack on the Dutch 'howse', or factory, at Pulicat in the summer of 1612 see *Golconda*, xxii, 4.

whereof hee partly is in a doute; and that which hee lamenteth above all the reste is that the shipp *der Goes* hathe taken a shippe under Ceylon belonging to one Mir Mahumad Tair,[1] the principall Moore in Musilpatam, comming from Tenesserin; which shipp was commanded by a Portingall, who was accompanyed with dyvers other Portingalls, whome they lette go with the shipp, taking the goods oute of hir, whereof parte they discharged in Musilpatam.

Newes from the coaste off Choromandell,

Afterwards the aforesayd Portingalls arryved there, challenging theyr goods, where they had greate assistance of the aforesayd Mir Mahumad Tair, giving theym letters of recommandation to Golconda, whether also the Captain Warner [*i.e.*, Wemmer] van Berchem[2] is gone. But before the Hollanders coulde heare any newes from him, came the Gouvernour of Musilpatam, fetching with force the Portingalls goods oute of theyr howse, and restoring it into the Portingalls hands; who were not therewith contented, but desired interest and dammages which hereby they had susteyned. Which proces was not ended in September laste, so that the Portingalls kepte theymselves verye hautye and proudly, and the Hollanders were muche perplexed; so that they, to witte the factorys of Musilpatam and Petapoli, resolved together to sende a man for Atchin and to go from thence to Bantam, to certifye the Generall of all things paste, to which the aforesayde Labistrate was ordayned. Which resolution is confirmed by Warner van Barchem in Golconda, who had bought there 2 very fayre horses to bee sente to the King of Atchin, which hee had undertaken himselfe, being in Atchin; with which sayde horses and one other Hollander being imbarqued in a *taure*,[3] hee wente for Atchin; butt by reason of

where the Hollanders are badly used.

They sende Labistrate for Atchin and Bantam to complaine to the Generall.

[1] The name is presumably Mir Muhammad Tāhir. According to *MacLeod* (i. 123), the vessel was searched because there were Portuguese goods on board, and only those goods were taken out of her.

[2] Wemmer van Berchem reached Java from Europe in 1610, bringing official news of the twelve years' truce between Spain and Holland. Shortly after, he was chosen to be Director on the Coromandel Coast; and on his way there he stayed for some time at Achin, where he established friendly relations with the King. He served on the Coast from 1612 to 1615; and at this juncture he was at Golconda, negotiating an arrangement for compounding for the customs at Masulipatam (*van Dijk, passim*).

[3] A type of sea-going vessel used in South India, sometimes of considerable burthen (*Dalgado, s.v.* Taurim).

contrary wyndes they fell in Keda, where the sayde Labistrate is in greate miserye, att greate charges withoute helpe or money, the other Hollander being deceased by the waye, having had no meanes to wryte hether till hee had layne fully 2 months in Keda, the letter having bene 36 dayes in the waye, wryting to bee supplyed with 200 R8. Neyther can hee departe thence till hee bee supplyed from hence, for the shipp that hee came in stayeth there in Keda, and will nott go for Atchin, so that hee muste hyre a junck or praw to go for Atchin. So that hee hath done loste labour, in that hee commeth to late to go for Bantam, the junckes being ready to departe att the ende of this month or the beginning of February, and hee shall nott bee able to gette from (thence) Keda before Marche. This is the right content of Labistrates letter, butt seeing hee knewe not who was residing heere in Patania, hee was the more briefe in his wryting. Whereuppon Hendrick Jansen and I, being greate friendes, parted, to have some more circumstances of this heavy newes. *Falleth in Keda.*

The estate of the Hollanders is very muche altered of late, for when wee fyrste arryved uppon the coaste with the *Globe* they did theyr beste to keepe us oute, as they did in Paleacatte, butt in other places where we were better knowen they coulde effecte nothing, and nowe are they not muche better then putte oute. Butt I do not so muche lament theyr losses as I feare the villanye of the inhabitants, which are not to bee trusted; howbeit, I have many poynts wherewith I coulde accuse the Hollanders, which for dyvers considerations I overpasse heere with silence. By reason of the warres in the Moluccos and Manillas, I feare me the Generall[1] will have butt small meanes to redresse this dishonour, butt tyme will shewe all.

With this *caffala* [*i.e.*, caravan] commeth the sone of the Malim[2] with whome Labistrate is to go for Atchin, with some 4 other persons more, not bringing in all 40 corges of all manner

[1] *I.e.*, Pieter Both, or Bott, the Dutch Governor-General in the East, who was at this time resisting the attempt of the Spaniards in the Philippine Islands ('the Manillas') to recover the Moluccas. Particulars of the position will be found *passim* in *Saris*, who was in those waters in March and April of this year.

[2] Arabic *mu'allim*, the officer next to the *nākhudā*, or captain, of a ship.

of sortes, who are to sell theyr goods with the fyrste,[1] and to returne to Keda; and by the recommandation of the sayd Labistrate, Henrick Jansen was buysie in buying the same, butt not being able to aggree, they shoulde sell their goods abroad,[2] and yf they coulde not gette in their moneys, then Hendrick Jansen was to paye theym their moneys and take in or receyve their dettes, and that onely for to dispatche theym with the fyrste posseble. Yett notwithstanding for wante of buyers they cannot sell theym, and in regard that att this tyme there bee no commodities heere wherin they can imploye theyr capitall, the aforesayd persons are resolved to staye heere till the comming of the junckes from China.

Clothes come from Keda and Bordelongh causeth a fall.

Heere are aryved some 4 or 5 balaos[3] or prawes from Bordolongh, which bring a small percell of cl[o]ath; among the reste 8 or 10 *tsulias* and *calynders*,[4] whereof eache one bringethe a corge or lesse of dyvers sortes, running with this thorough all the contrye, giving the goods so good cheape that it is to bee admyred att, onely to receyve a copan for to buye ryce for theyr bellies; so that I cannot sell one cl[o]ath, butt muste attend the tyme. Those of Bordelongh bring suche meane goods as is scarce to bee written; I sawe yett[5] yesterdaye, with the Orancaio, *pattas*

[1] The word 'corge', *i.e.*, score, indicates that the goods were cotton cloth, which was commonly handled by the score of pieces. 'With the fyrste' must represent Dutch *met den eersten*, which means 'as soon as possible'; so with the words 'with the fyrste posseble' just below. The locution was, however, apparently admissible in contemporary English; the *OED* (*s.v.* First) renders it 'among the first, hence chiefly, especially', but some of the illustrative quotations make better sense when it is rendered 'as soon as possible'.

[2] *I.e.*, they should find purchasers in the market for themselves.

[3] 'Balao', or 'baloon', is Malay *balyanw*, a kind of rowing-boat. Bordolongh has not been found on any map. H.M. Vice-Consul at Singora suggests that it may be Patalung, on the west side of the Inland Sea, about 75 kilometres north-west of Singora; the place can still be reached by boat, but local tradition says that about this period it was actually on the coast.

[4] Indian pedlars. *Chulia* (*Hobson-Jobson*, *s.v.* Choolia) was formerly applied in the Malay Peninsula to Indians, mainly Moslems, from the country round Negapatam. The word *Kĕling*, or *Kling*, is discussed in *Hobson-Jobson*; in the Peninsula it denoted an inhabitant of South India generally. As has been said above, Floris commonly dropped the final *-g* of eastern words, and the Dutch often added the suffix *-der* to denote the inhabitants of places ending in *-n*, as Japander, Achinder, etc.; 'calynders' appears to have been formed from Kĕling in this way.

[5] Dutch *nog*, which in this context would mean 'only'.

and black *salala*,[1] with other Maleys clothings, of the lengthe of 6½ *hasta* [*i.e.*, cubits], 4 spannes broad, the fynesse and *tsaia*[2] accordingly, which hee bought for 20 ma. the corge, our Maleys cloth being more then cento per cento better, understanding in lengthe and bredth, in coullour and fynesse.

Butt a greate oversight hath bene committed in the bespeaking of the foresayd Maleys cloth, to witte, the *pattas*, *dragans*,[3] *salalus* and theyr sortes, for they have all of theym, to witte, the Petapolishe cl[o]ath, a little narrowe white edge, and the upright[4] Maleys cl[o]ath muste bee withoute it, as the cl[o]ath of Paleacatte was; wherein those of Maleys are so curious [*i.e.*, particular] that they will not once putte foorth theyr handes to looke uppon theym;[5] and, yf I had not nowe founde it by experience, I had never believed it, that so small a faulte shoulde cause so greate an abatement in the pryce; and although I can nowe call to mynde that theyr came order with the *Concorde*[6] to cause none more to bee made uppon the coaste, yett that nowe is remembred to late. Those of Maleys saye they bee Siams sortes, so that I shalbee compelled to sende theym thether, as also the red yarne, which will no kynde of waye vente heere. Yett I will staye till the comming of the junckes of China, and trye then what can bee done; in the meane tyme, expecte the tyme. *A greate oversight in the Malveis cloth.*

Having expected very long and no alteration happening, yea, Adi 18 *Martii.*

[1] *Pattas* may be for *dopattas*, or wraps; *salalas*, or *salalus*, were Coromandel goods woven in colours (*Terpstra*, 196).

[2] 'Fynesse' is for 'fineness'. *Tsaia* is the red dye made from chay-root (*Oldenlandia umbellata*), which was employed on the Coromandel Coast.

[3] 'Dragans' represents Malay *dragĕm*, meaning 'purple' or 'dark brown', but the exact nature of the cloth is uncertain. 'Petapolishe' is a Dutch adjectival formation, denoting goods obtained in Petapoli.

[4] 'Upright' probably represents Dutch *recht*, in this context 'proper', or 'correct'.

[5] This conservatism of the Eastern markets was a most important feature of the trade; as George Cokayne wrote from Macassar, "They will not be brought out of their accustomed manner of clothing, and yet every several country must have particular sorts according to their fashion" (*Letters Received*, iii. 139).

[6] *Concorde* is here a translation of *Eendracht*, the name of a Dutch vessel which came from Bantam to the Coromandel Coast in 1608, and brought detailed instructions along with samples of the various goods required for the consuming markets (*Terpstra*, 62). The English ship *Concord* is mentioned further on.

yett small appearaunce of any, and the junckes of China staying theyr comming, I have, according to the resolution sente per Adam Denton, Bat. [*i.e.*, Bartholomew] Churcheman and Plurbier, the 14 of February for Siam in the juncke of the ambassador, this daye sente the shipp for Siam, with suche cl[o]athe as more att large appeareth by the factorye,[1] seing that in a long tyme it woulde not bee solde heere, and do not fynde it good to loose any longer tyme; for having no other meanes, neyther receyved any letters from Siam, I muste in this followe myne owne mynde, committing it to God, who sende us a good successe.

Adam Denton sente for Siam. The Globe *sente to Siam.*

Touching the matter of Mr Johnson, Mr Skinner and others, as also the gouvernment, I referre myselfe to the letter written from Siam[2] to Mr Lucas, wherein I wrote my mynde att large, and so for reasons passe it heere in silence.

This question to bee seene more att large in my letter [blank] *Siam to Mr Lucas.*

The King of Pahan[g], having marryed the younger sister of this Queene of Patania, and they not having seene one the other in 28 yeares, this Queene hathe sente dyvers tymes stately ambassadors, requiring that hir sister might once bee sente hether, that shee might once see hir before hir death, both being of a good age, this Queene 60 yeares of age. Hetherto the King of Pahan[g] hath refused to send hir, but delaying it still with one excuse or another, which now att laste hath angerd this olde woman very muche, so that shee helde upp all the junckes that came from Siam, Camboja, Bordelongh, Lugor [*i.e.*, Ligor], or any other places, being laden with ryce for Pahan[g], and sente foorthe all hir power by water, consisting of aboute 70 sayles with aboute 4000 men, sending theym for Pahan[g] under the commaunde of Maha Raia Datoe Bessar and Orancayo Sirnora, with order to bring hir sister hether, either in friendshippe or by force; so that Pahan[g] shall have muche to do by reason of the great dearth, the burning of his howse, ryce and barnes, as also

Cause off the question betweene Patania and Pahan.

[1] 'Factorye' here represents Dutch *factuur*, 'invoice'. The sentence is awkward: Denton and his companions, carrying the resolution, had already left for Siam by the junk, and the *Globe* now followed under Essington. It will be noticed that there is a gap of nearly two months at this point of the Journal.

[2] This must be a slip or mistranslation; read 'to Mr Lucas in Siam'; the letter is not extant. 'Gouvernment' must mean the command of the ship.

by the warres of Joor, who, as it is sayde, maketh a greate preparation to go in his owne person for Pahan[g]; and the King of Borneo maketh preparation to go to the succour of Pahan[g]. To conclude, every one is upp in armes, and tyme will shewe the successe [*i.e.*, result].

Heere arryved a juncke from Siam belonging to Pahan[g], which, as aforesayd, is arrested heere. With this juncke I receyve a letter from Mr Lucas, wherein [he] maketh mention that as yett hee was butt in a meane estate, and cannot come to the making of the pryce for the Kings cl[o]ath. For which cause the other shopkeepers dare not bee so bolde as to buye one piece of cloth till the King bee furnished and his price aggreed; which tyme will shewe. Adi 4 *Aprill*

Arryved heere 2 juncks of Camboja, being fetcht in by the Patanian fleete, being laden with ryce and bounde for Pahan[g]. 6 *&* 8 *ditto*

Commeth newes of the arrivall of a China juncke in Lugor [*i.e.*, Ligor]. 9 *ditto.*

Arryved heere a juncke of China, having bene 25 dayes in the waye; 15 dayes before his departure 2 junckes were departed hetherwards, of whome as yett there is no newes; bringing further newes that there were yett in lading 4 juncks for Siam, 3 for Bantam and one for Songora [*i.e.*, Singora], all very richely laden. 11 *ditto.*

Arryved the second juncke of China 14 *ditto.*

Another, being the third. These foresayde 3 junckes bring greate store of fyne perseleyn [*i.e.*, porcelain], aboute 150 piccoll[1] rawe silke, very fyne goods, a fewe and meane damasts, velvetts, taphaties, and suche lyke. 17 *ditto.*

Arryved the juncke of China in Songora. 20 *ditto.*

I receyved a letter from Siam, wherein hee [Antheunis] writeth of the arryvall of 2 juncks of China, 2 of Japan, and of Adam Denton with his company, with better newes of the trade, and was come to beginne the sale of his goods, whereof hee then had solde a good percell, also sent a persell of goods for Xamoi [*i.e.*, Chiengmai], with a sure hope to assiste me with a capitall of 15 in [*i.e.*, or] 20,000 R8. Which was no small joye for mee to understand. The King, not lyking the pryses of the taken 25 *ditto.*

A letter receyved from Siam with good newes.

[1] The picul, of 100 catties, was about 130 lb.

goods, hath given it all backe agayne, after having kepte it above 2 months in his howse. A pittifull case when Kings become marchants, butt this is used thorough all the Indies.

Adi 18 *and* 23 *May.* *Divers letters received. Trade for Japan from Siam.*

I receyved dyvers letters from Siam, wherein hee [Antheunis] writethe of the good successe and arryvall of the *Globe*, with other more particulars, whereof I referre mee to the sayd letters. Hee was then buysye to sende a cargason for Japan with the juncke of Jacob Joosten,[1] the cargason consisting in sapon,[2] for which the sayd Joosten, comming to Japan, shall paye cento per cento to Wm. Adams, or in his absence to Melchior Van Sandtwoort.[3] The sayde sapon Mr Lucas hath boughte of the King att 6 months tyme, so that hee onely bearethe the venture of the sea. God graunting a safe voyage, it wilbee good profite. From Siam greate trade maye bee done for Japan, both in the foresayd sapon as also in skinnes, waxe and other suche lyke goods, as also lacquers [*i.e.*, lac]; butt the mooste of the capitall consisteth in deare-skinnes. This yeare there were arryved 2 from Japan, butt having more goods then they coulde lade, eache Nachoda [*i.e.*, captain] bought yett another juncke for to serve their marchants turne; and in [blank] Apprill arryved yett another juncke from Japan, which muste winter there.

Hee also thoughte to sende Mr Martins for the Xhamoi [*i.e.*, Chiengmai] to gather there a capitall, and so to come downe the *primo* of Auguste, and, if all were not solde, then to leave Thomas Samuell[4] there, thinking so to dispatche the shippe by the 15 of Auguste. Butt as hee complayneth in his letters of 11 of Aprill that, though 3 China junckes were arryved there, yett fewe or no

[1] Jacob Joosten was one of the Dutchmen who reached Japan along with William Adams on the *Liefde*, and established himself there as a merchant; his name appears in various forms such as Youssen, Yozen, etc. An account of him will be found in *De Reis van Mahu en De Cordes* (Linschoten Society, 1925), iii. 28 ff.

[2] *I.e.*, sappan wood (*Cæsalpina sappan*), a dye-wood produced largely in Siam.

[3] Melchior van Santvoort was another of those who reached Japan on the *Liefde*, and, like Joosten, established himself as an independent merchant (*op. cit.* iii. 33 ff.).

[4] While Samuell was at Chiengmai the place was captured by the King of Burma; Samuell was made prisoner and taken to Pegu, where he died (*Golconda*, 44). Apparently he was a member of the crew of the *Globe*, taken by Antheunis for business on land.

goods were to bee had, hee giveth mee order to stretche credit to the summe of 10,000 R8, which hee will sende mee with the shipp. Butt afterwards in his letter of the 22 hee wryteth of the arryvall of a Portingall juncke of Macau,[1] thinking hir to bring very good goods, therefore giveth mee warning not to bee to hasty in the taking upp of 10,000 R8 as aforesayd; butt yett in all manner of meanes hee woulde sende me 4 in [*i.e.*, or] 5000 R8, whereuppon I might make a sure accounte. Which hee afterwards confirmeth in his letter of 29 Aprill, notwithstanding that there was yett another juncke arryved from Macau. *Mr Lucas ordeyneth me to take upp money heere.*

After that I had heere overcaste my reconing in what manner to disburthen mee of the cl[o]ath, to imploye the capitall in China wares, I knewe no better meanes butt to offer the sale thereof to the Queene att very reasonnable pryses, with this condition, that, comming agayne the nexte yeare and having any cloth unsolde, to take the same backe agayne att the same pryce, allowing hir a certayne present for the disbursing of hir money. Butt this projecte woulde not bee, excusing hir selfe dyvers wayes, butt offered mee that yf I woulde have any money att interest, that shee woulde lette mee have the same att reasonnable intereste, and that I shoulde seeke my selfe the mooste of my cloth.[2] Whereuppon I woulde advyse myselfe; and so wee parted. *Seeke to deal with the Queene butt in vaine.*

After mature deliberation, seing that the China wares wente well of from the hande, and myselfe being butt meanelye provyded with money, my dettes which were extant to come in very slowly, and that the cl[o]ath att this tyme coulde not stande mee in any steede, I resolved to take upp some money of the Queene to the valewe of 3000 R8, with condition to repaye the same within 3 or 4 months, att 6 per cento for the tyme to the Queene and 1 per cento to the treasurer, so that with the gifte and all it amounteth to 7½ per cento; and although Mr Lucas had written to mee of 5000 R8, yett I durste not go to the uttermooste, leaste it might have fallen oute otherwyse. The Hollanders tooke upp 13,000 R8 with condition if they repaye the same within a month att 5 per cento, if in 3 months att 6 per *Adi 5 June.* *Money taken off the Queene att interest.*

[1] Macao, at the mouth of the Canton river, where the Portuguese had been allowed to establish themselves.

[2] Presumably this means 'seek to make the most I could'.

cento, and within a yeare att 10 per cento, besides 1 per cento to the treasurer and the gifte. So that nowe wee fyrste doe fynde the wante of ready money, butt it is to late for this tyme; it maye bee prevented another tyme.

8 *ditto.* Arryved heere the juncke of Nachoda Hascan,[1] which wente awaye the laste yeare thinking to have gone for Jambi, but was driven downe with the streames [*i.e.*, currents] and fallen in Jortan [*i.e.*, Surabaya]. From thence hee wente to Bali, and in his returne putt on Succadama, thinking from thence to have gone for Jambi. Falling sicke by the waye, hee changed his resolution, comming directly to Patania. With this juncke I receyved a letter from Succadama subscribed by Soshoni Cozucke and Hugh Greete,[2] for the account of the 6th Voyage, wherein they recite very briefly that there had bene that yeare 8 Englishe shipps att Bantam, whereof 3 were gone homewards, 1 for the Moluccos, 1 for Japan and one for the coaste of [blank], making no mention of the reste, nor of any other newes, att which I wonder very muche. They wryte for 3 or 4 packes *dragams*, butt forasmuche as wee have none of those sortes att this tyme, wee att this tyme can sende theym none.

Receyve a letter from Succadama.

—*ditto.* Arryved heere the juncke of the Orancaia Maha Indeva[3] comming from Atchin, who in his returne had called in att Bantam and layne there 9 dayes. Bringeth no letters, neyther Dutche nor Englishe, butt sory newes, as that Campachina[4] hath twyce bene burned, the greate Englishe howse, being full of cl[o]ath, wholly burned, as also the Hollands howse, with a mightye losse. Moreover that there laye a greate Englishe shippe att Poulu Paniangh[5] very muche distressed, and greate mor-

[1] Probably Nākhudā (Captain) Hasan. Bali is the island next to Java on the east.

[2] See *Letters Received*, i. 201; ii. 28. In November, 1612, it had been decided to send Sophony (*not* Soshoni) Cozucke, along with a jeweller, to establish a factory at Sukadana, the diamond market in South-West Borneo. Cozucke was still there, along with Greete, the jeweller, when the *Darling* called in April, 1614.

[3] 'Indeva' should be Indĕra, or Indra, as the name is spelt in other passages; in the Dutch script of the time one form of *v* is almost identical with *r*.

[4] *I.e.*, Kampong China, the Chinese quarter at Bantam.

[5] Purchas gave in the margin the name of the ship, the *Trade's Increase*; her disastrous story can be read in *Jourdain*, 302. Pulau Panjang is an island

talitie; as also that the Englishe had taken 13 sailes of Gusarettes, being very richely laden; as also that dyvers Dutche shippes were gone to the Moluccos. Butt all withoute muche circumstance, onely that there was gone a shippe with cl[o]ath for the Moluccos, and another for England; and although they had loste muche cl[o]ath by the fyre, yett they had another lodge full of cl[o]ath att Pulo Panjangh where the shipp laye, so that, with this, for some yeares the trade in the cl[o]ath is att an ende.

Heere arryved 2 junckes belonging to Joor [*i.e.*, Johore], who were going from thence to Bantam. In the waye in the Straite of Palimbam they had mette an Englishe shippe[1] going for Choromandell, having wante of water, so that these junckes lette theym have 30 potts, letting theym go withoute any hurte. These junckes confirme the newes from Bantam. From thence they wente to Damao[2] in Java, and, having laden ryce, thoughte to returne to Johor; butt, comming neere Barra Bouquit,[3] they understood that those of Atchin[4] had so closely besieged Johor that no man might passe in nor oute; which newes hathe bene currant heere some 14 dayes agone, butt yett withoute any certaintie. They lykewyse affirme that there is a Hollands shippe in the river, who soughte to aide theym of Johor, shewing enmitye to theym of Atchin. What the ende wilbee tyme will shewe.

23 June.

The James *in the Straight off Palumbam*

Those off Atchin besiege Johor.

at the entrance to Bantam Bay, which was a convenient place for repairing ships; the name is sometimes so spelt as to cause a risk of confusion with Penang, or Pulau Pinang. 'Gusarettes' is for Gujarātīs, another reference to Sir H. Middleton's operations in the Red Sea.

[1] The *James*, for the ninth Voyage, having failed to get round Sumatra, attempted to go through the Straits in order to reach the Coromandel Coast, but was unable to do so, and returned to Bantam, eventually sailing outside Sumatra (*Purchas*, I. iv. 441).

[2] Demak, 15 miles north-east of Samarang (*Eredia*, 190).

[3] Berbukit, a port on the east side of the Johore estuary.

[4] A footing in the Straits had for long been an object of the policy of Achin. This siege was successful, and the fleet returned to Achin in triumph (*Purchas*, I. iv. 464); further details are given below under 12th July.

[CHAPTER VII

PATANI (*continued*)]

By reason of these former tydings I, of anewe, knowe not what to do with the cl[o]ath, for withoute doute they muste bee fallen very muche in the southerne places, suche abundance of theym being surprised,[1] which lykewyse wilbee soone felte heere, so that I fynde it beste to transporte the cl[o]ath I have remayning for other places, concluding with this newe following proposition.

A NEWE PROPOSITION.

Seing little good is to bee done in the spices, and the cotton clothes lykewyse oute of requeste, I have made this newe proposition and calculation, to witte, that wee by Gods helpe being able to bestowe the summe of 20 in [*i.e.*, or] 25,000 R8, both heere att Siam as also that which is expected from Maccasar, which according to the common computation oughte to yeelde uppon the Coaste 40, 45, in [*i.e.*, or] 50,000 R8, butt reconing cleere 40,000 R8, which there shoulde bee imployed in these goods following:—

40 candi[2] indigo att 80 Pa. the candi	R8 4300	25,000 R8
400 fardi[3] white yarne @ 24 R8	9600	
80 packs with dyvers sortes of cloth	11,100	
300 candi iron att 4½ Pa. the candi	1800	15,000 R8
to imploye for Siam, Patani &c.	13,200	

[1] 'Surprised' may be read as 'surprising'; or may mean 'captured' (*sc.* by Middleton in the Red Sea); or possibly may stand for 'brought over', *i.e.*, 'imported'. Each of these meanings would fit the context, and it is impossible to make a confident choice between them.

[2] The candy contained 20 maunds, each of about 26 lb. at Masulipatam. 'Pa.' stands here for pagodas, but, on p. 79, the same abbreviation represents packs, or bales, of cloth.

[3] 'Fardi' presumably represents the Portuguese plural, *fardeis*, of *fardel*, 'bale', a word common to Portuguese and English. The 'calculation' below shows that the bale of yarn was 150 lb., the usual weight at Masulipatam.

Then there woulde bee enough remayning in Siam for

300 piccoll benjamin[1] att 20 R8	R8 6000	7200 R8
130 barres lacquere att 10 R8	1300	

in Patany

100 piccoll benjamin att 20 R8	R8 2000	4400 R8
200 barres of pepper @ 12 R8	2400	

So that according to this computation this capitall might bee imployed for England in

40 candi indigo @ 80 Pa. the candi	R8 4300	25,000
400 fardi white yarne @ 18 Pa.	R8 9600	
80 Pa. [*i.e.*, packs] dyvers sortes of cl[o]ath valued	R8 11,100	
400 piccoll beniuni [*i.e.*, benzoin] @ 20 R8	R[8] 8000	11,700
400 piccoll lacquere @ 10 R8 [per bahār]	R[8] 1300	
200 barres of pepper @ 12 R8	R[8] 2400	
		36,700 R8

being aboute 280,000 lb. waighte, amounting, att 1200 lb. per tunne,[2] 233 tunne, which our shippe oughte to carry with ease; and this might yeelde in England aboute[3]

Calculation.

20,000 lb. indigo @ sh. 6 sterling the lb.	*li.* 6000
60,000 lb. white yarne @ sh. 4	*li.* 12,000
80 packes of cl[o]ath by estimation	*li.* 10,000
4800 lb. benjamin @ sh. 4 & 6	*li.* 10,800
4800 lb. lacquere @ sh. 3 & 6	*li.* 8400
8000 lb. pepper @ d. 14	*li.* 4500
Somma	£51,750.

[1] *I.e.*, benzoin, the resin of *Styrax benzoin*, used as incense. The word seems to have puzzled the translator, for it appears below as 'beniuni' and 'benivin'. 'Lacquere' is used for lac, the resin produced by *Coccus lacca*, an insect parasite on trees. The 'barre', or bahār, was in Siam usually 3 picul, or nearly 400 lb. The total of these two items should be 7300 R8.

[2] *I.e.*, the shipping ton, not the unit of weight; the weight of a measured ton varied, of course, with the nature of the goods.

[3] The last three items in this table seem to have been misread by the translator. Apparently Floris worked in Holland pounds, which were 9 per cent. greater than English, and took the picul as 120 of those pounds, which is very nearly correct; similarly, he took the candy of indigo as 500 Dutch pounds. There were thus 48,000, not 4800, pounds of benzoin and of lac, which would give the money-value entered. The 200 bahārs of pepper would represent about 80,000, not 8000, pounds, which at 14*d*. would be worth 4666*l*.; to get the total of 51,750*l*., which is repeated below, and is therefore

Summa: by calculation woulde yeelde in England 51,750*li.* sterling, of which I substracte 10,000*li.* for charges in England, so there woulde reste 41,750*li.*, besides some China silkes and other curiosities; and then woulde bee remayning heere att Siam and Bantam no lesse then 30,000 R8, which, being imployed especially from Siam for Japan, bearing the adventure,[1] ought to yeelde in England, all misfortunes excluded, no lesse then 120,000 R8 or 25,000*li. de claro.*[2] So that, according to this calculation, this capitall woulde bee woorth in England aboute 66,000*li.*, which for this present tyme is the beste and mooste convenient waye that I can imagine, and the rather because the Hollanders have not shipped any benivin [*i.e.*, benzoin] or lacquere these 3 yeares, so that in these wares no other can bee in oure waye. And for to putte this resolution in practize, I have resolved to sende some goods to Camboja, to have benjamin, lacquere, getta,[3] mandu or cardamum backe agayne for a returne;

Adi 2 *July.* *A cargason sente to Camboja per Nachoda Sanqua.*

and accordingly have this daye aggreed with Nachoda [*i.e.*, Captain] Sanqua that I shall deliver him a percell of goods, which hee shall seeke to sell for my mooste profite, for which hee is to have 10 per cento for his provision [*i.e.*, commission], with condition that I shall paye no fraighte, neyther going nor comming, nor custome nor any other charges, as more att large appeareth by the contracte made with the sayde Nachoda Sanqua; and have delivered unto him suche goods as appeareth by the receyte, amounting together 80 lyeell[4] golde Patania coyne. God graunte all maye succeede well.

6 *July.* Nachoda Sanqua departed for Camboja. Hee is a man of good

probably correct, we must assume that Floris valued the pepper at 4550*l.*, perhaps allowing something for wastage. *Somma* is the Italian book-keeping term for 'total'.

[1] Dutch *avontuur*, used at this time in the sense of the risks of a voyage.

[2] *I.e.*, 'net'. *Clarum* is defined in Ducange's *Glossary* as "what remains over after debts have been paid".

[3] Malay *gĕtah*, a gum or resin. Guttapercha, now the most familiar *gĕtah* of Cambodia, was not used in Europe at this period, and the reference is probably to the resin of *Garcinia Hanburii*, which yields the pigment gamboge, and was also used medicinally as a cathartic (Guyot and Raffalovitch, *Dict. du Commerce*, ii. 544). The word 'mandu' may represent Malay *munggu*, 'cardamom'.

[4] Apparently the translator's misreading of tael.

estate. I have had my mooste dealing with him. Hee hathe his howse, wyfe and children heere, so that his person is not to bee feared. *Nachoda Sanqua departeth for Camboja.*

Departed the juncke of Datoe Laxmanna for Siam, with whome I writte to Mr Lucas att large, as more att large appeareth by the coppye booke, whereunto I referre mee. *9 ditto.*

Heere arryved the King of Pahan[g] with the Queenes sister and 2 sonnes, who, after many sendings to and fro, commeth hether muche agaynste his will, leaving his countrye in greate povertye, in hunger, warre, and withoute howse or forte, all being burnt upp. Hee broughte certayne newes that the Atchiners had taken Johor, and carryed all the ordinance, slaves and other things along with theym, Raja Boungson[1] with his childeren taken prisoners, and the King of Johor fledde to Bintan[g]; so that it is to bee wondered att so auncient a kingdome to bee so overrunne, which in former tyme hathe endured greate sieges both of the Atchiners and the Portingalls of Malacca. They saye it hath bene besieged 29 dayes. Of the Hollanders the reporte is very differente,[2] butt it seemeth that the principall poynte is that the shipp was in the river of Johor before the comming of the Atchiners, and, the marchant of the shipp being on shoare, the Atchiners came stopping the passage betweene the shippe and the towne, lying [blank] leagues upp the river, and that the Hollanders shoulde have sente for some 30 muskettiers to aide of the forte; whereof some in the fight were slayne, and afterwards, the fort being yeelded with accord, the Hollanders thinking to passe thorough the countrie to come to theyr shipp, the which being knowen of the Atchiners, they were pursued, some slayne, some fledde into the woods, and some taken prisoners. The shippe having knowlege thereof wente doune oute of the river till Barra Bouquit [Berbukit], from whome no more since hath bene hard; a further certayntie dayly will bee knowen. *12 ditto.*

[1] Raja Bongsu, the King's second brother, and the effective administrator of the kingdom; for an account of him see *Eredia*, 183. Bintang is the large island south of Johore.

[2] *I.e.*, "the reports are very discordant". The facts regarding the Dutch ship, the *Hoop*, or *Hope*, are given below under 21st October, when she at last reached Patani.

13 ditto. The King [of Pahang], with his whole fleete, passing hard by along our howse, wee gave him a welcome in shooting of some chambers,[1] which did so please him that hee caused mee and Hendrick Jansen to bee called in his praw, giving us many thankes for oure good wills, desiring us to come oftentymes to see him, and [asking] why wee came not as well to trade in his countrye as in other places. Whereuppon hee was served,[2] being but homelye fetcht in, which did grieve him very muche, for no body of the greateste came to bring him in, onely all the doggs were killed for his sake, because hee can endure none.

16 ditto. Heere arryved the little pinnasse, being called *Little Enchuis of Bantam*, sette upp heere by the shipp *Bantam*, which wente from hence in company of the juncke of Empan, with whome I sente John Persons for Maccasar, and from thence to Ambona and Banda, from thence returning to Maccasar and so to Bantam, and commeth from Bantam in 12 dayes hether. With this pinnasse commeth Abraham van den Broeck,[3] who lykewyse wente from hence in hir; hath mette in Banda the Generall Gouvernour, Pr. de Bott [*i.e.*, Pieter Both], who hathe absolved him of his former offence, sending him expresly hether to redeeme [*i.e.*, relieve] Hendrick Jansen and to supply this place, to the greate admiration [*i.e.*, surprise] of many. This pinnas bringeth newes that the juncke of Empan shall not come hether this yeare, being

Abraham van den Broeck commeth with a little pinnass in Patana.

[1] The *OED* defines 'chamber' at this period as "a piece of ordnance; especially a small piece used to fire salutes"; but according to the contemporary *Seamen's Dictionary* (Navy Records Society, vol. lvi, 1922), "chamber is a charge which we put in at the breech of any murderer or fowler".

[2] Presumably in the sense of 'waited upon', or attended, by the officials whose duty it was to 'fetch him in' to the Queen.

[3] Abram van den Broeck came out on Matelieff's fleet in 1605, and was one of the party who established the first Dutch factory in Japan. After a visit to Holland, he came out again on Brouwer's fleet of 1611; and at Bantam, in February, 1612, he was condemned to death for the manslaughter of a quartermaster. The sentence was commuted, but he was still in disgrace when he came to Patani in that year. When he visited the Spice Islands on the *Little Enkhuizen* early in 1613, he was reappointed to the Company's service on his former salary; this must be the absolution of his former offence referred to in the text. He got into fresh trouble with the Governor-General a month after this entry was made, but served for some time longer in the Spice Islands; and he is probably the 'Abraham Vanderbrook' of *Letters Received*, iii. 62. Eventually he was ordered home by the Directors, and left the East in 1616 (*Ijzerman*, 171–4; *Bouwstoffen*, i. 34 ff.).

resolved to go to the Moluccos. The 13 of June John Persons was yett in Maccasar, where hee had boughte a little balauwe or prawe, to go with hir to Succadama and from thence hether; had almooste solde all his cl[o]ath excepte onely some *gobars*[1] and redd yarne; [they] saye that the steele was very well solde there, though there had bene tenne tymes as muche; butt having no letters from him I muste expecte [*i.e.*, await] his comming. *Newes from Maccasar,*

The *Darling*[2] hath bene in Loe, and there gotte some fewe cloaves, aboute 70 or 80 barres [*i.e.*, bahārs], butt hee was forbidde to trade by Capt Hitoe, so that nothing else hath bene done. It seemeth some difference is risen, butt can heere butt little certaintie. *&*

The *Cloave*,[3] with John Sayers, hath bene under the forte Mackjan to have refresshing, which, according to his saying, hee had there, and so to further theyr voyage for Japan. Moreover, that 3 Englishe shipps are gone homewards laste yeare, among whome are named the *Hector*, the *Peppercorne*, and the *Salamander*.[4] The *James*, being twyce returned to Bantam, once aboute the Straighte and once thourough, nowe for the thyrde tyme, having the very harte of the monson, hathe for the third tyme assayed hir voyage for the coaste in the ende of January, and withoute all doute will have a hard voyage. They saye, moreover, that the fayre and costely shipp, the *Trades Increase*, lyeth a grounde att Bantam, withoute maste, with 33 men, the greatest parte being sicke. The shippe is doubbled [*i.e.*, sheathed] on the one syde butt not on the other. In the sayde shipped [*sic*] are deceased some 100 Englishe men, and more Chinesians, which wrought for dayly wages, as also 8 Dutche, some plague or other mischievous sicknesse being come into the shippe; and, *Bantam.*

[1] Malay *gĕbar*, 'sheet'.

[2] A detailed account of the *Darling's* voyage to Hitu in Amboyna and Luhu (Loe) in Ceram will be found in *Jourdain*, 244 ff. 'Capt Hitoe' is the Captain, or Governor, of Hitu.

[3] The *Clove*, Captain John Saris, belonged to the eighth Voyage; her passage through the Moluccas to Japan is described in *Saris*, and also in *Purchas*, I. iv. 355 ff. Makian is one of the Moluccas; the fort was at this time held by the Dutch.

[4] The *Hector*, *Peppercorn* and *Solomon* (not *Salamander*) sailed for home early in 1613; the *James* was to go from Bantam to Masulipatam (*Letters Received*, i. 288; *Purchas*, I. iv. 441).

as it is reported, the Divell hathe kepte a foule rule there. Sir Henry Middleton dyed the 24th of May, mooste of hartesore. This in truethe is a grievous newes, the death of so many men, and the perishing of so costly and famous a shipp. Moreover, they certifye the taking of dyvers Gusarette shipps,[1] as also the 2 greate terrible fyrings, and that our howses where the cloths laye are burned, butt what is become of the cl[o]ath I cannott learne, seing I have no letters; although att this present there bee 3 English howses,[2] the one hath nothing to do with the other, and all 3 vente cl[o]ath, which seemeth very strange to mee, for eache spoyleth the others markett as much as they can, being the right waye to bee made to forsake the Indies. Neyther do I knowe why they have sente the *James* for the coaste to fetche more cl[o]ath. God give theym joye all. The fyrste fyre was in November laste paste, and the laste fyre was in May, 3 dayes after the death of Sir Henry. God Almightye requite it with some prosperitie in another.

The estate of the Dutche is, that by Captain Schott they have taken the castle and iland of Solor,[3] and there gotten a greate quantitie of sandelwood, and sente the Portingalls to Malacca. *Newes from Bantam.* In the Moluccos the Generall hath taken the forte[4] and iland of [blank], lying betweene Tidore and Ternate, a place of importance for the Spaniards and theyr galeys. Also the Generall hathe given defiance to the quarter of the Spaniards because of the evill intertaynement of the Dutche prisoners. So that there wilbee a hoate warre on both sides, for the Viceroy of Mexico

[1] The reference is to Sir Henry Middleton's operations at Mocha, summarised in *Letters Received*, i. Introd. xxxiii ff. 'Fyrings', both accidental and intentional, were frequent at Bantam; see *Scot's Discourse*, in *Purchas*, I. iii. 167 ff.

[2] The lack of cooperation between the representatives at Bantam of the different Voyages is noticed in *Jourdain*, lix ff.

[3] Solor is one of the most easterly of the chain of islands which runs from Java to Timor. The Portuguese were established there mainly for the trade in sandalwood; in April, 1613, their fort surrendered to the Dutch under Apollonius Schott after three months' siege. Schott was drowned in the following November while bathing near Jakatra; Coen wrote of him to the Directors that he was "as valiant a soldier, as skilful a man, and loyal an adherent of Your Excellencies as anyone in India" (*van Dijk*, 76).

[4] Pieter Both captured the Spanish fort of Marieko on Tidore early in February of this year (*Saris*, xli). 'Defiance to the quarter' means, perhaps, 'had notified that no quarter would be given'.

and the Gouvernour of the Manillos [*i.e.*, Philippine Is.] are gathering greate forces, agaynst which the Generall laboureth with greate diligence, and hathe gathered the whole fleete together, being att this present of 22 sayle, and with theym gone to the Moluccos to spye an advantage from the Spaniards before they can come together. The tyme will shewe the effecte. They expecte yett this yeare 14 shipps more, and there is butt one to goe homewards. Moreover, there bee 4 shipps gone for the coaste of Choromandell, 2 from Bantam and 2 from Holland. The shipp the *Hope* sette sayle from Bantam in Marche with 70,000 R8 in silver and 10 in [*i.e.*, or] 12,000 R8 in cl[o]ath of cotton, with charge fyrste to putte on Johor, and then to come hether to discharge the capitall heere, of which capitall the factories of Siam, Songora and Succadama shoulde bee furnished, butt, as aforesayd, commeth not. Shee is a shipp of 300 laste or 600 tunne, provyded with 24 peeces and 80 men. God knoweth where shee abydeth. For [? Hir] not comming wilbee a greate entertayning[1] of the Dutche, (being) sitting in these foresayde places withoute goods or money. This shipp the *Hope* was ordeyned to go for the Moluccos, therefore this pinnas bringeth nothing with hir.

The newes of Europe is that the Emperour Rudolph is deceased, and Matthias chosen in his place; the King of Poland to have taken Muscow, and the King of Dennemarck to have warres with Sweden; the reste of the kingdomes to bee in good peace.[2]

I in company of Hendrick Jansen and Abraham van den Broeck wente to see the King of Pahan[g] with a present, which was very acceptable unto him, promising to come and see us in our howses. As yett hee is butt little esteemed heere. *21 July.*

[1] This may possibly be sarcastic, but more probably the translator took the wrong meaning of a verbal noun derived from the ambiguous *onderhouden*. This verb, reckoned in the larger dictionaries as two, means (1) 'to underhold', that is, support, maintain, entertain, etc.; (2) 'to hold-under', that is, depress, oppress, etc. Floris probably meant that the non-arrival of the ship would be a great blow to the Dutch.

[2] The Archduke Matthias was elected Emperor in June, 1612, in succession to Rudolf II, who had died in the previous January. The activities of the Northern Powers here referred to can be studied in chapter v of the *Cambridge Modern History*, vol. iv.

—ditto. Arryved a juncke from Siam. I receyved letters from Siam of 29 Aprill. Mr Lucas writethe mee that hee had delivered His Majesties letter[1] to the King of Japan to Melchior van Santvoort to bee delivered to William Adams, and by him to bee delivered to the King, yf hee shoulde so fynde it good; butt is of no greate importance, because it is thoughte John Sayers [*i.e.*, Saris] will have bene there before him. For the reste, confirmeth his former letter, and that as yett hee coulde nott gette leave to sende Mr Martins to the Jangomai [*i.e.*, Chiengmai]: whereby the knaverye of this countrye may bee perceyved.

Letters receyved from Siam.

25 ditto. Abraham van den Broeck departed with the pinnas for Songora, there to dubble [*i.e.*, sheathe] hir and to take in some goods.

—ditto. Departed the laste juncke of China, the fyrste being departed the 15 and the 2nd the 23 ditto, having for theyr lading aboute 300 barres [*i.e.*, bahārs] of pepper, with many buffe [*i.e.*, buffalo] and other beasts skinnes, rottan, and byrds or foules heads. They have broughte this yeare aboute 150 piccoll raw silke and 50 picoll of throwne silke, which Hendrick Jansen did take in barter against elephants teethe [*i.e.*, ivory]; the teeth @ 65 R8 and the silke att 220 and 225 R8 the picoll. The rawe silke att 180 the beste; other according to their goodnesse. Of silke wares fewe or none that was good.

Adi *27 July.* Nachoda Hadsie [? Hājī] wente for Siam, with whome I have written att large of all what is passed heere.

I write for Siam.

28 ditto. Came the Ambassador of Pahan[g], who had layne 8 months in Malacca, bringing newes howe those of Malacca made greate preparation, fearing the increasing power of the Atchiners.[2] As also that 3 greate shipps and a barque were gone for China this month.

3 Portingall shipps go for China.

31 ditto. The King of Pahan[g] came with greate state to our house, making greate promises that wee comming into his countrie shoulde have kynde intertaynment. Whereuppon I woulde fayne have made a contract with him, butt, the Patanishe gentilitie being present, hee putte it of till another tyme, that somebodye shoulde come into his countrye, and then hee woulde yeelde to

The King off Pahan commeth to oure house.

[1] Printed in *First Letter Book*, 426.

[2] Achin laid siege unsuccessfully to Malacca in 1615 (*Letters Received*, iii. p. xxiii).

us in all what shoulde bee founde reason. And after wee had had some fewe woords together, and having given some presents of clothings to him, his two sonnes and some of his principalls, hee departed with great contentment; for hee oftentymes was hearde to saye that hee was receyved in better sorte of us, being strangers, then of the Pataniers theymselves; and, to saye the truethe, it was homelie enough.

The Queene sente for us to the courte, whereas was a greate feaste in honor of the King of Pahan[g]; and there was playde a commedye all by women, to the manner of Java, which were apparrelled very antickly [*i.e.*, grotesquely], very pleasaunte to beholde, so as I doute not to have seene the lyke in any place. Adi 2 *Auguste.*

Arryved heere a juncke from Bintam, confirming the newes of the taking of Johor, and that the King nowe keepeth himselfe att Bintam; butt can saye nothing of the successe [*i.e.*, fate] of the Hollanders, and the shippe is not yett to bee seene, for since it was driven oute of the river no newes hath bene heard of hir. 5 *ditto.*

Heere arryved a juncke of Pahan[g] confirming all the former newes. Adi 6 *Auguste.*

Departed the King of Pahan[g], having bene heere rather as a mockeng stocke then otherwyse; and the Queenes sister, for whome all the sturre had bene, woulde nott leave him, but returned backe with hir husband, and in lieu of getting many greate presents had almooste spente all that shee had. 9 *ditto. King of Pahan departeth.*

Arryved heere a juncke of Maccasar, by whome I receyved a letter from Thomas Brette with simple[1] newes, fyrste, that they were come to a dead markett; secondly, that John Persons is growen franticque; and that they had boughte a juncke thinking to have come awaye the 12 of July; butt in the meane tyme the *Darling* came thether,[2] being full of clothing, to settle a factory there, and in regard they were freshe men and unacquainted there, they kepte upp the juncke there till they should bee settled. And nowe the monson drawing neere to his ende, I am in very greate doute, and marvayle very muche that they of the *Darling* shoulde bee so bolde as to keepe upp the juncke till the 16 *ditto.*

[1] Presumably in the eighth, obsolete, sense given in the *OED*, 'wretched', 'pitiful', 'dismal'. Brett had accompanied Persons to Macassar.

[2] For the visit of the *Darling* to Macassar see *Jourdain*, 292 ff.

ende of the monson, to putte the voyage in a doute; and not one of theym all to bee so kynde as to wryte a woorde. Surelye wee maye well take paynes in planting newe places to keepe correspondence with all places, to leave remembraunces and instructions; butt wee have nott hitte on the right men, and so muste take patience. Butt yf the junck speede otherwyse then well, those of the *Darling* shall answere for it; for my instruction and order was to returne backe with the fyrste [*i.e.*, as soon as] possible, and they to the contrarie keepe him upp till the very laste, yf not to to late. Tyme will shewe the reste. Butt concerning the trade hee [Brett] writeth nothing att all, as not knowing any thing himselfe.

Adi 8 *September.* *The arrivall off Raja ndra Mouda from Banda.* Arryved heere the juncke of Raja Indra Mouda, which wente from hence the 25 October; had bene fyrste at Maccasar, and from thence to Banda,[1] where hee came to a good merte [*i.e.*, market] and made good profitte, especially the castle having no money, so that those of the castle had no meanes to buye his ryce and other things, so that hee was licenced to deale with Ortatan and other places and Bandameses,[2] whereby hee gott good store of mace and cloaves, which those of the castle coulde not forbidde to bee transported, for theyr wante of money, as also that the juncke belonged to Patania. Shee brought aboute 200 sockles[3] mace, and a greate percell of nuttmeggs which shee had solde to the Portingalls in Maccasar.

Adi—*ditto.* *Richard Welden.* Orancaio Raja Indra Mouda broughte me 2 letters written in Banda by one Rychard Welden,[4] butt nothing butt complements, withoute mentioning any thing; butt I understoode by the sayd Nachoda that hee was sente thether by the King of Buton as

[1] The Banda Islands were the only source of nutmegs and mace. At this time the Dutch occupied a fort or 'castle' on the island of Neira, but they had not yet subdued the islanders (*Letters Received*, iii. p. xxx).

[2] 'Bandameses' should be Bandanese; Ortatan was a market on Lontor, or Great Banda.

[3] Sockle, suckell, etc., was the name given to the packages in which mace was transported; the weight varied from 120 to 140 lb. The suggestion in *Hobson-Jobson* (*s.v.* Catty) that the word is a misreading of picul is negatived decisively by various Dutch commercial records.

[4] Richard Welden sailed with David Middleton on the fifth Voyage, was left in this region, and entered the service of the King of Buton, an island lying south-east of Celebes (*Jourdain*, 274 *n.*; *Letters Received*, iii. 308).

ambassador, touching certayne wrongs which the sayde King had receyved of the Hollanders, and after hee had delivered his message hee departed for Pulo Wai.[1] This is all that I coulde learne concerning this matter. By the aforesayde Nachoda I learned the state of Banda. The Generall Pr. de Bott, being in Banda, hath settled reasonnable good orders, and ministred very *The state off Banda.* severe justice uppon some which onely had slepte in the watche, hanging theym presently on a gallowes hard by the castle, so that ii [two] hung thereon; which caused dyvers to runne over to the Bandanesians, whereas [*read* whereof] att his departure 10 were turned Moores [*i.e.*, Moslems], and, what meanes soever they of the castle used, yett they coulde nott gett theym into their handes agayne. So that those of the castle have no commaunde att all over the Bandanesians, onely that they can commaunde all the junckes to ryde under the castle, as also the shipps; whereby the[y] bee commanders of the sea, butt on lande they dare not give a bad woord to the Bandanesians, neyther maye they once prate[2] oute of the castle.

The sayde Nachoda in his returne backe putte on Maccasar *—ditto.* agayne, arryving there the 9 of Auguste, where hee solde all his nuttmeggs to the Portingalls, excepte some 40 barres [*i.e.*, bahārs] which were in the bulster,[3] att 22 and 23 R8 the great barre. *Newes from John Persons.* And after having layne there 14 dayes, hee came in 26 dayes to Patani, and broughte mee newes howe that the *Darling* and John Persons juncke were gone awaye the daye before his arrivall, and that in hir running in in the morning hee had seene theym both in Maccasar in an Englishe howse with 5 persons. The chiefeste speakes very good Persianishe,[4] and the sayde Nachoda hath bene twyce in theyr howse. Also they have kepte with theym Ibrahin the Gusarite [*i.e.*, Gujarātī] whome I had sente with John Persons, who sendeth his commendations to mee. Butt

[1] Pulau Ai, or Wai, is one of the smaller Banda Islands.

[2] In the MS 'prate' has been substituted for 'peepe forth'; the latter makes better sense, but the original may have been *praten*, which means 'to speak', not necessarily 'to prate'.

[3] Dutch *bolster* or *bulster*, the outer covering of a nut. The meaning here is 'in the shell'; nutmegs were usually shelled before export.

[4] 'The chiefeste' must be John Jourdain; he had been in India from 1609 to 1612, and presumably acquired fluency in Persian during this period.

yett, notwithstanding all the former recited occasions, it hathe not pleased those of the factorye to sende any one woord by wryting, neyther of theyr successe and planting of theyr factory, nor of the departure of the *Darling*, nor of John Persons, nor his sicknesse, nor his dealings, nor any other circumstance; neyther in the meane tyme doth John Persons come to sight. Wee maye well go and plante newe factories, discover newe places, give instructions and leave advyce for all places where wee come, butt wee fynde not the men with whome wee have to do; att leaste yf they did butt lette our things in quyet and trouble theymselves with theyr owne, for they are an occasion of John Persons staying oute a whole month longer after hee was readye to departe; what a months tyme is in these countries, where a man muste travayle by the monson, I referre to the judgement of others who are skilled in that matter and by experience have had triall thereof. In the meane tyme I expecte with devotion what wilbee the ende, and whether hee can come within these 15 dayes.

[CHAPTER VIII

PATANI (*continued*)]

Aboute noone wee sawe a shipp over the Sabrangh, butt being rainye wether both wee and the Dutch sente a praw to knowe what the shipp was, who returned aboute 7 of the clocke saying that shee was the *Globe*, and had bene very neere hir, butt having bene turned over with the praw hee woulde go no further, being very ill and almooste drowned. Adi 21 *October. I thinke this should bee September.*[1]

I wente in the morning to seeke the shippe, but could not spye any shipp, and so returned home withoute doing any thing. 22 *ditto.*

In the morning wee sawe the shippe agayne, comming directly from the sea towards the roade, and knewe hir to bee our shipp. Wherefore I wente presently aboorde, and founde the company in reasonnable good lyking. By the letters of Mr Lucas I understood that hee did sende mee 13,000 R8 both in golde, silver and other marchandize, and that it was impossible for him to do any more, not having receyved any newes from the cargason sente to Jangomay [*i.e.*, Chiengmai], because the passages were stopt because of the warres intended betweene theym of Awa [and] theym of Lanjangh,[2] so that all the wayes are shutte upp. It seemeth that this yeare they will go to it. God defende us from harme. The King of Awa is sayde to have taken Siriangh[3] and to have caused the Xenga to bee slayne. The young King of Siam 23 *ditto. The* Globe *arriveth from Siam.*

[1] The marginal correction, whoever made it, is obviously correct.

[2] Awa (Ava) here stands for Burma. Anaukpetlun, the reigning King, first established himself in the north, and then extended his rule southward to Pegu. He conquered Chiengmai in 1614, but it does not appear that Lanshan was involved in that particular war.

[3] After Philip de Brito (Xenga) had defeated the Arakan flotilla, as mentioned in a previous note, he was for a time practically independent, and defended himself successfully against his neighbours; the Viceroy of Goa recognised him as Portuguese Governor of Syriam, but could not control him effectively. In 1612 he marched north, and sacked Toungoo. Anaukpetlun then besieged Syriam, captured it, and executed de Brito (*Harvey*, 185–9; *Journal*, Burma Research Society, August, 1926, pp. 101 ff.).

doth expecte him with greate forces, setting good watche uppon his borders. The successe [*i.e.*, result], tyme will shewe. For the reste, I referre myselfe to the letter [*not extant*] of Mr Lucas, wherein hee discourseth att large both of the traficque and state of the countrye, especially touching the disorder in the shipp, which according to his wryting and thinking was by him alayde, butt I founde it muche otherwyse.

Reference to Mr Lucas his letter.

Adi 24 *ditto.* Wee wente to the Queene to certifye hir of the arryvall of the shipp, and that wee were readye to paye our dette, asking whether wee shoulde paye in golde or silver. Whereuppon shee answered shee was content to take golde. Whereuppon wee wente home to fetche the golde from aboord. In our waye Mr Essington asked mee whether [*read* whither] I was resolved to sende the shippe; whereuppon I answered, for the coaste of Choromandell according to our fyrst resolution. Butt hee, having no great mynde thereunto, tolde mee of many difficulties, to witte that the shipp was very leacke, the men unwilling, and that it were better that the shipp wente home to certifye the Company of all matters, and that then the shippe might bee sette foorth agayne for the same accounte. Which prepositions being strongly urged by him sounded very strangely in my eares, and nowe did see very well that Mr Lucas had written to mee nothing but trueth; butt giving him suche satisfaction and shewing the contrary with suche good reasons, that hee had nothing to saye agaynst it. And so wee came home, desiring Mr Essington to go aboord and to fetche the golde, butt nothing came of it, putting it of till the nexte daye.

Butt something else laye hidden under it, for att night, sitting att supper and discoursing of the running awaye of James Pieters and other disorders of the shipp, wherewith I was not a little discontented, wisshing the sayde Essington henceforward to bee more warye, and not to beginne any thinge so obstinately of himselfe, butt according to the Companies commission to rule all things with counsell and advyce, and so to prevente all disorders; which hee, as seeking some occasion, tooke very ill, calling me a disloyall servaunte of the Company, that I soughte to diminishe his autoritie, and that I was a maynteyner of traytors and villaines, and hencefoorthe woulde not knowe mee

Very dangerous contention between Essington and mee

in any thing, with many suche lyke termes and speeches. All which I sawe and bore in presence of dyvers persons, and perceyving both by the writing from Siam and the ill gouvernment of the shipp what hee intended, I coulde not refrayne, butt turned stifly to him agayne, hoping to bring him to reason; butt all was in vayne, so that I thoughte it beste to go to my chamber and to see howe it woulde bee in the morning, which accordingly I did.

In the morning there was almooste no rule with him, for hee packed his cheste and luggage and wente aboorde; and although I had sufficient meanes to arreste both him and the boate, yett I woulde not go that waye, butt lett him alone, hoping that when hee shoulde bee come aboord hee woulde bethinke himselfe. Butt to the contrary, comming aboord hee fell to sclaunder mee, with so many greate and false lyes that during my lyfe the lyke hath not happened to mee. Then perforce hee woulde go home, making there a certayne writing, and all suche as woulde not subscribe it were for villaines sente ashoare; and although hee playde many prankes, which all did tende to the hurte and hinderance of the voyage, yett for certayne waightie reasons I will heere passe theym over with silence, and make no mention howe hee kepte William and Robert[1] aboord, howe the boate was sente armed on shoare, the Dutche pinnas did arme hirselfe, and all the towne runne to armes, howe I by the counsell of some good friends did arreste the skiffe, and so came to a parley, till the 31 ditto that wee were reconciled together againe, after that a verye foolishe peece of service was paste, and I having gotten on my syde dyvers of the shipps company, that they were nott able to waye their ancker. All these proceedings I referre to the acte [*i.e.*, record] which is made thereof, hoping it shall nott bee needefull to remember the same any more.[2]

25 ditto.

31 ditto. The differen is pacified.

[1] 'William' is presumably Floris' cousin, William Ebert, who is mentioned below under 21st October; and 'Robert' is Robert Littlewood, the purser, who was left with Ebert at Patani when the ship sailed for Masulipatam.

[2] The 'acte' is not extant; but one paper bearing on this dispute, printed in *Letters Received*, i. 296, shows that on 27th September Essington intended to sail for home *via* Bantam, leaving the factors at Patani. This was directly contrary to clause 11 of the commission (*First Letter Book*, 385), under which this was a question to be decided by the chief merchants, not the captain.

Adi 4 *October.* Being the fyrste daye of Lente in the Moorishe style,[1] aboute 8 of the clocke in the morning, there rose a mightye fyre in the towne, or rather forte and courte, of Patania, and in regard of the strangenes of the matter I will particularly recite it. Datoe Besar and Datoe Laxmanna, dwelling amoost neere one to the other, and, excepte Raja Schey, the richeste in slaves of Javanians,[2] it chanced that Datoe Besar had bene threatned of his Javanian slaves to kill him, Laxmanna, Raja Sitterbangsa and others; which being presented [*i.e.*, reported] by dyvers, att laste it came to the eares of the foresayde persons. Wherefore Datoe Besar, calling his Javanian slaves together, asked theym howe the matter was, who did denye it. Neverthelesse, hee caused 2 which were suspected mooste to bee bounde, which the Pongoulu[3] of the slaves woulde not suffer. Whereuppon Datoe Besar, being angry, drew his cryce[4] or weapon, and thruste thourough the sayde Pongulo. Whereuppon the other Javanians playde amock,[5] and it wanted not muche butt they had gotte Dato Bezar into their handes, butt with the helpe of his other slaves hee escaped. Whereuppon the Javanians slewe all that came in theyr waye, and presently sette the howses on fyre. The Javane slaves of Laxmanna, not being farre from thence, seing theyr contryemen in trouble, even in sighte of their master Laxmanna [and] notwithstanding all his threatnings, ranne to their ayde, setting all on fyre, gathering together some 100 persons, more or lesse, the exacte number nott being justly knowen; and so ranne to the greate gate called Puntu Gorbangh,[6] setting all on fyre on bothe sydes as they wente, so that the whole towne, excepte some fewe, as the Queenes courte, Orancaio Sirnora, Dato Bandara, and the Meskita,[7] was burned; and the Javanes going along the long streete tooke the beste bondwomen

Fire and tumulte in Patania.

[1] *I.e.*, the month of Ramadhān, or Ramazān, as the name is pronounced in Persia and India.

[2] *I.e.*, 'the richest in Javanese slaves'.

[3] Malay *pĕnghulu*, 'headman'.

[4] Creese, Malay *kĕris*, 'dagger'.

[5] Dutch *amok spelen*, 'to run', literally, 'play, amuck'. The word 'amuck' is discussed at length in *Hobson-Jobson*.

[6] Malay *pintu*, 'gate', and *gerbang*, 'great' or 'main'.

[7] Bandara is Malay *Bĕndahara*, which with the prefix Dato' would mean Lord of the Treasury, or Warehouse; the term was however generalised, and the precise functions of the *Bĕndahara* in Patani at this time are not on record. Meskita is Portuguese *mesquita*, 'mosque'.

that they founde along with theym, and there they stayed till one of the clocke after dinner, dominering very lustely, not anybody being so bolde as once to come att theym.

In the meane tyme wee were not withoute feare in oure quarter, for the Javanians did reporte that they woulde fall uppon our houses. Wherefore wee, together with the Hollanders, kepte strong watche, sending aboorde to have as many armed men as was possible; which came in very fitte tyme, for they being landed and things sette in order, wee resolved to go to visite theym and to stop theym the waye, which wee did, even juste as they were comming awaye to go downewards; butt understanding by theyr spies that wee were so strong and comming towards theym, they durste nott meete us, butt retyred thwarte[1] to the fielde, and fledde to Quale Bouca, and so forward to Bordolongh, Songora, and so into the contrie; wee receyving nott any other hurte by theym, butt onely that wee gott the name of defenders of the strangers. The Javanes were followed afterwards, but to no purpose, getting onely 3 or 4 sicke men prisoners, which were fayne to paye for all. What became of the reste was not yett knowen att our departure. This is the thirde tyme that Patania hath bene burned; twyce by the Japanesians and once by the Javanes. A strange thing to see and incredible to bee tolde.

Departed the pinnas *Little Enchuisen* for Bantam, with whome wee had obtayned so muche that John Johnson, who was so muche in disgrace of the shipp, might go in hir as passenger, seing wee coulde nott by any meanes obtayne his receyving agayne into the shipp. With him wee wrote briefly to the Company, for in regarde of the former brabblings not knowing what to wryte, and since the pacifying having no tyme to wryte, hereof I will speake no more, butt putt it to the account of reference. With this pinnas departed Cornelis Van Niewrode and John Van Henseden, William Jansen being master in hir. Shee wente for Bantam to certifye the retarding of the *Hope*. Written[2] also for helpe and assistence, for were muche indetted to the Queene and others.

—ditto.

The pinnas Enchuisen *departeth.*

John Johnson sente with hi[r]

Cornelis Van Niewrode departeth.

[1] *I.e.*, 'turned aside into the fields'.

[2] We should perhaps read "...retarding of the *Hope*, writing also for helpe", etc.

Adi 21 October. Having dispatched our buysinesse as muche as was possible for mee, receyved the dettes extant, and imployed the capitall of Siam, payde the Queene and taken leave of hir, which in this troublesome tyme was in homelye manner enough, giving to me and Mr Essington a golden crys [*i.e.*, dagger], wee were nowe readye to departe; and therefore wente to sette order for oure howse, who shoulde tarry there as well to vente [*i.e.*, sell] the goods that were remayning and to take order for the goods sente abroad, as also to keepe the howse, to sende advyce to Mr Lucas in Siam, and to leave a good foundation for the Englishe shipps. Wee coulde not aggree who shoulde bee lefte heere, and notwithstanding myne excuses,[1] yett William Ebert is thereto ordayned, for I am verye loath to misse [*i.e.*, spare] him. Wherefore the greateste question rose nowe, that hee was unwilling to go from mee, for yf hee shoulde bee lefte there and wee perhapps not come againe, and I comming to dye, hee having no wages, and having bene foorth these 3 yeares, after 7 or 8 yeares service might returne home and nott have gotte a penny; therefore hee refused to staye there unlesse hee knewe in what manner and for what. Which all of us understood sufficiently to bee true. Yett wee were very scrupulous, as not having any commission for to do so or the lyke; yett notwithstanding, the Companies service so requyring, and having none butt Adam Denton, of whome I shoulde stande in neede uppon the coaste, and Robert Littlewood,[2] who was altogether unfitte because of his greate sicknesse, not having as yett gathered his senses, nor John Persons foorthcomming; wherefore wee resolved to leave William Ebert heere, allowing him the wages of

Take leave off the Queene.

Why William Ebert is lefte heere.

[1] 'Excuses' is here probably an echo of the Portuguese sense of 'refusal' or 'objection'. William Ebert, a cousin of Floris, came out with him on the *Globe*, but not, apparently, as an employee of the Company, for he had no wages. He stayed at Patani for nearly a year, and, as mentioned later on, came to Bantam on the *James*; he returned to England on the *Globe*.

[2] Littlewood was purser on the *Globe*; as recorded below, he died in 1614 on the *James*, just before she reached Bantam. The commission authorised the employment as factors of the purser and his mate, but gave the merchants no power to employ anybody else; Persons, the mate, having already been employed, it was necessary to go beyond the terms of the commission. The *Court Minutes* of 9th November, 1617, show that the Company granted Ebert, for his services at Patani, "the some of 50*li* besides the 25 dollers formerlye receyved by him in the countrye".

John Persons, namely 50s. sterling a month, hoping the Company will take it in the beste, and that hee will carry himselfe so as that hee shall well deserve it; and because of the sicknesse of Robert Littlewood wee have lefte him and Raphe Cooper with him, setting the sayde Robert in the commission with Wyllyam, as more att large appeareth by the aforesayd commission and instruction lefte heere with theym, according to the which they are to rule theymselves. I also wrote a letter for Siam to Mr Lucas, wherein I wrote of all things what was paste, to rule himselfe accordingly. The goods which are remayning heere are to bee seene by the bookes and by the receyte of William Ebert and Robert Littlewood. Thus having sette all things in good order, wee resolved to go aboord in the evening, for to (bee ready to depart) sette sayle in the night with the land wynde.

The Hope *arriveth.*

In the afternoone, wee being ready to departe, heere arryved the unhoped for shipp, the *Hope*, which had bene expected so long and no newes had of hir, the historie whereof is this: that they comming from Bantam into the river of Johor, the Fiscall[1] and others wente upp to the towne, and, before they coulde come agayne aboord, the *armade* [*i.e.*, fleet] of Atchin was before the towne to besiege it; wherefore they sente a letter aboorde to have 30 armed men sente theym by lande, and to come into the river as highe as they coulde with the shipp, for to fight agaynste the Atchiners; the which, in regard of the sholes of the river, they coulde not do high enough, so that they coulde not hinder the Atchiners, butt that after 29 dayes siege the towne was yelded upp unto theym by aggreement, by which meanes the Atchiners gott 23 Hollanders prisoners, and 12 persons came aboord. Among the prisoners were 6 of the lodge [*i.e.*, factory] and 17 of the shipp, among whome were the Fiscall, the master, under-merchants and others. Bockholt[2] of Johor and those of the *Hope*, seing no other waye, resolved to go to Patania, nobody of commaunde being lefte butt onely the masters mate and one assistent. Being gotte oute of the Straighte and comming by

23 Hollanders carryed prisoners to Atchin.

[1] Dutch *fiskaal*, an abbreviated form of *advocaat-fiskaal*. The *fiskaals* employed by the Dutch Company usually appear as engaged in either legal or diplomatic business; in this case the mission was presumably diplomatic.

[2] Bockholt had been senior factor for the Dutch at Johore for some time, and a successor to relieve him had come on the *Hope* (*Bouwstoffen*, i. 59).

Pulo Tiaman, [they] gotte a greate storm oute of N.W., whereby they drove uppon the corall grounde of Borneo and were att 7 faddem; then the wynde grewe larger, and putting over [they] fell with Pulo Condor,[1] so as it was not possible to gette to Patania, but were compelled to seeke a place for theyr refresshing, which was in the Warellas,[2] where indeede they were in a good baye butt in a leane kitchin, the people being their enemyes. In suche manner they came to Patania, having 48 men aboord, whereof the mooste parte laye in their cabbins in a very pittifull plight; and this was the cause of their long staying. Shee brought 70,000 R8 and 29 packes with Indie cl[o]ath. In the evening wee suppt with the Dutchemen in presence of the masters mate and assistent called Jan Janss. du [blank]. After supper wee parted, and aboute midnight came aboord, setting sayle in the morning.

The Hope *in greate miserie.*

Wee departe with the Globe.

[1] Pulau Condore, off the mouths of the Mekong river in Cochinchina.

[2] Linschoten's map shows 'Avarella' as a town on the east coast of Cambodia, close to Cape Varella, in 12° 52′ N. The term *varella* is discussed in *Hobson-Jobson* and *Dalgado*: probably it represents Malay *bĕrhala*, 'an idol', but it was used by the Portuguese in the sense of 'temple' or 'monastery', and also as a place-name.

[CHAPTER IX

THE VOYAGE TO MASULIPATAM]

Wee were sydewards of the Poynte of Barwas,[1] being aboute [*October*]
8 (miles) leagues from the roade of Patania N.E. by N. and N.E. Adi 22 *ditto.*

In the morning wee were with the southerlieste ilands of 25 *ditto.*
Ridangh, and in the evening wee sawe and came by the Iles of
Capas. These Ilands of Ridangh are aboute 18 or 20 in number, *Ridangh.*
lying uppon 6 degrees; the middlemooste and greateste lye from the Poynte of Barwas S.E. [as] well as E. aboute 20 (miles) leagues, and Pulo Capas and 3 little iles lying S.S.E. from Ridangh aboute 13 (miles) leagues, and aboute 2 leagues from the firme land.

In the evening wee sawe Pulo Tyamon, which lyeth S. and S. Adi 26 *ditto.*
by E. from Pulo Capas aboute 28 (miles) leagues.

In the morning wee were by Pulo Tyamon, and being very 27 *ditto.*
calme all the daye wee drove aboute [*i.e.*, towards] the S.E., and sawe Pulo Pisan and Pulo Tingi aboute 7 leagues from Pulo Tyamon S. by E. Att the north syde of this ile Pulo Tyamon lyeth an ile aboute a league from Tyamon and 2 small iles by the same iland; and on the south syde of Tyamon lye dyvers little iles. In the evening wee gott a blaste or cake [*i.e.*, squall] from the W.S.W., and with the same wee ran N.W. towards the iland of Tyamon, and caste ancker att 29 faddem aboute 3 (mile) leagues from the iland, and had a hard streame running aboute [*i.e.*, towards] the S.E. towards Borneo.

Wee laye att ancker all that daye. 28 *ditto.*

Being calme and little wynde, wee ranne towards Pulo Tingi. 29 *ditto.*
In the evening wee caste ancker att 19 faddem. Pulo Pingi [*read* Tingi] is a high picke; from hence towards Pedra Branca the course is S. by W., and yf you keepe att 18 faddem withoute

[1] Tanjong (Cape) Bruas, or Barrawas, on the coast, almost due east from Patani. The various islands mentioned below had been passed on the outward voyage.

comming any nearer to the firme land, you neede not to feare anything but what you maye see with your eyes.

[THE PASSAGE OF THE STRAITS

A few words of introduction will make it easier to follow on the sketch map the narrative of the ten days spent in passing the Straits. The traditional view used to be that at this period European ships used only the narrow channel winding round the north of Singapore Island, and known as Sĕlat Tĕbĕrau, and this view is represented in the alternative name Old Strait, found on some modern maps; the latter name is, however, ambiguous and dangerous, for, as is explained below, at least three Old Straits can be distinguished in the literature. Colonel Gerini gave fresh currency to the traditional view in his *Remarks on Ptolemy's Geography of Eastern Asia* (London, 1909), a work which was followed by the editor of *Mundy* (iii. 144, 146). Meanwhile the erroneousness of this view had been established conclusively by W. D. Barnes in his paper on *Singapore Old Straits and New Harbour* in the *Journal* of the Royal Asiatic Society, Straits Branch, December, 1911. The primary authority is chapter XX of Linschoten's *Reys-Gheschrift*, where the regular route taken by the Portuguese is shown to have kept close to the south of Singapore Island, passing through two distinct straits. The eastern strait, called at that time the Strait of Sinca Pura, is now known as Keppel Harbour; but for part of the distance there are alternative routes separated by the small island of Brani, north of which runs the eastern part of the harbour, called by Floris the New Strait, while to the south is his Old Strait, now known as Sinki Strait. The western strait, called First on the voyage eastward, and Second on the voyage westward, is now known as Sĕmbilan Strait, running between the south-west coast of Singapore Island and the chain of the Sĕmbilan Islands which lie close to it.

Floris, who, as the text shows, relied entirely on Linschoten, reckoned three straits in all. His 'Strait of Johore' is the passage between Cape Romenia, his 'Point of Jantana or Johore', and the island of Bintang; his 'First Strait of Sinca Pura' is Keppel Harbour; and his 'Second Strait' is the Sĕmbilan Strait. The passage ends at the opening between Great Kĕrimun Island and Cape Bulus, the 'Tanjang Bouro' of Floris, where the long Straits of Malacca begin.

The map of the Straits given in *Eredia* (Plate III) shows the Old Strait to the north of the New, which reverses Floris' nomenclature. The names Old and New do not occur in Linschoten, so Floris

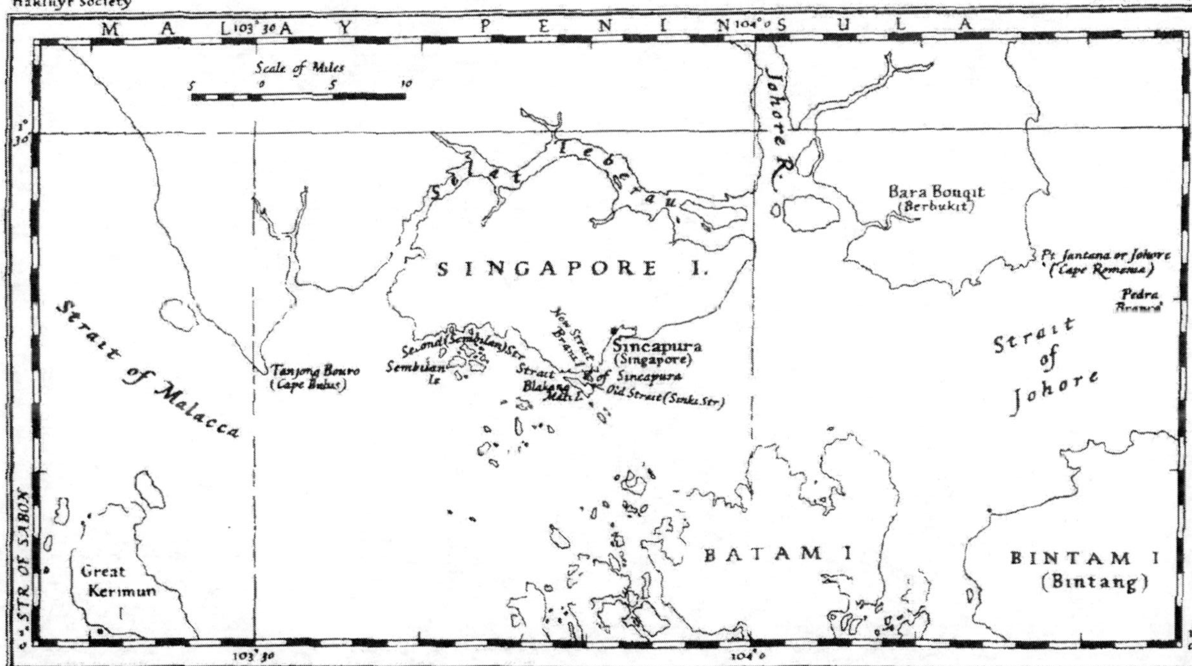

THE PASSAGE OF THE STRAITS

most probably obtained them from the Saletter, or sea-gipsy, whom he employed as pilot; and in the absence of other contemporary authorities the question remains open whether Eredia or the pilot made a mistake. The observation in Linschoten that the passage now known as Sinki Strait "could be used only by small foists" suggests that it may have been older (in this sense) than the other; but this consideration is not conclusive, and the fact remains that the name Old Strait is applied by Eredia to Keppel Harbour, by Floris to Sinki Strait, and in later maps to Sĕlat Tĕbĕrau.

The question when, if ever, the route north of the island of Singapore was in general use is one of some interest, but it does not arise in connection with the text, since there is no doubt that Floris took the route to the south, and his Old Strait is Sinki Strait, not Sĕlat Tĕbĕrau.]

Being Mondaye. Wee sawe the poynte of Jantana or Johor,[1] and the mounte uppon the Iland of Bintam [Bintang]. These 3 dayes wee advanced butt little. Adi primo *November.*

In the morning, having sette sayle, and the wynde W., wee came in the sight of Pedra Branca S. and S. by W. from us, being aboute 3 leagues from the poynte of Johor. And aboute 10 of the clocke wee came to the dangerous riffe [*i.e.*, reef] which falleth of from the poynte of Johor 4 (miles) leagues into the sea, and wee were not above 2 leagues from the little iles which lye from the poynte of Johor, having a very uneven grounde from 6 to 9, 11, 7, 6, 8, till wee came to 12, 14 and 20 faddem; then wee were passed the shole, not withoute danger. Wee had the poynte with the 3 little ilands W.S.W. from us, so that John Hugens[2] doth describe this shole very well; [it] is aboute the bredth of ½ league, therefore it is good to keepe towards the sea till you bring the little iles shutte in with the pointe of Johor, and Pedra Branca open with the Ile of Bintam, and then you neede not to feare. Wee, having broughte Pedra Branca with the Ile of Bintam, the wynde being W. and W.S.W., with a strong ebbe comming oute of the Straighte running aboute [towards] the E., came to an *2 ditto.*

[1] The extreme south-east point of the Peninsula, marked on modern maps as Cape Romenia. The name Jantana is Malay *Ujung*, 'point', and *tanah*, 'land', and was properly applied to the extremity of the Peninsula, though it was also used more loosely (*Eredia*, 87).

[2] *I.e.*, Linschoten, in the *Reys-Gheschrift*.

ancker att 20 faddem good grounde aboute 31 leags[1] from Pedra Branca.

3 *ditto.* With the flood and W. wynde wee sette towards the Straight of Johor, passing by Pedra Branca, being butt a rocke full of fowle and bedungd, which causeth the toppe to bee white, whereof it beareth the name. Wee came att an ancker under Bara Bouquit [*i.e.*, Berbukit].

4, 5, 6 & 7 *November.* Wee were buysie every daye in turning upp with the flood, till wee were paste the river of Johor, and came aboute 2 leagues from Sinca Pura.

8 *ditto.* Dyvers prawes came aboorde of us hard by the Straight, being of the Salettes[2] under the King of Johor, which for the mooste parte keepe [*i.e.*, live] in the prawes with their wyves and childeren, living chiefely by fishing. By these Salettes wee understood howe the King of Atchin had sente the yonger brother of the King of Johor, Raja Boungsoe, backe agayne with greate honoure, in companye of 30 prawes and 2000 Atchiners, for to build upp agayne the forte and cittie of Johor, with good store of ordinance and other necessaries, having marryed him to his sister; and was gone for Bintam some 14 daies ago, saying that the olde King shoulde bee deposed, and hee sette upp in his place. Newes from Malacca wee coulde learne none, onely they sayde that some 4 or 5 dayes agone there was paste by a shipp comming from the Manilles [*i.e.*, Philippine Is.]. Heere wee tooke a pilott[3] to bring us thorough the Straighte of Sinca Pura for 7 R8; and hee counselling us to go thorough the newe straighte, wee followed his counsell; which wee entered aboute the noone tyde, after they had fyrste sette of with beacons the hidden rockes,[4] which lye verye dangerous and are very perillous

The firste Straight, off Sinca Pura. The newwe Straite.

[1] So in the MS, but a glance at the map will show that the figure must be a mistake, probably for 3½ leagues. Fractions appear in various forms in the Dutch script; in the MS of Pelsaert's *Remonstrantie* in the Rijksarchief (foot of folio 1), 3½ is written 3l, which could easily be misread as 31.

[2] Usually written Saletters, from Malay *sĕlat*, 'strait'. The name was applied by the Portuguese to the sea-gipsies who inhabited the Straits.

[3] Since there is no mention of any intercourse with the shore, it seems that the pilot must have been one of the Saletters; and the rest of the party would be 'they' who marked the dangerous places with 'beacons'.

[4] These would include the Tembaga shoal, shown on the Admiralty Chart 2023 at the east entrance to Keppel Harbour, which Floris called the New Strait.

to passe, [the channel] not being paste ⅛ of an Englishe mile broad. And the flood being done, which runneth heere very strong, wee were forced to come to an ancker, juste by the rocke which lyeth in the middest of the Straighte,[1] att larboord aboute 1½ faddem under water; and although wee did not touche it, yett were wee not 2 faddem from it, having in the middle shipp 5 faddem and in the fore parte 9 faddem. Butt in regard it was very fayre wether and calme, the danger was the lesse, the ebbe running so strong that wee coulde not carrye oute a warping ancker. Heere wee rode till the ebbe was spente, being 12 of the clock att night, the ebbe having lasted heere 12 houres. Then wee sette thorough the Straighte, not being paste ½ Englishe myle in lengthe.[2]

In the morning, being passed the fyrste straighte, wee made N.W. for the second, passing by the olde Straighte of Sincapura,[3] which wee coulde see from ende to ende, being betweene 2 high ilands and very narrowe, so that the newe straighte is better for greate shipps to passe. Taking thus oure course towards the second straighte wee discryed a sayle, in fashion muche lyke a carvell, which stood aboute [*i.e.*, towards] the easte, butt wee spake not with him. Aboute 9 wee came to an ancker in the 2nd straighte, aboute 7 leagues[4] from the fyrste, the flood being spente and having a continuall W. wynde. This second straighte is longer and broader then the fyrste. Heere wee wente upp to an iland to seeke freshe water, butt wee gotte none, butt some palmites[5] trees, which wee cutte downe and ate the pith; which

9 ditto. Olde Straighte.

2nd Straighte.

[1] At first sight this might be either the Meander shoal at the west entrance to Sinki Strait, or the north edge of Berdaun Island, about half a mile farther west. Captain J. A. Edgell, R.N., who has kindly studied the text, concludes that it was the latter: the soundings given in the Journal point to Berdaun rather than Meander, while a passage just below shows that the *Globe* must have passed Sinki Strait in the daytime, that is before reaching this anchorage.

[2] Berdaun is approximately ¾ mile from the west entrance to Keppel Harbour.

[3] As indicated above, this is Sinki Strait; its mention here must be an afterthought, since the details in the text show that the *Globe* passed it on the previous day. The statement that they could see it from end to end indicates that they passed the entrance by day, not by night.

[4] The distance between the two straits is in fact only six or seven miles, and perhaps 'leagues' is a slip.

[5] Portuguese *palmito*, 'a palm tree'. Mr I. H. Burkill, F.L.S., informs me

did us no good, for all that had eate of theym fell sicke, casting all the night long. The nexte daye it was paste; which was very strange, for the palmite trees bee eaten thourough all the Indies, butt these had a kynde of a bitter taste, and muste needes bee of another kynde.

10 ditto. In the morning wee sette sayle to turne oute of this straighte, which att fyrste stretcheth N.W. and W., being aboute the lengthe of 2 leagues, the south syde being full of ilands; and in the middeste of the 2 laste there lyeth a rocke under water,[1] being juste in the middst of the channell, uppon which unknowing wee had almooste hitte, nott lying 1½ faddem under water. One muste passe by it att the N. syde, whereas cometh a poynte of read earthe juste over the rocke, which poynte being paste, then the straighte openeth, and then one maye see the greate Iland of Carimon and the long poynte of Tanjang Bouro[2] aboute 6 leagues W. from us. This passage is so well described in the 20th chapter of the *Deroutes* of John Hugens van Linschoten that it cannot bee mended, for wee have founde all juste as hee hath described it, so that a man needeth no other judge or pilote butt him.

12 ditto. Wee were att an ancker betweene Carimon and Bouro; there a juncke paste by us, butt wee spake not with hir.

13 ditto. Yett lying att an ancker. Wee gott a hard blaste or cake [*i.e.*, squall], so that our streame cable brake, by which meanes wee drove aboute a league eastward, and then came to ryde att our greate or sheat ancker.

14 ditto Our cable and ancker were become foule and wee drove, wherefore wee wounde upp the ancker and cleared it. Hadde

that there is no record of the species of palms now to be found on the Sembilan Islands, but various species are probable, some of which would have a bitter taste, while others would produce 'casting', a term which, according to the *OED*, might denote either vomiting or purging; the most probable species is *Areca catechu*, the betel-palm, which has both characteristics.

[1] The Admiralty Chart shows a sunken rock just south of the deep channel between the two most westerly islands of this group, which are marked as P. Sembilan and P. Pisee.

[2] The island of Great Kėrimun, and Tanjong (Cape) Bulus on the mainland. The name *Deroutes* comes from the long sub-title of the *Reys-Gheschrift*, which begins *Sommige Derouten*; probably it represents Portuguese *derrota*, 'course of a ship'.

many hard blastes oute of the W.N.W. and N.W., and wee were fayne to lye still. Heere is the stillest water, and heere meete the tydes of W. and E. as also S.

A juncke passed aboute [*i.e.*, towards] the E., wee lying att ancker, butt did not speake with hir. 15 *ditto.*

In the night the wynde came to the N.E. and wee sette sayle. 16 *ditto.* This iland of Carimon is a high and greate ile, and lyethe in the waye of 3 passages, the passage for Sinca Pura, Sabon,[1] and Malacca, which 3 straights do meete heere.

In the morning wee were by the iland Pulo Picon [*i.e.*, Pisang], 17 *ditto.* lying 3 (miles) leagues E. and W. from Tanjangbouro; hathe 2 little ilands close to it towards the sea, lyeth aboute a league from the mayne.

Wee were 3 leagues paste Rio Fermose,[2] which wee passed in 18 *ditto.* the night, being aboute 6 leagues from Picon, N.W. and S.E. The whole daye it was calme and wee came to an ancker. After sunnesetting the wynde came to the N.E., and wee sette sayle.

In the morning, the ebbe being spente and very calme, wee 19 *ditto.* came to an ancker aboute 2 leagues paste Malacca, and sawe the little iles, *as Islas* [*read* Ilhas] *dos Naos*,[3] lying before Malacca, butt had butt little intelligence from the castle and towne, being paste it in the night. Understoode nothing of any *armada* [*i.e.*, fleet], and sawe butt onely a small sayle under land. Aboute noone, the ebbe comming on and the wynde being N.W., wee sette sayle, to have by daye light good knowledge of the Cabo Rachado.

Wee were N.E. by N. from Pulo Parselar, all this tyme having 23 *ditto.* a contrary wynde and calmes, so that wee coulde butt woorke with the ebbe, till wee were paste Cabo Rachado and within 3 leagues of Pulo Parselar. Rachado lyethe from Malacca aboute *P. Rachado.* 10 (miles) leagues, att 2½ degrees. Pulo Parselar lyeth uppon *P. Parselar.*

[1] The Strait of Sabon is described in the *Reys-Gheschrift* (ch. xxv) as running south between Great Kĕrimun and Sumatra, and being the ordinary route from Malacca to Java. The name was taken from the island formerly known as Sabão, but now named Kundur (*Eredia*, 198). Most of the places mentioned below are merely sea-marks, and will be found on the map facing p. 30.

[2] The river now known as Batu Pahat; the correct form of the Portuguese name was Rio Formoso.

[3] The name is Portuguese, meaning 'the islands of the ships'.

3 degrees, N.W. from Cabo Rachado. Pulo Parselar is a high mountayne standing uppon a lowe poynte of grounde, differing from the high land towards the land syde, so that it seemeth afarre of as yf it were an iland, butt it is firme land.

24 ditto. Towards the evening the wynde came N.E., and wee broughte P. Parselar E.N.E. and E. by N. from us aboute some 2 leagues, and so wente N.W. by W. and W.N.W. towards the Ilands of d'Aru [*i.e.*, Aroa], being aboute 12 leagues, differing W.N.W. and E.S.E. from Pulo Parselar.

25 ditto. Att noone wee were asyde of the Ilands of d'Aru, lying large att 3 degrees. In the evening wee gott the wynde S.E. with a gale. Tooke our course N. and N. by W. towards Pulo Sambilan.[1]

26 ditto. In the morning wee sawe the Ilands of Sambilan, lying uppon 4 degrees, and the Ile das Jartes [*i.e.*, Jara] which wee lefte seawards from us. Heereaboutes is firme land till Keda; thare [? there are] marvaylous high mountaynes. There is a riche myne of tinne called kalein,[2] in the Maleys tong *tinna pute*, (whereof) from whence the Portingalls cause greate quantitie to bee broughte, and furnishe all the Indies with it.

28 ditto. Wee came to an ancker under Pulo Pinao [*i.e.*, Penang] att the W. syde att 10 faddem, being a greate iland, and founde the description of John Hugens to bee very true as well of the Straighte of Malacca as of this iland; for by his direction wee founde freshe water, being a little ile att the S. syde of the greate sand baye, and right over agaynste the little iland southward is a small baye besette on both sydes with rockes, and is full of oysters, and by this baye is verye fayre water and easye to bee fetched. Wee sente our boate and skiffe ashoare to fetche water. Wee were come to an ancker to farre from the shoare, aboute 1½ leagues, for wee mighte have come att 6 and 7 faddem, a good muddy grounde, within ½ league of the shoare.

[1] The name Pulau Sĕmbilan, or 'Nine Islands', was applied to at least three groups of islands on this route—those which form the Sĕmbilan Strait mentioned above, those now mentioned, lying off the Perak river, and those mentioned below under 6th December.

[2] Portuguese *calaim*, 'tin'. 'Tinna pute' is Malay *timah putĕh*; the first word covers both tin and lead, while the second, meaning 'white', marks the distinction between the two metals.

I wente myselfe ashoare, and the oysters being so fayre and good I ate as many as made mee sicke. Heere wee founde a Portingalls name, P° do Carvallo, a° 1596 Auguste, cutte in a tree; whereuppon wee also cutte *Globa van* London, 1613, 29 November, for a signe. This iland lyeth uppon 5¼ degrees. *29 ditto.*

Wee sette sayle with a N.E. wynde, taking our course N.N.W., having a fayre depthe. Wee were no lesse then 6 in [*i.e.*, or] 7 leagues from any shoare, att 28 faddem muddy grounde, and sawe perfectly the Ilands of Buton [*i.e.*, Butang]. These ilands bee all high land, yett not so high as the mayne land. Wee had very fayre wether, and yett notwithstanding, uppon a suddayne, wee gotte a great leake in the shipp; for during the whole voyage wee never pumped paste 15 in [*i.e.*, or] 18 inches in 12 houres, and nowe wee had 24 inches every 4 houres. Wee coulde not learne where the leake was, fearing that it was worme eatings. Tyme will shewe it. Primo *December.*

Wee were E. and W. aboute 2 leagues with the S. ende of Buton, lying att 6 degrees. These ilands of Buton are commonly called the Ilands of Keda, and are a greate many, and of strange formes or fashions of rockes, towers, &c., lying close one under the other. Wee wente thorough as is usually done betweene the rockes in Norwaye,[1] having for the mooste parte 18 to 12 faddem softe grounde. *2 ditto. P. Buton.*

Wee sayled betweene the foresayd ilands in the night tymes, being a N. and N.E. wynde. And in the daye tyme, the wynde comming from the sea W. and N.W., wee used all possible diligence to gette the height of 8, 9 or more degrees before wee were willing to go from the coaste, for to passe northward by the ilands, yf it were possible, to meete the northern wyndes, and so to assure our voyage. Att this tyme wee were att 7 degrees. 3, 4 & 5 *ditto.*

Wee had fayre wether with a little wynde, and came in sight *6 ditto.*

[1] This phrase has been examined by Vice-Admiral H. P. Douglas, R.N., in consultation with the Netherlands Hydrographer. It does not appear to denote any specific method of handling the ship, and presumably it is a personal reminiscence; Floris or some of his companions may have remarked, as they felt their way through the islands, that it was like sailing along the coast of Norway.

of the Ilands of Pulo Sambilan.[1] In the night wee gott a N.E. wynde, and sette our course N.W. and N.W. by W. towards the (westerlieste) westermost ile of Pulo Sambilan.

7 ditto. In the morning wee were hard by the ilands att the S.W. syde, att $7\frac{3}{4}$ degrees. These iles bee greate, and a great many of little iles lying rounde aboute theym. Heere wee came to an ancker *P. Sambilan.* because of the tyde and calme, sending our skiffe ashoare to fetche oysters, which growe there in greate quantitie by the rockes. Heere uppon a little ile wee founde a greate percell of broken porseleyn of all manner of sortes, among which were greate fyne langerys.[2] From whence it was come wee coulde not knowe, for wee sawe no signe att all of any junckes or shipps which might there have bene caste awaye. This morning there was a tumulte in our shippe because [? of] the cobion[3] of a quartermaster, which was not come to service [*i.e.*, duty] or prayers, butt laye sleeping in his cabbyne, and yett the other officers woulde not laye hande on him; wherefore the captayne kepte backe theyr breakefaste, and the folkes refused to pumpe. I, lying in my bedde, and having taken a purge, sente for 2 or 3 officers, and having contented theym with reasons, all was quyeted.

8 December. Wee had the ayre close and the wynde N.E. by E. and E.N.N.

[1] The map in Linschoten's *Reys-Gheschrift* shows a group of islands named Pulo Sambilaom, close to his Junçalao (Puket, or Junk Ceylon), which he erroneously placed on the mainland. From the latitude given, the reference must be to The Brothers Islands, shown on the Admiralty Chart between 7° 30′ and 7° 45′ N.

[2] The word 'langerys' has not been found elsewhere, and Mr R. L. Hobson, the Keeper of Ceramics in the British Museum, who has kindly studied the problem of its meaning, is unable to offer a final solution. It is tempting to equate the word to *langelijs* ('long Elizas'), a Dutch trade-name for Chinese porcelain decorated with tall female figures; it is doubtful, however, if this particular decoration was in use so early as 1613, while the word *langelijs* has not been traced back beyond the year 1760, and, if it existed, it is not likely that a Dutchman would have misspelt it. More probably 'langerys' is a corruption of some Chinese term; and conceivably it may represent *lung-wêng*, 'dragon-jar', that is, large stoneware oil-jars decorated with dragon designs; here as elsewhere, the *r* may be read as *v*, which Portuguese speakers would substitute for *w*, and there are other instances of final *-ng* being absorbed in a Portuguese nasalised vowel.

[3] Apparently this represents Italian *cobio*, which is applied to various species of small fish; the name is commonly given to the loach, which is proverbial for sluggishness, and so would be appropriate in this context.

Wee resolved to passe the Ilands of Andemas att 11 degrees,[1] therefore wee sette our course N.W. In the night wee (hadd) gotte a great rayne, which afterwards brake oute into a storme.

9 December. Wee had the storme continuing from the E.N.E. with darke wether and rayne. Wee made little sayle and tooke of our bonnetts,[2] lying the whole daye and night in the wynde.

10 ditto. The wether cleered upp, yett the wynde being freshe, wee wente on N.W. by N. and N.N.W. In this storme the shippe grewe very leake, so that wee pumped 20 inches every 2 glasses;[3] butt yett after the storm it ceased a little, so that nowe wee pumpe 16 in [*i.e.*, or] 17 inches every 4 glasses. In the evening, seing no land and guessing [*i.e.*, reckoning] to bee att 11 degrees, wee runne on W.N.W. and W. by N.

11 ditto. In the morning att 9 of the clocke wee sawe (a greate breache) a great shole or a shorte breaking of the sea.[4] Wee made towards it and were not ½ league from it, and putte in the wynde and passed by att 14, 16 and 18 faddem northwarde hard grounde. *Note this breach.* Wee coulde butt even discerne the blackenesse of the rocke, and was not passing a shipps lengthe where the sea did so breake, a mooste dangerous place yf wee had fallen thereon in the night tyme. The rocke lyethe in 11 degrees, the neareste of all, and lyeth from the Ilands of Andeman aboute 18 leagues. Att noone wee had the perfecte heighte of 11 degrees and 5 or 6 minutes; and aboute 2 of the clocke sawe the Ilands of the Andemas, where canniballs bee.[5] Towards the evening wee sawe an opening

1 This would be by the Duncan Passage, between Little Andaman and South Andaman.

2 *I.e.*, pieces of canvas laced on to the sails to increase their size.

3 The hour-glass was the usual device for reckoning time at sea.

4 Probably the south end of the large bank which lies east of the Duncan Passage.

5 This statement represents the common belief of the period. In 1885 Mr E. H. Man wrote that no trace could be discovered of the practice of cannibalism in the Andamans, even in far-off times; but some of the tribes still believed the story of others (*The Aboriginal Inhabitants of the Andaman Islands*, p. 45). Mr A. R. Brown suggested (*The Andaman Islanders*, Cambridge, 1922, p. 110) that the belief may have originated in the custom of burning the bodies of slain enemies: "We can well imagine that when, as must often have happened, sailors venturing to land on the islands have been killed and the survivors have seen the bodies of their companions cut up and placed on fires, they would readily conclude that they were witnessing a cannibal feast".

of 5 leagues broad, thourough which wee passed in the night with a greate pace, having 14, 16, 18, 20 and 26 faddem.

12 ditto. Wee were oute of sighte of these ilands, yett wee sawe the mooste westerlye ile[1] of the Andemas N.E. from us. Wee steered N.W. by N. to gette the height of 16½ degrees, having the wynde att easte, with a good gale. Att noone wee were oute of sighte of all the ilands, att the heighte of 11⅝ degrees.

16 ditto. The wynde being betweene N.E. and E., wee were att 15 degrees and 12 minutes. Wee wynded [*i.e.*, steered] N.W. by N. according to the compas, which, because of the variation, helde but N.W.

17 ditto The wynd and our course as aforesayd. Wee were att 16 degrees and 5 minutes, having every daye very fayre wether and a standing gale; yett notwithstanding our men were not in healthe, complaining muche of a badde stomacke, which I thinke tooke a beginning of the oysters and palmites.

18 ditto. The wynde and course as before. In the night, aboute 2 of the clocke in the morning, wee came att 12 faddem, wherefore wee tooke in all our sayles, hulling till the daye.

[1] The North Sentinel Island The latitude of Masulipatam is 16° 9′ N., so the course was set, according to the usual practice of the period, to get the right latitude while well to windward of the destination.

[CHAPTER X

MASULIPATAM]

In the morning wee sawe the land, and were right before Narsapur Peta.[1] Wee runne along this coaste W.S.W.; and aboute 4 of the clocke in the afternoone discryed the roade of Musilpatam and sawe 5 shipps att ancker. Att 7 of the clocke att night wee came to an ancker, and shotte of 7 pieces. Wee were welcomed of 3 shipps, and, presently after, the *palewares*[2] or fishermen comming aboord according to custome, wee understoode the one to bee an Englishe shippe, and 2 Hollanders, the fourthe to bee the Kings shipp going for Mocha, and the fifth a *tauri*. Wee lykewyse understood that Mirsadardi was oute of his gouvernment, and that Atmachan and Busebullerau[3] did nowe gouverne; wherefore wee founde it good to sende a letter on shoare, and to sende for the captaine or marchant to come aboorde of us, for to conferre with theym touching the estate of the countrie and of theyr voyage.

[December] 19 ditto.

Arrive in the roade off Musilpatam.

In the morning the shippe the *James*,[4] taking knowledge of us, welcomed us with 7 peeces, uppon which wee answered theym agayne. Aboute noone the *James* hir boate came aboord of us, and another, being sente from the Gouvernour, in which came Capt. Edmund Marlowe, Mr John Gourney, Mr John

20 ditto.

[1] Narasapur, on the south mouth of the Godāvari, was the principal shipbuilding centre on the Coromandel Coast.

[2] This is probably for *paravas*, the Portuguese name for a caste of fishermen on the South Coromandel Coast (*Dalgado, s.v.*), applied to fishermen in general.

[3] Atmachan appears in *Letters Received*, iv. 33, as Etmoatach[an], which may safely be read as Itimād Khān. The second name is perhaps Bāsu, or Vāsu, Bali Rao.

[4] The *James*, with Edmund Marlowe as captain, John Davis, or Davy, of Limehouse, as master, and John Gurney and Richard Cobb as factors, left England for the ninth Voyage in February, 1612, and, after many delays, reached the Coromandel Coast from Bantam in June, 1613. The Journal of the voyage is in *Purchas*, I. iv. 440; and Gurney's account of it in *Letters Received*, ii. 80. The commission for this Voyage is not extant.

Davis and Mr Rychard Cob; by whome wee understood what had happened to theym and what passed heere on the lande, as also that they were sente expresly to second us in our voyage, desiring of us our instruction and information, shewing us their commission to the same effecte, delivering to mee certayne letters from England and Holland, whereof 2 were from Sr. Thomas,[1] who lykewyse desired the same of us; I accepting the same very willingly, and comming ashoare to caste theym a direction, offering withall to sende Adam Denton along with theym and to keepe George Chancye with mee.

Mr Davis, seing our shipp to bee so leacke, and understanding that wee mynded to bringe hir into the river of Narsapur Peta, sayde that wee were fooles, and that it was not possible to bringe the shipp over the barre, saying there was butt 9 foote water, and that himselfe had sounded it when the Kings shipp[2] came foorth; which made us in a greate perplexitie and knewe not what to answere, onely I thoughte that where the Kings shippe had paste, there the *Globe* lykewyse might swimme, and that it were better to give a better courage to our men and not to make theym afrayde.

All the *tapés* [*i.e.*, skirts] which wee lefte att Bantam were solde, and the provenu [*i.e.*, proceeds] for the 7th Voyage came to [blank in MS] R8, which there were lefte by Mr Spalding with Mr Wyllyam Sheppard[3] to imploy the same in China wares; which hath not bene done this yeare, because of the dealing of Sr. Henry Middleton, who boughte upp all, and the reste muste sitte and looke on.

Adi 21 *December*. I wente on shoare with Mr Gourny, Adam Denton and Rychard Cob, the sea being very greate, yett came well ashoare;

[1] Sir Thomas Smythe, Governor of the E.I. Company. The words 'to caste theym a direction' probably mean to draw up directions for their guidance. George Chauncey had been left at Bantam, as mentioned above, and had there been taken aboard the *James*.

[2] *I.e.*, the pilgrim ship for Mocha, fitted out by the King of Golconda. The pilgrim ships were much larger than the ordinary run of Indian vessels.

[3] Sheppard probably came out on the *James*, and was left at Bantam, where he made a fortune by private trade, and was in consequence recalled (*Letters Received*, iii. 315). Sir Henry Middleton, on the *Trade's Increase*, had reached Bantam in the autumn of 1612.

whereas wee were mette by Wentacadrae,[1] sonne to Busebullerau, with the Sabander and other Moores [*i.e.*, Moslems], and were well receyved, giving dyvers *tesseriffes*[2] to us, as also to the Directour, Warner [Wemmer] Van Berchen, giving to eache of us both a very fayre horse; and although I made greate refusall, fearing their treacheries, yett att the laste I was compelled to accepte of it, hoping to bee free with paying for it.

Being on shoare and there fynding the Serpent Master[3] of the *Greene Lyon*, who lykewyse had bene with Mr Davids in Narsapur Peta, I asked him what depth was uppon the barre. Hee answered mee to have founde 11 foote, the water having begunne to fall, not douting butt att a full sea to fynde 12 foote; which gave me a little more courage, and thereuppon I sente for Mr Essington to come on shoare.

I tooke a *caule* or safeconducte att 4 per cento, according to my olde custome, giving foorthwith order to land the goods, making the boats readye for it, which were buysied in lading the shipp of Mocha.[4] *22 ditto.*

Mr Essington comming on shoare in company of Captain Marlowe, who had had some strange counsell together, as appeared by all their actions, and inticed or sette on by others, att all which I wincked, I charged Mr Essington foorthwith to go for Narsapur Peta with Job Palmer, and so to go to the barre and see with theyr owne eyes, whereunto they might truste, being aboute 40 Englishe miles from Musilpatam. Whereuppon they departed the 23th [*sic*].

Mr Essington wrote me from Narsapur Peta that they had founde 10½ foote, hoping with the full moone to fynde no lesse then 11 foote, and that they were buysie to take a *caull* according to custome. *27 ditto.*

Mr Essington returning, wee resolved to discharge the shippe [1614 *N.S.*] *1 January.*

[1] In later entries the name is given as 'Wencatadra', which probably represents Venkatādri.

[2] Arabic *tashrīf*, used in India to denote a complimentary present, usually of apparel.

[3] *I.e.*, the master-gunner; 'serpent' was used as a synonym for serpentine, a type of gun commonly carried by merchant vessels. His ship was the Dutch *Groene Leeuw*.

[4] This would be the 'King's ship' mentioned above.

heere as soone as possibly wee coulde, to bee brought into the river, and that hee shoulde go thether agayne to make provision of timber, plankes, and other necessaries, also to make a bangsall[1] or storehowse for to laye the shipps provision, that all things might bee readye againste the comming of the shipp, for to make all possible haste that the shipp might bee oute of the river agayne before the S.W. wyndes do blowe, which causethe a very rough sea. Whereuppon Mr Essington departed the 2 of January.

5 *ditto*. A leake was founde in our shippe, behynde in the sterne, where the water was hearde to come in mightely, being under water, so that none coulde come att it; and although it coulde not bee stopped, yett it was a greate comforte to us, for Mr Davids and others sayde it [*i.e.*, the cause] was worme eatings, and irrepayrable. But God confoundeth my enemies.

8 *ditto*. Being buysied in discharging of our goods, and the Gouvernours, understanding our shipp to bee so leake, and that wee were mynded to sende the shipp for Narsapur Peta, there to bee (dubbled) sheathed, did thinke nowe to bridle mee, as many tymes theymselves had made triall and caused to bee tryed by others, that I shoulde inter into a contracte with theym for 5 in [*i.e.*, or] 6000 P^as^, they being very scant of money for the dispatching of the shipp of Mocha. The which I playnelye refused, calling to mynde howe in former tyme I had bene used of the Gouvernours, making foes of friends, and that ever to my losse and discredit. Neyther had they delte butt meanely with Mr Gourny, and yf it had not bene for my comming [he] should hardly withoute losse have come from theym. Butt yett what I woulde nott do with my will I have bene fayne to do againste my will, for these Gouvernours soughte all possible meanes to bring mee to it, and seing they had none, tooke holde of this. They sente for mee in the custome howse, where they tolde mee that they understood that wee were mynded to bring the shipp into the river, and to that effecte had already sente a man thether to make a bangsall, butt that wee shoulde proceede no further

[1] This is the South Indian meaning of the word 'bangsall', which is discussed at length in *Hobson-Jobson*. The other meaning, 'custom-house', appears below, under 24th November.

till wee had a *firman*[1] from the King, as not being in their power to give us leave, seing there had never an Englishe shipp bene in the river, and therefore shoulde go fyrste to the King to seeke it, offering their service to wryte in my behalffe. Butt this made mee to suspecte something else, the rather that this Atmachan and Busebuleraw had lykewyse the gouvernment of Narsapur Peta, having farmed oute onely the revenews[2] to a Bramene called Apagie, who had no power nor autoritie to withstande theym, for else they woulde soone have putte him oute; and although hee had already graunted a *caull* to Mr Essington, that was onely concerning the custome; with the reste hee had nothing to do. So that I was muche perplexed. For to go to sollicite to the King, besides the greate losse of tyme, woulde have coste me no lesse then 3 in [*i.e.*, or] 4000 R8 to gette a *firman*, and yett I muste have stood to the discretion of the Gouvernours; so that to go to the King I lyked nott att all, and to give a present heere to the Gouvernours I founde it not good, for I shoulde never have bene ridde of the knaves. So that I helde it beste to enter into a contracte with theym for 5000 P^{as}, to deliver theym in dyvers sortes of marchandizes according to the course of the markett, to paye me the same within 4 months in indigo, cotton yarne, iron, and other things according to the contracte, and for that to promise mee to free mee of all molestations which mighte bee layde uppon mee, and to helpe and assiste mee with carpenters, pilotts, smiths and others. Also that yf the King shoulde bee discontented, then they to take the faulte uppon theym. This mee thoughte to bee the readyeste and fitteste waye that possibly I coulde use, for, the woorste comming to the worste, I shoulde alwayes have founde some one meanes or other to come to my owne with a little losse. And after having advised with Mr Essington, Mr Gourny, Adam Denton and others, I delivered to the Gouvernours the sayde summe of 5000 P^{as}, taking a strong writing under theyr hands, wherein I also comprehended that yf they did not paye mee in 4 months that then

[1] Persian *farmān*, in Indian official parlance an order issued by the King personally.

[2] That is to say, the Governors had sublet the farm of Narasapur to a brāhman named Appajī.

I shoulde bee assigned to 4 committies,[1] who from this tyme bounde theymselves to it, so that I thoughte I was reasonably well assured and well hedged in agaynst these greedye wolves. God graunte all for the beste.

17 *ditto.* The Kings shipp departed for Mecca [*i.e.*, Mocha], for which I came in very fitte tyme, for I solde a greate parcell of lacquere, benjamin, sapon [*i.e.*, sappan wood], and porseleyn, with other things. Shee had laden muche ryce, iron and Indie cl[o]ath, being a reasonnable riche shipp.

25 *ditto.* The *James* departed for Petapoli, Mr Gourny yett remayning heere to cleare his things. With greate admiration [*i.e.*, astonishment] I have seene heere the evill gouvernment of the *James*, not possible to bee described, so that I, thinking the *Globe* to bee the woorste gouverned shipp, sawe heere muche otherwyse. Among other things they had 2 howses on shoare, one for Capt. Marlowe and another for Mr Gourney, eache carrying greater state then the other; and Captain Marlowe had spente above 1500 R8 whereof hee woulde give no account, butt would do it to the Company.[2] Moreover there was a threefolde contention among theym, whereof Cob and Davids were the principall causes and instigators, to the greate confusion of the Companies service. Among the reste it was also tolde mee that I had betrayed the *James* and the *Globe*; neyther coulde I have any other amends butt that Davids afterwards came to aske mee forgivenesse. Howbeit Mr Essington was the principall cause hereof, according as some have tolde mee that heard him speake it. Butt in regard I am not come abroad to accuse others or to note other mens faultes, I will passe this heere in silence, and rather make reporte thereof by woord of mouth, yf neede so requyre, then to fill my journall with it.

Marlow 1500 R. spente and woulde give none accompt of it.

20 *ditto.* The 2 Holland pinnasses departed for Paleacatte, having a greate floate of beames and timber dragging behynde theym,

[1] *I.e.*, Komatis, members of the principal commercial caste in this part of the country; the meaning appears to be that four merchants stood security against the Governor's default.

[2] The marginal note is in a different hand, and was perhaps made by someone in the Company's office. The *James* was not a 'happy ship'; various accounts of the relations between captain, master, and factors will be found in *Letters Received*, ii. 64, 89, 312, etc.

which they had bought att Narsapur for a fortification and building of theyr forte and howse in Paleacatte. The Directour, Werner Van Berchem, wente along with theym. I have kepte good correspondence with him, not regarding the contention betweene him and Captain Marlowe.[1] Hee keepeth himselfe heere very stately both in apparrell and otherwyse, and is a very fitte person to keepe these proude Moores [*i.e.*, Moslems] and gouvernours in awe.

Mr Gourney, having dispatched his buysines heere, departed for Petapoli, after I had assisted him heere and cleared his reconing with the *Lingua*, Callopa[2] and the Gouvernour, having disbursed 1000 Pa. for him, for which hee delivered mee some gilte plate and some extant dettes; the reste hee was to paye me in course *tapés* [*i.e.*, skirts] which hee had bought att $2\frac{1}{2}$ Pa., butt because I can nowe buye the same att $1\frac{1}{2}$ and $1\frac{3}{4}$ Pa., wee aggreed that I shoulde take the same att $2\frac{1}{2}$ Pa. and that hee shoulde carrye theym with 6 or 7 packes of *tapechinders*[3] in the *James* to Bantam, withoute paying any fraighte. Captain Marlowe made muche ado to carry the same, yett hee carryeth over Moores and their goods for fraighte, and hee with the company of the shippe have above 600 corges of *tapés* besides other cl[o]ath for theyr particular [*i.e.*, private] account. Att laste, after some protestations, hee condiscended to it. I sente this cl[o]ath expresly to Bantam, there to bee bartered against pepper, and to have the same ready againste November nexte, hoping then to bee att Bantam, as more att large appeareth by the instruction sente along with Adam Denton. I have wholly nowe given over the voyage[4] for Petania, seing that nowe those factories wilbee sufficiently **Primo *February*.**

[1] This contention is not mentioned in the English records, but from what we know of their dispositions it is most unlikely that the two men could have been long in the same place without quarrelling.

[2] As the text stands, 'Callopa' might be either the interpreter (*lingua*) or some other person with whom Gurney had business, the punctuation of the MS not being precise; subsequent entries, however, indicate that he was a merchant.

[3] This word usually appears as *tapechindos*, and probably means skirts of some particular type of printed cloth; *chindos* represents the Indian name *chit*, or *chint*, as modified in Portuguese usage.

[4] The original plan had been to make a second voyage to Patani (*First Letter Book*, 428).

seconded and provided by the *James*, resolving therefore to imploye the whole capitall heere in Choromandell commodities to bee sent for England, and so to lade the resté of the shipp with pepper and other returnes of Siam, Patania, Maccasar, &c., and so to proceede homewards, and so to committe it to God, not being able to do more then Hee will graunte unto us, praying Him to turne all to the beste. I keepe George Chancy with mee and sende Adam Denton in the place; also I have given an instruction to Mr Gourny according to the Companies order.

7 ditto. The *James* departed from Petapoli for Bantam. God sende hir a prosperous voyage.

18 ditto. I wente to Marsapur Peta [*i.e.*, Narasapur], to take some order there with Captain Essington touching the shipp and some other matters; and the 19 att night I came to Peta, when a little before the shipp was come into the river, to the greate joye of us all, and confusion of ourc enemies, who woulde fayne have seene it otherwyse. Shee came over uppon $10\frac{1}{2}$ foote, drawing $9\frac{3}{4}$ foote. God bee praysed for His mercies.

22 ditto. After that wee had taken order together, I wente backe agayne to Musilpatam, where I arryved the 23, from whence I presently dispatched the peon of Suratte, wryting to Mr Aldwoorth,[1] sending withall the letters of the *James*. I kepte this peon heere thus long because I might wryte a certaintie of the getting over of our shipp into the river.

23 ditto. *Newes from Pegu.* Heere arryved a navette of Pegu, wherein also came one Cornelis Francke,[2] by whome wee understood that it was certayne that the King of Awa [*i.e.*, Burma] had taken the fort of Siriangh [Syriam], and slayne all the Portingalls, and that Xenga or Philip de Britto was either spitted or soulathd.[3] This was done

[1] Thomas Aldworth was now in charge of the English factory in Surat. Floris' letter to him is recorded in *Letters Received*, ii. 19, but the text is missing.

[2] Cornelis Franckx was a Dutch factor employed in Johore and the neighbourhood in 1607–9. No later reference to him has been found, but it is improbable that a Dutch factor would have travelled on a Portuguese vessel, and possibly he was now an independent trader.

[3] 'Spitted' (Dutch *gespit*, Portuguese *espetado*) meant at this time 'impaled': 'soulathd' has not been found elsewhere. The words in the original Journal, as read by the translator, must have been *ofte gespit ofte gesoulath*, but final *-th* is so exceedingly rare in Dutch transliteration of the period that it

in Marche laste. The King had given order for the building upp again of the olde towne,[1] calling all the Peguers together, and making many fayre promises. Himselfe wente forward toward Tenesserin, where Banga Dela[2] came to him with 50,000 Peguers, who before had bene under the King of Siam; all which is not withoute danger. The Moores [*i.e.*, Moslems] heere in Musilpatam rejoyce greatly att this conqueste, hoping nowe to gette the trade of Pegu into theyr handes agayne, and prepared 2 shipps to sende thether in September nexte. Tyme will shewe what will become of it.

Arryved in Tenagapatam [*i.e.*, Tegnapatam] the shipp called *der Goose* [*der Goes*], bringing greate store of marchandises in very good tyme, when I had almooste solde all myne, or else woulde have come to a bad marckett. *28 ditto.*

In this month there came newes overland from Goa that *Martius.*

may well be a misreading, and it is permissible to read *-ch*, pronounced as a guttural, because in the Dutch commercial script *c* is nearly identical with one form of *t*. Suggestions deriving 'soulathe' directly from Persian and Hindi *sūlt*, 'impaling-stake', have proved phonetically impossible, and the choice lies between the Mon verb *salòh*, 'to dismember', and the Malay verb *sulakan*, 'to impale'. Mr R. Halliday, the compiler of the standard Mon dictionary, writes that *salòh* (second vowel pronounced as in 'fall') is used in the *Razadarit Ayedawpon* of dismemberment ordered as a punishment by Razadarit, who was King of Pegu from A.D. 1385 to 1423; so that this word makes good sense, but it does not account for the final *-th* in the text. Malay *sulakan*, on the other hand, fits in precisely with the text, emended as suggested above, but does not make obviously good sense, for the translation shows that the two words denoted alternatives. From what is known of his record of service it is probable that Franckx, the narrator, would use Malay rather than Mon terms, and it is possible that he was alluding to two different methods of impalement. Dr C. Otto Blagden informs me that in the usual Malay procedure the culprit was pierced with a shoot of the *nipah* palm, but as an alternative a living bamboo was allowed to grow up the rectum; and possibly the phrase in the text expresses uncertainty as to which of these methods was adopted in de Brito's case. In the absence of illustrative passages it is not possible to decide which explanation is correct. It may be added that the method of de Brito's execution is not altogether certain. The statements in modern works that he was impaled all derive from Faria y Sousa's *Asia Portuguesa* (III, 238 of the Lisbon edition 1666–75), where the authority seems to have been hearsay; it is, however, probable enough in the circumstances.

[1] Anaukpetlun was now restoring the capital, Pegu, which had been laid waste in the years before his accession, as described in the Introduction.

[2] See above, in the Description of Siam, where the name appears as Bangade Laa. Binnya Dala, the Siamese Governor of Martaban, submitted to Burma in 1613. Anaukpetlun's attempt to recover Tenasserim from Siam was unsuccessful (*Harvey*, 189; *Wood*, 164)

11 shipps were arryved there, 8 from China and 3 from Malacca, which broughte suche quantitie of all sortes of marchandizes that all the marketts of the Indies fell in the ashes. In a happy houre had I almooste solde all my goods so tymely.

1614 13 *Aprill.* After that wee had had great trouble and toyle to keepe our ordinance aboute the shipp, for the Gouvernours woulde have it carryed into the Kings howse, fearing that wee mighte caste upp a forte, as the speeche wente among the Moores, and that it might come to the Kings eares, and so to bee layde to their charge, whereby they might come in the Kings disgrace: againste which wee did very muche, butt all in vayne: att laste, after muche sending to and fro, wee lette go 3 peeces, and by intercession of the Admirall Duriachan[1] the reste remayned in our bangsall [*i.e.*, storehouse], and the 3 peeces returned backe agayne, for it had not bene possible to carine our shipp withoute helpe of the ordinance; and although I overrunne this heere slightly, yett notwithstanding it is passed with muche labour and charges, as more att large appeareth by the letters [*not extant*].

17 *ditto.* Atmachan departed for Golconda to give upp his accounte, the yeare comming to an ende, as also to renewe his gouvernment, which came very well to passe for him; for the King deposed the greate treasurer, and made Malick Tusar[2] treasurer, who was a greate friende of this Atmachan, which caused greate joye in the commonaltie, hoping for a better gouvernment. This also came well for mee, for by this Atmachan was assured of his gouvernment, whereof before hee was in greate hasard, and thus my dette also was secured, for as long as they bee gouvernours there is hope of payement, butt being once putte oute there is

[1] Dariyā Khān, meaning 'sea-lord', is here probably not a proper name, but the designation of the officer who had charge of the port and dockyard; the term 'admirall' is misleading, for Golconda had no fighting fleet. In order to careen a ship, that is, to lay her over on one side, it was necessary to throw extra weight on that side, and the ship's guns were especially suitable for the purpose.

[2] Sir Wolseley Haig informs me that the extant chronicles of Golconda are unsatisfactory for this period, and do not record the administrative change mentioned in the text. 'Malick Tusar' probably represents *Malik-ul-tujjār*, 'lord of merchants', a title which was occasionally conferred on prominent members of the mercantile community, and there are other instances of a merchant being appointed 'greate treasurer', *i.e.*, Chief Minister; it is not recognisable as a proper name.

butt small appearance to recover anything. A desperate case, and needfull once to bee purged with a sharpe purge.

The markett howe lying heere wholy under foote, and no marchants comming downe to buye anything, butt going all to Goa, and I yett having a percell of porseleyn, resolved to sende the same to Golconda to bee quitte thereof. Which accordingly I did. Howbeit it was solde muche under the former markett, and yett it was the beste meanes, and by this trick [*i.e.*, expedient] I solde all my porseleyn and gotte ready money into my handes, whereof I stoode in greate neede, because of the greate charges of the shipp, our howse, and having lente so muche unto the *James*; yett I thanke God I ridde myselfe thorough. *30 ditto.*

Heere arryved the shipp *der Goose* [*der Goes*], having been in Paleacatte and Petapoli, and discharged some goods and taken in some packes; the reste shee was to discharge and take in heere. The Director, Van Berchem, came also along in hir. *13 May.*

Att night I receyved a letter from Mr Skinner, dated the 17 in the afternoone, wherein hee wrote me that Mr Essington was verye sicke, fynding it good that I shoulde come thether. And ½ houre after I receyved another letter, that yf I woulde see Captain Essington alyve I muste presently come thether. And scarce having read the letter, I receyved the 3rd letter, wherein they wryte of the decease of Thomas Essington uppon the 17th *stanti* [*i.e.*, instant], att 5 of the clocke in the evening, of a suddayne heate, having yett att noone eate his dinner att the table. Hee had some byles [*i.e.*, boils] aboute him, which att this tyme of the yeare are very common, among which was one verye greate one uppon his shoulder, which woulde not breake, and this was thoughte to be the cause of the heate. This so suddayne newes did amaze mee very muche, and wente yett the same night for Narsapur Peta, leaving George Chancy to looke to the howse. *18 ditto.* *The death of Thomas Essington.*

In the evening I came to Narsapur, and, muche contrarye to my opinion [*i.e.*, expectation], I founde all the company verye glad of his death, not hearing any one man to bewayle him, which broughte mee into no small suspition of his suddayne death, yett never coulde learne anything. The common people of the countrie sayde that the Gouvernour had bewitched him, *19 ditto.*

being very greate enemies, butt there was no grounde to bee taken holde of. Hee was a man more hated then beloved of everyone, being very mistrustfull, and fearing [*i.e.*, suspecting] eache one to bee desirous of his lyfe, which caused him to beare a true harte to nobody. So lykewyse hee had his spyes everywhere, which carryed him tales of all what was done, which made him to bee very suspitious and disquieted in mynde, especially a little before his death. God bee mercifull to him and graunte him a joyfull resurrection, and to us all when wee shall followe.

Hee was muche behynde hande in his bookes and wrytings, so that I have enough to do to order the same. So lykewyse I founde his estate very intricate, and almooste eyther more or lesse indetted to everybody, so that I muche marvayled hee shoulde so have intangled himselfe, the rather because that during his lyfe tyme I never have heard of it. And after that I had payde his dettes and solde his goods, which came to a reasonnable summe, I fynde that hee giveth no account of [blank] R8, which in Patania and Siam hee kepte in the shipp, which hee promised mee to do as soone as wee shoulde come uppon the coaste; for I cannot fynde in all his papers that hee hath payde oute anything of this money, onely that some saye hee hath payd it in Petania for damasts and velvetts, which hee hath solde att Narsapur Peta. Howbeit I do not fynde it in his casshe when I tooke the same to mee in presence of Mr Skinner and other officers; yett hee was no publicq spender, so that I marvayle the more what is become of this money, and howe hee shoulde bee so deepely indetted to the folkes, though some saye that hee broughte nothing with him oute of England. Butt I referre this to God and every mans conscience; for my parte I have not founde it otherwyse then heere I doe sette downe.

After I had cleered all thinges heere, and reconed with the woorkemen, I was sore troubled with whome to leave the gouvernment, Mr Skinner being to greate a drunckard, Mr Martins nott beloved of the folkes, George Chancie to young, and I of force muste bee att Musilpatam to have care of the buysines there. Therefore, calling the folkes together and to knowe their opinions, they all cryed they were not desirous to accepte of any butt of mee; which seemed very strange to mee, so muche to abase myselfe, and to treade in the place of myne undermarchaunt. Wherefore I putte them in good hope that, as soone as they shoulde come to Musilpatam, I woulde take suche meanes and rule in hand that withoute my disparagement they should receyve good contentment. In the meane tyme I committed the gouvernment to Mr Skinner, hoping that nowe hee will a little more refrayne from drunckennes, feeling this burthen uppon his necke, according as I intreated him, and hee lykewyse promised to mee. The shipp being almooste right upp att the second syde, so that the mooste parte of the buysines was come to an ende; and after having thus ordered the matter, I returned for Musilpatam. Primo *Junii.*

[CHAPTER XI

MASULIPATAM (*continued*)]

2 June. I arryved att Musilpatam, where I founde all things in good order. I gave fayre woords to everyone, uppon hope that whosoever carryed himselfe beste shoulde have the fyrste place, thinking that thereby every one woulde stryve for to do beste, butt yett it fell nott oute altogether as I had thoughte. Heere I founde some 3 persons which were arryved heere some 3 dayes agone, which sayde that they were sente with letters from Obiama,[1] Queene of Paleacatte, Jaga Raija, Gouvernour thereaboute and of St. Thome, [and] Apa Condaia, Secretary of the greate King Wencatadraja, wherein they sente mee woord that yf I woulde come thether they woulde graunte mee a place right over againste the forte of Paleacatte, with all suche privileges as wee shoulde desire, and other greate promises besides. Butt I, considering howe I and the *James* had bene intertayned there,[2] coulde beleeve butt little; yett att laste wee aggreed that one of theym shoulde staye with mee, and the reste shoulde departe with one of my folkes, who shoulde carry the letters to the foresayd persons, as also one to the King; wherein I repeated the bad intertaynment which wee had att Paleacatte, and yf nowe it pleased him that wee shoulde come into his contrye, then to sende us his *caull* or safeconducte, to which wee might perfectly truste, with other circumstances. Wherewith they departed the 5 of June.

Ambassadors off the greate King off Velur come in Musilpatam to seeke my friendshippe.

[1] Obājamma, one of the wives of King Venkata, who held Pulicat for what may be called her privy purse. Jagarāja was the King's brother-in-law. The Secretary's name is apparently Appa Kondayya. The form of the King's name given here represents Venkatādri Rāja. The designation 'King of Velur', given in the margin, is discussed in the *Journal of Indian History*, April, 1932 (pp. 114 ff.). Strictly speaking, 'King', or 'Emperor, of Vijayanagar' would be more appropriate, but his prolonged periods of residence at Vellore seem to have brought the other designation into popular use by this time.

[2] The *James* had had the same experience as the *Globe*, being confronted with the Dutch monopoly at Pulicat (*Letters Received*, ii. 83).

I receyved a letter[1] from Mr Aldwoorth from Baroche [Broach], with musters of indigo. Which letter I answered the 25th ditto. 10 *June*.

I had certayne newes that our men lived in greate disorder, in drunckennesse and fighting one with another, so that I was forced to go thether [*sc.* to Narasapur] in my owne person to see what the matter was. Butt comming thether they were so quyette that I coulde scarce learne what had passed; yett att laste I understood howe that, among other quarrells, Job Palmer and Rychard Bisshopp had challenged one the other to the fielde [*i.e.*, a duel], and had bene in the fielde, the one receyving a wound above his eye, and the other having loste almooste 2 of his fingers. Whereuppon I called the other officers together, laying before theym the danger of this action; who answered mee that they coulde not helpe it, butt prayed mee not to conceyve an evill opinion of theym all, but of him that deserved it, and to lette him beare his well deserved punishement. Therefore, considering with myselfe that this was the fyrste tyme of all the voyage that suche a fight had bene, and that very strong articles were made againste it, I founde it good to punishe this faulte to the uttermooste; and therefore condemned theym both thryce to bee drawen under the shipps keele, and then to bee nayled with a knyfe thorough theyr hand att the mayne maste,[2] and there to stande till they pulled it quite thoroughe their handes, and yett [*i.e.*, further] to loose 6 months wages besides. Thus being resolved to have the execution done the nexte daye, I wente downe to the shipp, and being buysied in reading of the judgement to the folkes, there came to mee the Admirall called Duria Cham [*i.e.*, Dariyā Khān], a man of greate porte [*i.e.*, position] and my olde acquayntance, who having heard of the justice, and being a friend to Job Palmer because hee did instructe him in the building of shipps, came expresly to intreate for theym; wherein I made very greate refusall, yett at length, being aggreed Adi primo *July*.

[1] In *Letters Received*, ii. 59, there is a letter dated 17th, not 25th, June, from Floris to Aldworth, acknowledging one of 10th May with 'musters', *i.e.*, samples, of indigo.

[2] A similar punishment is recorded by Jón Ólafsson as imposed by the naval regulations of the King of Denmark (*The Life of Jón Ólafsson*, Hakluyt Society, 1932, ii. 43).

because of his greate importunities, and the company promising mee not to take any exceptions against mee, butt all of theym very earnestly intreating to harken to the Admiralls requeste, I have yeelded to it, with a solemne protestation not to lette hereafter the lyke passe withoute punishement.

Nowe by this tyme the shipp was wholly dubbled [*i.e.*, sheathed], the rudder being sore eate[n] so that wee were buisie to hang in the niewe, hoping within 2 or 3 dayes to come to the barre with the shipp, and so to take holde of the fyrste opportunitie to come over the barre. So that, having sette all things in good order, I departed agayne for Musilpatam.

15 *July*. Understanding that Mr Skinner, muche contrarie to myne opinion [*i.e.*, expectation], kepte very bad rule, being drunk every daye and att extraordinarye expenses, as per his rekening is to bee seene, muche neglecting the going downe of the shipp,[1] contrarie to his promise, I have bene compelled to sende George Chancy thether to looke to the howse and the expenses, and commanded Mr Skinner to go aboord, and foorthwith to fall downe with the shipp towards the barre, for to take the fyrste convenient opportunitie; and had it not bene for the greate negligence of Mr Skinner, the shipp might before this tyme have bene before the roade of Musilpatam, for I putte it to the judgement of all mariners whether a shipp oughte to lye 6 months in a river to bee dubbled [*i.e.*, sheathed], where all things are so abundante, and paste 25 carpenters and calkers for woorkemen, besides 24 lascares and 60 coulis or labourers which dayly did woorke aboute the shipp. Butt I see with whome I am shipped. Patience is the beste I can use, having no other meanes to prevente it.

Great disorder att Narsapur, so that I sende G. Chancy thether.

29 *ditto*. Heere arryved 4 persons as ambassadors, with my man Wengali, from the greate King of Narsinga or Velur, bringing to mee a full answere and *caull* or safeconducte, with his *abestiam*,[2] being a white cl[o]ath where his owne hande is printed in sandall or saffran, as also one of the Queene of Paleacatte, and dyvers

[1] *I.e.*, taking the ship down to the bar of the river.

[2] Dr Krishnaswami Aiyangar informs me that this is probably for *abhayahastam*, a term used in religious symbolism to denote a particular pose of the hand which expresses the idea of protection.

letters from Jaga Raja, Tima Raja, Apacondaia, and others. The Kings letter was written uppon a leafe of golde, wherein hee excused the former faulte done to us in Paleacatte, desiring that nowe wee woulde come into his countrie and chuse a place to our beste lyking, and that there wee shoulde builde a howse or castle according to our owne lyking, with other privileges more mentioned in the same. Hee gave mee a towne [*i.e.*, village] of aboute 400 Pa. yearely revenue, with promise to do more att my comming thether. The Hollanders had wroughte muche againste it, butt att this tyme theyr woords were not of suche force as in former tyme they had bene, the inhabitants nowe seing every yeare Englishe shipps comming, and to passe by their haven withoute any profite to theym; which hath bene the onely cause—namelye the commons complaynte—that the King doth nowe call us in such friendly manner. I tooke all in consideration, and kepte the ambassadours with mee, allowing theym theyr dailye charges, till the shipp shoulde bee come hether on the roade, and then to see what tyme will do. My man Wengali had bene in person before the King and spoken with him, the King laying his hand uppon his head, presenting him with a *tesseriff* [*i.e.*, complimentary gift], so that I am sufficiently assured that there is no deceyte in this.

Ambassadors off Velur come againe with good newes.

Departed the shipp called *der Goes*, having taken in aboute 800 packs of cl[o]ath and 300 farden[1] indigo; and understanding by this shipp that Generall Beste[2] had broughte the 3 howses att Bantam into one head, I knewe not nowe howe to truste to my formerly ordayned lading. Wherefore I wrote a letter[3] to the Principall in Bantam, praying him to provyde 2000 sacks of pepper for mee, for so muche it was adjudged that the shipp might well carry, and by all manner of meanes to make a dispatche of my cl[o]ath sente him by the *James*, according to my

Adi 7 Auguste. The shipp der Goose *goeth for Bantam.*

[1] 'Farden' is perhaps the translator's misreading of *fardeis*, the plural of Portuguese *fardel*, 'a bale', which appears above as *fardis*.

[2] Thomas Best commanded the tenth Voyage. In November, 1613, he arranged that John Jourdain should take charge of all the business at Bantam, thus putting an end to the rivalries and disputes between the different Voyages (*Jourdain*, 312–14).

[3] Printed in *Letters Received*, ii. 40. The date is there given as 10th July, but the last paragraph refers to the *der Goes* having been delayed, and reads like a later addition.

order given to Adam Denton; and yf the same were not sufficient, then to speake to the cargason[1] lefte with Augustine Spalding; or else, yf that were sente home already, I woulde do it him good att my comming there, as more att large appeareth by the coppy of my letter. I also sente a letter to my brother Hans, which I gave to P[r] Gillis,[2] my speciall friend, repeating briefly myne estate [*i.e.*, condition], butt durste not venture to Sr. Thomas Smith, for feare it might not come to his hands.

Greate upper-water att Narsapur.

In this month was in Narsapur Peta and thereaboutes the greateste (upperwater) overflowing[3] that the lyke had not bene seene in 29 yeares, to see the river so overflowing in suche manner that whole salte hills, townes [*i.e.*, villages] and ryce drove awaye, and many thousands of men and cattle drowned; so that our shipp, ryding aboute that tyme before the barre, had enough to do to ryde oute the same, butt lying within a poynte or nooke it was a greate helpe for the ancker and cable to holde; dyvers men travailing on horseback by the waye coulde not escape it butt were drowned. The water was att the leaste 1½ faddem above the common highwaye, a matter altogether incredible, and yf I had not seene it myselfe, I coulde not have believed it, because of the knowledge which I have had of the countrye these 11 yeares. In Golconda, where the river passethe by, or rather to saye a braunche that runnethe into this greate river,[4] being drye in the summer or butt a kreeke, there were aboute 4000 howses washed awaye. Twoo stone bridges which go over the river, the one of 19 and the other of 15 arches, as artificially [*i.e.*, skilfully] made as the lyke maye scarce bee seene in Europe, in my judgement att leaste 3 faddem high above water, these were 2 *hasta* [*i.e.*, cubits], being 3 foote, under

[1] Dutch *aanspreken*, literally 'to speak to', is used in commerce in the sense of 'have recourse to'. 'Do it him good', just below, is Dutch *goed doen*, 'to make good' or 'indemnify'.

[2] Pieter Gilliesz van Ravesteyn, who, after six years' service in the Dutch factory at Petapoli, sailed for Bantam on the *der Goes* (*Golconda*, xlii).

[3] Dutch *opperwater*, 'floods'. 'Salte hills', just below, presumably means the mounds of salt stacked after manufacture.

[4] At this point the description passes from Narasapur on the Godāvari to the Kistna. Golconda is on the Mūsi, a tributary of the Kistna, the 'greate river' of the text; but the stone bridges mentioned are in Hyderābād, the recently built capital, not the older city.

water; whereof, of the bridge of 19 arches, 6 arches were washed awaye. Yf anybody shoulde have tolde mee this 7 yeares ago I shoulde hardly have believed it, for then I was uppon this bridge[1] and behelde it with admiration, and might very wel bee compared to the bridge of Rochester; and although it is not my custome to make of a little a greate, yett this mee thinketh to bee one of the strangest things of the worlde. Others which shall see it heereafter wilbee able to confirme the same. By this high water att Narsapur the barre was stopped; for whereas before was 10 and 11 foote of water, there was nowe no more then 7 or 8 foote, so that there was no hope of the shipps getting over till this high water was done. And att a suddayne the barre openeth with a greate depthe, which tyme muste bee expected with patience.

In this meane tyme I was buysie in getting in of my dettes, which were reasonnably many and came in very slowlye, the tyme of 4 months being already paste; and although I feared [*i.e.*, distrusted] none butt the Gouvernour, yett I muste take patience, for theyr generall answere was that, the shipp being come over the barre, I shoulde not staye for their payements; whiche answere I muste bee content withall, for else they might have returned the goods uppon mee, uppon which they loste att leaste 30 in [*i.e.*, or] 40 per cento, so that I muste take that for contentment. And seing heere were 2 shipps to go for Pegu by halfe September, I made no doute butt the shipp would bee over the barre by that tyme, and then I would have arrested these 2 shipps till I had bene fully payde. Wherefore I tooke all in the beste. In the meane tyme I writte to Mir Mahumim[2] and Malick Tusar complayning of the Gouvernour because of his badd payement, for I feared [*i.e.*, distrusted] him mooste; who indeede gave mee a kynde answere and made greate promises, butt nothing else did followe, and till the shipp was come over the barre I durste nott utter my meaning.

[1] Floris had accompanied Paul van Soldt on the Dutch mission to the Court at Hyderābād in 1606, eight, not seven, years before the date of this entry. Peter Mundy noted the "very faire stone bridge" over the Medway at Rochester, described by Defoe as "the largest, highest, and the strongest built of all the bridges in England, except London Bridge" (*Mundy*, iv. 34).

[2] Mu'min Khān, who appeared in an earlier entry as Masunim.

Adi 11 *September*. I receyved letters from Suratte[1] from Mr Aldwoorth, being an answere unto myne, as also letters to the Companie, and musters [*i.e.*, samples] of indigo, butt [we] were not of one opinion. I kepte the messenger till the shipp might bee over the barre, and then to dispatche him. This month of September had very foule wether, the wyndes for the mooste parte being att S.S.W., which bloweth right into the river, so that the shipp muste attend better wether. In the meane tyme the 2 shipps wente for Pegu the 16 ditto, whereby I loste a good paunde[2] for my dettes, neyther had I nowe to expecte any other butt onely the shipp of Mocha,[3] which was uncertayne; wherefore I made my complaynte to the courte for the second tyme, to do mee justice, or by defaulte thereof I woulde go seeke my payement somewhere, the waye of the Redd Sea being sufficiently knowen unto mee, where the proude Moores of Suratte had once bene well fetcht over,[4] desiring theym to give mee no occasion thereunto, in regard I was their friende. Whereuppon they sente mee comfortable letters, butt yett I gotte nothing the more of my dettes.

29, 30 *ditto*. The wether began to bee somewhat more tractable, and I receyved letters from Mr Skinner that nowe hee was in greate hope to gette over with the shipp, and that nowe att leaste there was 10 foote of water, which made mee nott a little glad.

4 *October*. The wether continuing thus still and fayre, yett I heard no newes from the shipp, which made mee almooste madd, so that I resolved to go thether myselfe to see what the matter might bee. And being some 10 mile on my waye, I mette a peon with letters from Mr Skinner and George Chancy, wherein they wrote me the joyfull newes that the shipp was come over the barre yesternight att 5 of the clocke, withoute any hurte, knocking onely a little uppon the barre withoute any hurte. Wherefore in my harte I gave thankes to God for it, and so returned backe to Musil-

The Globe *commeth over the barre*.

[1] Printed in *Letters Received*, ii. 101.

[2] Dutch *pand*, 'pledge'.

[3] *I.e.*, the pilgrim ship returning from the Red Sea.

[4] 'To fetch over' bore the meaning, now obsolete, of 'to get the better of' (*OED*, *s.v.*). The allusion is to Sir Henry Middleton's reprisals on the Gujarāt ships in the Red Sea.

patam. And that daye it began agayne to blowe and to rayne, so that yf the shipp were not over there woulde bee little hope to gett over this month. God bee praysed.

This newes of the comming over of the shipp I did presently spread abroad, especially among my detters, that nowe the daye of payement was att hande, and althoughe I had bore patience thus long, yett nowe I coulde staye no longer; which sente mee answere that before the newe moone I shoulde have my payement of theym all. Yett I had a very hard opinion of the Gouvernoure; wherefore I writte to the courte the third tyme, giving knowledge that the shipp was come over the barre, and nowe I coulde not staye any longer lingering, this shoulde bee the laste that I was mynded to wryte to theym; they mighte looke unto it yf so they thoughte it good, for I woulde gette my payement, together with the intereste, will they nill they. Whereuppon they wrote unto Mir Masrasa[1] and the Sabander to looke by any meanes to it that I were contented of the Gouvernour, that I might not departe with discontentment.

The shipp lying att Narsapur Peta, and [having] taken in the mooste parte of hir lading, so that butt onely 2 boats were resting [*i.e.*, remaining], which very well gotte over the barre, there arose suche a suddayne storme that they coulde not come to the shipp, and came before wynde to Musilpatam, in greate danger of theyr lyves. That night it blewe verye hard, so that the shipp lost ancker by the breaking of a cable, so that they muste sette sayle till the nexte daye; whenas they came aboute 3 leagues eastward from Musilpatam and roade there till the storme ceased, which was the laste foule wether that was to bee expected that yeare. 17 *October.*

The shipp came into the roade of Musilpatam to my greate joye. I praye God to make us thankefull for all His mercies. As soone as the shipp was come into the roade, I tooke order for the shipping of the goods which were ready, for the more hastening of my debitors. 23 *ditto.*

[1] This is another instance where the translator at first misread Floris' *h* as *s*. The name appears below, under 24th November, first as Mah: Rasa, and then as Mahumad Raza; the position occupied by this Muhammad Razā is not on record.

25 *ditto.* *The King off Velur deceased.* Newes came that Wencatadrapa,[1] King of Velur, having raigned above 50 yeares, was deceased, and that his 3 wyves, among whome Obajama, Queene of Paleacatte, was one, had burned theymselves quicke [*i.e.*, alive] with the corps: whereby greate troubles are expected. The Hollanders were in greate feare of [*read* for] their castle in Paleacatte. Tyme will shewe the issue.

1 *November.* Heere arryved a shipp called the *Lyon with Arrowes*, in which came Hans de Hase, Visitator,[2] to make visitation of the coaste. He came from Bantam in halfe [*i.e.*, mid] Auguste, bringing newes that Gerrard Reynts came for Gouvernour Generall, also the casting awaye of the shipp *Bantam* in the Tessell [Texel], as also of the *White Lion* under St. Helena, with other particularities from our *patria*.[3] The *James* was well arryved att Bantam, and gone for Petania; whereof I was very glad, for nowe I made a sure building on my lading of the pepper, as having there nowe aboute 10,000 R8, which is enough for 4 in [*i.e.*, or] 5000 bags; so that nowe I am not mynded to receyve any more *tapés* [skirts] or Javane commodities, as I was mynded before. In this shippe came 155 men, among whome were 60 souldiours to lye in the forte of Paleacatte. The Visitator was mynded to plante a factory in Bengale, whereatt I have a greate ayme: looke further of this in my description [*not extant*]. Aboute this tyme came certayne newes that the Kings shipp comming from Mocha was arryved att D'Abull,[4] having made a good voyage; for which I was very

[1] This form of the King's name probably represents Venkatādri with the honorific suffix Appa. 'Fifty years' is an exaggeration, for he came to the throne in 1586; but, as has been suggested by a writer in the *Journal of Indian History*, 1931, p. 222, the popular figure may have included the period of his viceroyalty before his accession.

[2] The ship was the *Leeuw met Pijlen*. Hans de Haze, a member of the Council of India, was appointed in 1613 to inspect all the Dutch establishments in the East. He remained on the Coromandel Coast on this duty till June, 1615, and returned as Director of the Coast in April, 1616. His designation at this time appears variously as (French) *Visitateur*, (Portuguese) *Visitador*, and the hybrid *Visitadeur* (*van Dijk*, 43 ff.). Gerard Reynst succeeded Pieter Both as Governor-General in this year.

[3] *Ons patria*, 'our native land', was used frequently by the Dutch in the East in the sense of 'Home'.

[4] Dabhol, a port on the West Coast, whence the passengers and treasure could reach Golconda overland.

sorry, as being nowe destitute of all my pandes [*i.e.*, pledges] uppon which I might make any accounte. God helpe me.

I wente aboorde for the correction of some insolent fellowes, so that I caused 9 men, beinge mooste all officers, to bee caste from the yarde, and broughte 2 to the captayne; as more att large appearethe by the judgement given in that behalfe.[1] *—ditto.* *Justice.*

Seing no waye to gette in the Gouvernours dette, who still putte mee of from newe moone till the full, and from the full till the newe agayne, and in the meane tyme came in greate hazard of not going home this yeare, and yf it were not done this yeare it was to bee feared that the shippe woulde bee founde unfitte for ever getting home, besides seing no Moores [ships] to lye in the roade[-stead], and the Kings shipp, whereon I thoughte to take my warraunte, arryved att d'Abull [*i.e.*, Dabhol], I resolved to carry the Gouvernour[2] or his sone from the custome howse aboord, the which, though it was a dangerous matter to putte in practize, yett notwithstanding it seemed fesible. So that I sente for aboute 15 men of the principalls to come to mee, laying this enterpryse before theym, who all of theym did approove it, promising to live and dye with mee. Whereuppon I gave order for the boate to go aboord and bee well provyded, and to bring 6 musketts wrappt upp in the sailes, and so to lye in the custome howse till wee shoulde see our opportunitie. Moreover, seing wee maye not bring any weapons ashoare, I gave order that all our folkes shoulde staye within the howse, and to come to mee in the custome howse as soone as I shoulde sende for theym, and to take houlde of the souldiours pikes that were of the Gouvernours or his sonnes garde, and so presently to *18 November*

[1] 'Captayne' must be a slip for 'capstan'. According to *Boteler's Dialogues*, 17–18, the commonest punishments at sea at this period were ducking from the main yard-arm, and 'at the capstan'. In the first, the delinquent was bound with ropes, hoisted to the end of the yard, and let fall violently into the sea. In the second, he was tied in a painful posture to a capstan bar, sometimes with a weight hanging round his neck.

[2] Apparently there had been some change in the local administration. The loan was exacted by the two Governors, Atmachan and Busebullerau, jointly; while the entry of 17th April, above, shows that the former had secured a renewal of the appointment. His name does not, however, occur again, and from this point on Busebullerau appears as sole Governor. The nature of the change is not on record; possibly Atmachan had sublet the position to his former colleague.

enter the custome howse, which standeth hard by the rivers syde, and then to shutte the doore, so wee shoulde bee able to carry theym into the boate before ever the allarum shoulde rightly bee knowen in the towne; and having of theym butt once in the boate, wee neede not to feare the whole towne. Wherefore, this being so concluded, wee made ourselves ready as soone and as secretly as possible wee coulde, yett coulde not doe it so secretly butt those of the Hollands howse had intelligence thereof; who woulde not beleeve it, thinking onely itt had bene butt a bragge, and so revealed it to nobodye.

—ditto. I dispatched the peon of Suratte with letters[1] to Thomas Aldwoorth.

21 November. The Gentives had a feaste, which feaste is 3 tymes a yeare when the newe moone commeth uppon a Mondaye. Then the Gentives come, both men and women, and washe theymselves in the sea, which they take for a great indulgence; among whome also the Bramenes and Cometis are comprehended.[2] It happened that the Gouvernours sone Wencatadra came downe the river in a boate whenas our boate was not gone downe a cabells length before him; a matter which grieved me very muche, for wee might have taken him without any gainesaying or other knowledge of anybody; butt it was to late.

23 ditto. I thoughte to have putte it in execution, but there were to many Moores [*i.e.*, Moslems] in the custome howse, so that I founde it good to expecte a better occasion.

24 ditto. In the morning Wencatadra came into the towne and wente to Mir Mah: Rasa, and a little after came the Gouvernour himselfe, who lykewyse wente thether; and so I lykewyse wente thether, charging George Chancy and Mr Skinner to staye within the howse and to keepe all the folkes in a readinesse, and to come to mee in the custome howse as soone as I shoulde sende for theym. I comming att Mir Mahumad Rasas founde there the Gouvernour and dyvers Moores, and Wencatadra butt even

[1] Printed in *Letters Received*, ii. 164.

[2] The feast is usually known as Somwatī Amāwas. 'Gentives' is a Dutch formation from Portuguese *gentio*, the Anglo-Indian 'gentoo', and was used sometimes, as here, to denote all Hindus, and sometimes for Hindus other than brāhmans and komatis. 'Indulgence' is obviously used in the ecclesiastical sense of remission of the penal consequences of sin.

The Dutche shipp was ordayned to departe this night, butt att the requeste of the Moores it was stayed, as it seemed to keepe us in awe, and thus the foresayd van Berchem returned on shoare. Att his departure wee gave him 5 peeces. And thus this daye wente of with good successe, having undertaken as desperate a peece of service that the lyke hath not bene heard of heere.

The same sayde van Berchem with the Secretary Olives[1] came aboord of us agayne, certifying us that the Gouvernour was contented to paye his dette, butt of other dettes hee woulde take no notice. Whereuppon I answered that I asked no more of him then his dette and the dette of Callopa, for whome hee was become suretye, and the rather because, the sayd Callopa bringing some indigo for mee, the Gouvernour tooke it of him, and was afterwards the cause of his flying awaye, and therefore it was reason that hee shoulde do it mee good [*i.e.*, indemnify me]. As for any other dettes, I asked none of him, butt, hee being Gouvernour, I onelye came to him that hee might see mee payd, and to sende those aboord of my shipp that woulde not paye mee, and so I woulde holde myselfe satisfyed. Whereuppon, though they had nothing to saye againste it, they protested[2] againste mee of all dammages and interests which they had already borne and yett might beare because of my hostilitie. To which protest I answered by writing, shewing the nullitie thereof. Thereuppon they sente a *recado* [*i.e.*, message] to their shipp for to departe that night, not being desirous to loose any longer tyme for our sakes, for which I was not sory; and so they returned to the shoare. *27 ditto.* *The protestation off the Hollanders against me and my answere to the same. The shipp the* Lion *goeth for Petania.*

In the meane tyme the poore Wencatadra remayned aboord withoute eating or drincking, for hee, being a Bramene, maye neyther eate nor drinke in anybodies howse butt what hee hath dressed himselfe;[3] which made mee to pittye him, and made

[1] Raphael Olyva, or Oliva, came to the Coast as senior factor on the *Rooden Leeuw* (*Red Lion*); he was subsequently senior factor at Masulipatam (*MacLeod*, i. 135).

[2] A formal written protest was the regular etiquette among Europeans in the East, in cases where men of one nation acted in such a manner as to prejudice those of another: etiquette required also a written reply.

[3] Dr Krishnaswami Aiyangar informs me that this statement may be accepted as correct for certain classes of brāhmans in this part of the country, who are stricter in the matter of food than those of Northern India.

Offer made to Wencatadra. offer to him that, yf 2 Moores of any qualitie woulde come aboord in his place, I woulde then lette him go ashoare; but there coulde not one bee perswaded to that; so that hee was fayne to tarry aboord fasting. In the meane tyme the Gouvernour, nowe seing that neyther his knaveryes nor force woulde take any place, payd both his and Callopas dette, and made all the reste to paye excepte Miriabeck[1] and Datapa, which were in Golconda, and by mildenesse of George Chancy not being followed hard enough; and by the interlocutions of the Dutche the prises lykewyse sette higher then my order. Butt considering *I gette paiement off my debitors.* with myselfe that a little tyme att this present was more pretious then 3 or 400 Pa., I did accepte of it, to shewe thereby that though wee have the upperhand, yett wee will rather loose something then to seeke all to the uttermooste. Nowe was the question howe to make the change; hee woulde not truste the goods aboord, nor I my paunde [*i.e.*, pledge] on shoare, till att laste van Berchem was suretye for mee and Mir Mahumad Tair was suretie for the Gouvernour. Whereuppon the goods were laden in boats to the barre, and I sente Wencatadra also beyonde the breache of the sea, and so wee changed, to our greate contentment that in so shorte tyme I was come to my payement, being *30 November.* *The manner of the change.* the 30 November. In the meane tyme George Chancy stayed on shoar for to sende water, wood, ryce and other necessaries aboord.

Adi primo *December.* Hans de Hase and Werner [Wemmer] van Berchem wente over lande for Petapoli, to go from thence with the shipp for Paleacatte.

Divers Moores come aboord. After that thus wee were aggreed with the Gouvernour, dyvers Moores [*i.e.*, Moslems] and others came aboord to visite mee, promising to wryte to the King the very trueth of these proceedings, desiring mee not to hurte any Moores shipps. Whereuppon I answered I was satisfyed for this tyme, and had no reason to do it, butt that they shoulde take heede of giving the lyke cause to any Englishemen heereafter, for it shoulde not *write to the Courte off Golconda.* passe in this manner. I also sente letters to the Kings courte, wherein I wrote of all things that were paste, praying theym

[1] 'Miriabeck' probably stands for Mirza Beg, a Moslem merchant; the other debtors named were presumably komatis.

another tyme to give better hearing to Englishmens complaints or complaintife letters, and to doe theym quicke justice, or else more evill woulde followe of it heereafter.

The ambassadours off Velur dispatched.

From hence I dispatched the ambassadours of Velur, the tyme beinge nott fitte att this presente, in respecte of the shortenes of my tyme, as also because of the troubles that were in those places; yett I gave theym 3 letters for the firste Englishe shipps that shoulde arryve there, wherein I have declared att large the state of that place and my opinion of the same, as more att large appeareth by the coppye thereof [*not extant*].

The Sabandt sendeth some tapés *in our shipp for Bantam.*

The Sabander intreated very earnestly that I shoulde carry over some 10 or 12 packes of *tapés* [*i.e.*, skirts] for him, which in these conjunctions I woulde not refuse him, giving thereby to understand that wee were friends of the towne, and mynded to come agayne another tyme.

7th Decembe

Mr Chancie and all the reste came aboord, and then I woulde fayne have come ashoare to take an honest and friendly leave of the Moores, butt the Gouvernour was againste it, fearing that I shoulde wryte so muche to the courte by those Moores that hee might loose his office thereby, saying hee was ashamed to looke mee in the face, having made so good a friend a bitter foe. Thus seing heere nothing else to bee done butt losse of tyme, I sente my commendations to everybodye, and in the night wee sette sayle, and before daye saluted the towne with 3 peeces, and then tooke our course towards the sea S.E. by S., with a N.E. wynde. Adi 8 *ditto.*

By the negligence of George [Chauncey] there rested 190 Pa. not imployed; therefore I lefte theym in the Hollands howse, which did assigne mee to receyve the same in silver att Bantam. This I tooke to bee the beste waye, for else there woulde have bene muche loste by the pagades [*i.e.*, pagodas] att Bantam.

[CHAPTER XII

BANTAM]

[*December*] 22 *ditto.* Wee passed the lyne, and hetherto wee had a good passage.

29 *ditto.* Wee sawe the land of Sumatra att 4½ degrees. Nowe it was calme till—

[1615 *N.S.*] Adi primo *January* Wee sawe the Iland of Engano. The 2nd wee sette into the straighte [of Sunda], with rayne and wynde and darke wether, so that wee hulled till midnight.

3 *January.* *We arrive att Bantam.* In the evening wee arryved in the roade of Bantam, where wee founde the *James*, the *Hoseander* and the *Concord*;[1] also I founde my cousin William [Ebert], who was come with the *James* from Petania, bringing a reasonable cargason, whereatt I muche rejoyced. God bee praysed for His mercies and goodnesse.

In Bantam. Adi 4 *January.* Att my going on shoare, I wente fyrste aboord of the *James* to visite Captayne Marlowe, who was sickly, and comming to him hee tolde mee all what was done heere on shoare; and hee, hearing that wee had butt 38 men in our shippe, founde oute meanes for the furnishing of men, to witte, that the *Hoseander* or *Concord* shoulde bee layd upp and the men *pro rato* divided, which was sufficiently aggreed uppon, namelye that the *Hoseander* shoulde bee layd upp, and the *Concord* to bee sente for Amboina and Banda. Butt because Ed[ward] Christian, captain of the *Hoseander*, woulde not forsake his shipp, being for the 10th Voyage, neyther tarry any longer in the countrye, they coulde nott aggree. I, having heard all, tooke it in consideration till

[1] The *James*, of the ninth Voyage, had been at Masulipatam in the previous year, as recorded above, and had now returned from Patani; the *Osiander* belonged to the tenth Voyage; the *Concord* had reached Bantam in the previous September on behalf of the Joint Stock, which had now superseded the system of separate Voyages (*Letters Received*, ii. 144). The name of the second ship is somewhat puzzling. It appears variously as *Hosiander*, *Osiander*, *Oceander*, etc. 'Osiander' is the accepted spelling of the name of a prominent theologian, who in the sixteenth century founded a sect of German Protestants (*Allgemeine Deutsche Biographie*, *s.n.*), but it is not easy to see how his name can have come to be borne by an English vessel.

I came ashoare, and have taken more information, and so wente with the sayd Captain Marlowe ashoare.

Comming on shoare I founde heere Mr John Jourdayne,[1] Principall Factor in Bantam, who delivered dyvers letters to mee from Sir Thomas Smith, my brother Hans, Mr Lucas, Mr Gourney, Adam Denton, George Cockens, and others, by which I understood what passed in those quarters, which was a good helpe for mee.

Sir Thomas Smith wrote mee of the receyte of my letters written from Petania; moreover that the Companie was joynd in one,[2] so that all the remaynders whiche were remayning heere of eache particular Voyage shoulde bee praysed [*i.e.*, appraised] in this countries so as they might well bee woorth in ready money, and those goods shoulde bee delivered to the generall factor of the United Companie, for which the Company shall give a certayne profitte att home, to have in this manner a shutting[3] of all the particular Voyages: according to which I shall knowe to rule myselfe.

Mr Cockeyn wrote mee from Maccasar that hee had well receyved the cargason I sente him by William Ebert and Robert Littlewood, and had solde parte thereof, and other circumstances more.

Adam Denton and Mr Gourney[4] complayned of Captain Marlowe, [and] the dead markett, because of the warres, as appeareth by their letters.

Mr Lucas his letters were olde, declaring the miserable estate hee was lyke to come into because of the warres; butt in regard the *Darling* is gone thether I hope hee will shortely bee delivered and bee better comforted.

William Ebert hath done his buysinesse reasonnably well in

[1] Jourdain's *Journal* is not detailed for this period, and makes no mention of this visit of the *Globe* to Bantam. Cockens is George Cokayne, who had been left by Jourdain in Macassar (*Jourdain*, 294).

[2] That is to say, the system of separate Voyages had given way to the Joint Stock, as explained in the Introduction.

[3] The Dutch verb *sluiten*, 'to shut', was used regularly for 'closing the books', and so came to denote a settlement of accounts.

[4] Denton and Gurney were now in Patani, while Antheunis (Mr Lucas) was still in Siam. The 'warres' to which reference is made would be the capture of Chiengmai by Burma in 1614.

Petania, having beneficed[1] or solde all that was lefte there, gotte in the voyage of Cambosa [*i.e.*, Cambodia], and imployed the 3000 R8 which hee receyved of Mr Lucas, leaving in Petania nothing butt the howse and some small remnants, as appeareth by his bookes. Robert Littlewood dyed in the *James* even in the sighte of Bantam—a man that hath shortened his lyfe very much with drincking. Raphe Cooper stayed with Adam Denton in Petania.

Moreover I founde heere John Persons, whome att the firste I had sente to Maccasar, and bene from mee very neere 2 yeares. Hee coulde give no reason of his actions nor accounte of his bookes, alledging sometymes his sickenesse, and sometymes that Thomas Brett, whome I had sente with him and was deceased heere in Bantam, had cousined [*i.e.*, cozened] him. Att laste hee broughte mee a meere invented accounte, having neyther head nor tayle, and yett in this reconing hee commeth shorte above [blank] R8. Wherefore I was mynded to bring him over to make his answere to the Company, not knowing any other thing to bee done in this matter heere. Mr Jourdayne denyethe to have forced anybody to laye in wayte for him,[2] and this muste thus passe heere for currant payement.

I lykewyse founde heere Mr Johnson, whome wee had sente from Petania to Bantam; whome Generall Best refused to carry for England, butt sente him backe agayne to Petania with a letter to Captain Essington counselling him to receyve Mr Johnson agayne into the shipp as master, with some other threatning woords, wherein hee much forgetteth himselfe. Butt hee, not fynding the *Globe* in Petania, came back with the *James* to Bantam, whereas hee desired of mee that hee might bee receyved into the shipp as master; which I refused to do, for Mr Skinner having nowe served the mastershipp almooste 2 yeares, notwithstanding that hee also was a greate drunckard

[1] The Dutch verb *beneficeren* does not appear in modern dictionaries, but at this period it was used in the East in the sense of 'to sell'; it was perhaps formed from Portuguese *beneficio*, used in the sense of 'profit'. The Cambodia venture is recorded above under 2nd July, 1613.

[2] The reference is to the 'simple newes' recorded under 16th August, 1613, that Jourdain had delayed the voyage of the junk on which Persons was preparing to leave Macassar 'To laye in wayte' is presumably the translator's attempt to say 'to lie waiting'.

and no friend of myne, I coulde not fynde in my harte to thruste him oute att this tyme and to receyve the other agayne. Yett I woulde bethinke myselfe and see what occasions might happen, and then do what ought to bee done.

After I had infourmed myselfe of all things howe and in whatt manner meanes might bee founde to manne these greate shipps, and that the voyage for the Moluccos might go forward, which in my opinion concerneth the Company very muche, there was no other meanes butt that the *Hoseander* muste bee layd upp, and to make a repartition of those men; butt in regard shee was belonging to the 10th Voyage, and Ed[ward] Christi[an], being come foorth for purser in the *Dragon*, and by Generall Beste in this countrie made captain of the *Hoseander*, woulde not forsake his shipp and go passinger in another, neyther staye any longer in the contrye, so that I sawe all laye uppon him. I, seing there was no other meanes, gave him my woord that hee shoulde go home for captain in the *Globe*, notwithstanding that I had promised it before to my undermarchant George Chancy; yett I was to respecte the shipps service before the preferment of any particular person. My woord being paste to the sayd Christian, all stryfe was ended, and so a generall courte[1] was assembled, by whome it was founde good that the *Hoseanders* goods shoulde bee discharged into the *Globe*, and Ed[ward] Christian, captayne, and Nathanaell (Samuell) Salmon, master, and in liewe of this Mr Skinner shoulde go master in the *Hoseander*, and that in the *Globe* wee shoulde have 50 men, and in the *James* 55, the *Hoseander* 20, and 3 or 4 to keepe the *Concord*. Which accordingly was putte in execution. Yett I had greate trouble to gette Captain Christian into the shipp, being buysied 2 dayes before I coulde perswade the men. Att laste all was pacifyed and perfourmed. *9 ditto.*

After that I had overlooked the accounte of Adam Denton, I fynde strange proceedings with our capitall of 4700 R8, by Augustine Spalding lefte with Mr Sheppard, who settethe above 1500 R8 losse in accounte, and the reste bestowed in China commodities, which are so boughte in[2] as that Mr Jourdayne *Mr Sheppard*

[1] The proceedings of the Court are in *Letters Received*, ii. 284.

[2] Dutch *inkoopen*, which means merely 'to buy', not 'buy in'.

woulde not accepte of theym in payement of pepper. It is no marvaile that these marchants have their purses so well filled, and neede butt a yeares tyme to become riche, as these Sheppards are become. This I maye putte for a remembraunce [illegible] even in the butt see little else come of it.

The clath sente per the James *unsolde.* The cl[o]ath sente by the *James* per Adam Den[illegible] very much unsolde heere, being att the fyrste neglected by the sayd Adam Denton, and afterwards by Mr Balie,[1] to whome had bene offered 25 R8 for the *tapé chinde*, 12 for the *tapé* girdles, and 10 for the course *tapés*; butt Mr Jordaine woulde not suffer theym to bee solde unlesse they woulde take the whole percell of the *James*, so that, the percell being to greate, nothing did followe. In the meane tyme, expresly contrary to my order, the cl[o]ath lyeth heere unsolde, so I, that made accounte to have att the leaste 10,000 R8 in Bantam, have not a penny, so that nowe I am in very good case for the lading of the shipp. God helpe mee. It seemeth that these servants have joyntly bounde theymselves to hinder our good purpose, as in all our enterprises to to muche hath bene perceyved. Well, patience!

25 ditto. Aggreement for 4000 baggs off pepper. After muche brabbling and questioning, I aggreed att the laste with Mr Jordayne for 4000 baggs of pepper against the foresayd cl[o]ath and other which nowe I bring with mee, reconing eache as they are woorth att this present; so that I come of very fayrely, for the pepper which was boughte att 10 and 11 R8 was nowe come to 15 R8, the *tapé chindes* att 18, the *tapé* girdles att 9, and the course *tapés* att 4 R8 the corge, the iron att 4 R8, which shortely after hee solde for 6, so that they playde with mee as the catte doth with the mouse; yett I had no other meanes in the worlde, the tyme being so shorte as that I can neyther wynde nor turne myselfe,[2] so that I muste thinke myselfe yett muche beholding for this aggreement and the

[1] See *Letters Received*, ii. 120–2, for Denton's account of these transactions. When he left Bantam for Patani, he entrusted the unsold goods to John Baylie, 'a careful and diligent man', who had come out in the *Expedition*. Baylie died in Japan in 1616 (*op. cit.* iv. 163).

[2] Dutch *wenden of keeren*, meaning 'to twist or turn'. It would be possible to attach too much weight to these bitter comments on the bargain. Floris naturally wanted the best possible terms for his Voyage, while Jourdain wanted to do the best he could for the general interests of the Company, and there was obviously room for conflicting views.

greate discretion shewed unto mee. Well, looke to it better another tyme!

The *James* departed to go on before, and to staye a month att the Cape, and, yf wee came not by that tyme, then to staye [illegible] St. Helena, for to go home together in companie. 30 *ditto.*

After I had [illegible] the fyrste juncke of China, bringing newes that many [illegible]ore were comming which were very richely laden, bringing 400 picoll of rawe silke, &c. Seing the *Hoseander* coulde not so quickly bee made readye, and the monson beginning to bee farre spente, it is thought good that the *Concorde* shoulde go the voyage for Amboina, and the *Hoseander* to remaine lying heere till more supplye. Whereuppon the *Concord* departed, George Bale[1] going along in hir, and George Chancye for to staye in Maccasar, who was not nowe willing to go home, and seing Mr Jourdaine did so earnestly desire to have him I, though very loath, gave him leave. God Almightie give him good successe. —*ditto.* *The* Concord *goeth for Amboina.* *Mr Bale.* *Mr Chauncie.*

John Persons desired very earnestly that hee might staye in the countrye, and I was intreated by dyvers on his behalfe not to undoe him wholly, for yf hee shoulde bee sente home, hee coulde not then tell in all the world what to do; and although I had firmely purposed to carry him over, yett I was loath to bee a cause of his undoing, so that I have lefte him heere with Mr Jourdaine. Oure olde master, Johnson, I receyved into the shipp agayne as a passenger, to make his answere before the Companie; in the meane tyme hee might use his place of masters mate.[2] *John Persons.* *Mr Johnson.*

The [Dutch] shipp *Zelandia* arryved heere the 27 January from Japan, Henrick Brouwer comming along with hir, bringing a percell of copper and some silver, the reste laden with victualls, as meale, fleshe, latun[3] salted, verye good; and brought letters *The shipp* Zelandia *arriveth from Japan.*

[1] George Ball went out on the eighth Voyage. He subsequently became President at Bantam, but was recalled on account of his private trading (*Letters Received*, iii. 319).

[2] Johnson had been master's mate before his appointment as master. 'Use his place' means apparently that, as a member of the ship's company, he would draw rations during the voyage, which a mere passenger would not do.

[3] Apparently for Spanish *el atun*, 'the tunny fish'. In a list of exports from Japan to the Philippine Islands about this period there is an entry of 'salted tunny, which was fresh and tasty' (*Takekoshi*, ii. 402). The Spanish name would naturally follow the delicacy westward.

from Mr Cocks,[1] who wrote that Mr Peacock with the Hollanders was slayne in Cochinchina, and that Mr Adams and 4 other Englishmen were gone for Siam; touching the trade, little or nothing was to bee done.

Mr Jourdayne having yett a percell of silkes and silke wares which hee coulde not shippe in the *James*, I offered him to leave a percell of cinamon and white yarne there, and to carry over the sayde chestes for the Companies service, so that hee shall sende the sayde cinamon and yarne hether with the nexte shipps. Whereuppon att laste wee aggreed.

14 February. Captaine Middleton arriveth att Bantam with 3 shipps.

Heere arryved Captain David Middleton in the *Samaritan*, *Thomas* and *Thomasin*[*e*], the men being well and in good disposition.[2] Hee had spoken under Java with the [Dutch] shipp *Enchusen*, and bene att an ancker, Diricke de Vries being in hir. I receyved a letter from Sir Thomas Smith, being almooste of the same content as I receyved by the *Concord*. Which letter having read over in haste in Mr Jourdains chamber, wee were called to the table for our meate, and there laying the letter uppon the table I never sawe it since, neyther can I thinke who might have playde mee this tricke, for none or very fewe come in his chamber, and those being his familiar friends. Howbeit it is no great matter. Captayne Middleton, having understood the death of his brother Sir Henry Middleton, and the losse of the shipp called the *Trades Increase*, was wholy perplexed, resolving to go home. Wherefore hee called a courte to see [to] the disposing of the shipps and the manning agayne of the *Hoseander*. It was then founde fitting, according to the Companies order, to sende home the *Samaritan* with the very fyrste [*i.e.*, as soon as possible], the *Thomas* to Sumatra, and the *Thomasin*[*e*] for Amboina, for to succoure the *Concorde*, and the *Hoseander* for Petania and Japan, to visite the factories. The which being resolved was lykewyse

[1] Richard Cocks, chief factor for the English Company in Japan; his Diary was published by the Hakluyt Society in 1882 (vols. 66, 67). For Tempest Peacock's death see *Letters Received*, ii. 197. He was sent on a trading voyage from Japan, and joined a Dutch party on a journey to the capital; the whole party were murdered on the way. Adams sailed from Japan for Siam on a junk named the *Sea Adventure*, but she lost her voyage (*op. cit.* iii. 245, 249).

[2] The Journal of this Voyage is printed in part in *Purchas*, I. iv. 524.

putt in execution. Touching his owne person, no expresse commission being touching the same, hee might looke what hee was beste to do.

The [Dutch] shipps *Rotterdam* and *Zelandia* departed from Jacatra to the Moluccos. Adi 17 *February*

[The End]

LIST OF AUTHORITIES

Note. This list is not a complete bibliography, but is limited to the works which it has been found convenient to cite in abbreviated form.

ANDERSON. English Intercourse with Siam in the Seventeenth Century. By J. Anderson. London, 1890.

BEGIN ENDE VOORTGANGH. Begin ende Voortgangh van de Vereenigde Nederlandtsche Geoctroyeerd Oost-Indische Compagnie. Amsterdam, 1646.

(Each voyage is separately paged, so that it is necessary to quote the name of the Admiral in command.)

BOTELER'S DIALOGUES. Navy Records Society, vol. LXV. London, 1929.

BOUWSTOFFEN. Bouwstoffen voor de geschiedenis der Nederlanders in de Maleischen Archipel. Ed. P. A. Tiele and J. E. Heeres. The Hague, 1886–95.

(Issued in the form of a supplement to DE JONGE, OPKOMST, *q.v.*)

CAL. S.P. Calendar of State Papers, Colonial Series, East Indies, China and Japan. Vol. 2, 1513–1616; vol. 3, 1617–21. London, 1862, 1870.

COURT MINUTES. The MS volumes recorded in the India Office under this title.

DALGADO. Glossário Luso-Asiático. By S. R. Dalgado. Coimbra, 1919–21.

DE JONGE, OPKOMST. De Opkomst van het Nederlandsche Gezag in Oost-Indie. Ed. J. K. J. De Jonge. The Hague, 1862–88.

(See also BOUWSTOFFEN.)

ENGLISH FACTORIES. The English Factories in India, 1618–1669 (13 vols.). Ed. Sir W. Foster. Oxford, 1906–27.

EREDIA. Eredia's Description of Malaca. Tr. J. V. Mills. Journal of the Malayan Branch of the Royal Asiatic Society, vol. VIII. Singapore, 1930.

FIRST LETTER BOOK. The Register of Letters, etc. of the Governour and Company of Merchants of London trading into the East Indies 1600–1619. Ed. Sir G. Birdwood and W. Foster. London, 1893.

(Lettered on back, The First Letter Book of the East India Company.)

GOLCONDA. Relations of Golconda. Ed. W. H. Moreland. Hakluyt Society, 1931.

(Contains the relations of William Methwold, Antony Schorer, and (?) Pieter Gilliesz van Ravesteyn.)

HARVEY. History of Burma. By G. E. Harvey. London, 1925.

HOBSON-JOBSON. A Glossary of Colloquial Anglo-Indian Words and Phrases....By H. Yule and A. C. Burnell. New edition, ed. W. Crooke. London, 1903.

IJZERMAN. Cornelis Buijsero te Bantam. Ed. J. W. Ijzerman. The Hague, 1923.

IMPERIAL GAZETTEER. The Imperial Gazetteer of India. Oxford, 1909.

JOURDAIN. The Journal of John Jourdain. Ed. W. Foster. Hakluyt Society, 1905.

JRAS. The Journal of the Royal Asiatic Society of Great Britain and Ireland.

LANCASTER'S VOYAGES. The Voyages of Sir James Lancaster, Knt., to the East Indies. Ed. C. R. Markham. Hakluyt Society, 1877.

LETTERS RECEIVED. Letters Received by the East India Company from its Servants in the East. Ed. F. C. Danvers and W. Foster. London, 1896–1902.

LINSCHOTEN. The Voyage of John Huyghen van Linschoten to the East Indies. Ed. A. C. Burnell and P. A. Tiele. Hakluyt Society, 1884.

(See also REYS-GHESCHRIFT.)

MACLEOD. De Oost-Indische Compagnie als Zeemogendheid in Azie. By N. MacLeod. Rijswijk, 1927.

MUNDY. The Travels of Peter Mundy. Ed. Sir Richard Carnac Temple. Hakluyt Society, 1905–24.

OED. A New English Dictionary on Historical Principles (commonly called The Oxford English Dictionary). Oxford, 1888–1928.

PURCHAS. Hakluytus Posthumus, or Purchas His Pilgrimes. London, 1625.

(The references are to the original edition, the paging of which is given in the margin of the Glasgow reprint of 1905.)

PYRARD. The Voyage of François Pyrard, of Laval, to the East Indies. Ed. A. Gray. Hakluyt Society, 1887, 1889.

REYS-GHESCHRIFT. Reys-Gheschrift van de Navigatien der Portugaloysers in Orienten....By J. H. van Linschoten. Amsterdam, 1595.

SARIS. The Voyage of Captain John Saris to Japan. Ed. Sir E. M. Satow. Hakluyt Society, 1900.

SATOW. Notes on the Intercourse between Japan and Siam in the Seventeenth Century. By E. M. Satow, in Transactions of the Asiatic Society of Japan, vol. XIII. Yokohama, 1885.

SCHOUTEN. Beschrijvinge van de Regeeringe...des Coninghrijcx Siam. By Joost Schouten.

(Included in Beschrijvinge van het Machtigh Coninckrijcke Japan. Amsterdam, 1648.)

TAKEKOSHI. The Economic Aspects of the History of the Civilization of Japan. By Yosoburo Takekoshi. London, 1930.

TERPSTRA. De Vestiging van de Nederlanders aan de Kust van Koromandel. By H. Terpstra. Groningen, 1911.

VALENTYN. Oud en Nieuw Oost Indien. By F. Valentyn. Amsterdam, 1724–6.

(The Parts have separate paging; the references are to the Part dealing with Coromandel.)

VAN DIJK. Zes Jaren uit het Leven van Wemmer van Berchem. By L. C. D. van Dijk. Amsterdam, 1858.

(The volume includes also some notes on Japan, separately paged: these are referred to as *van Dijk* (J).)

VAN VLIET. Beschryving van het Koningryk Siam. By Jeremias van Vliet. Leiden, 1692.

WOOD. A History of Siam. By W. A. R. Wood. London, 1926.

WOORDENBOEK. Woordenboek der Nederlandsche Taal. Ed. M. de Vries, and others. The Hague, 1882–(in progress).

INDEX

Abestiam, 126
'About', special sense of, 2*n*
Abrolhos, the, 2, 3
Achin, kingdom and seaport, *passim*; Antheunis at, xlvii; Floris at, xli–xliii; conquers Johore, 77, 81, 97, 98; threatens Malacca, 86; trade of, 27
Adams, William, 35, 36, 74, 86, 146
Adi, term explained, 1
Administrative methods—in Golconda, xxii, 14–20, 114, 129–139; in Bantam, 23–26; in Patani, 33–38; in Siam, 46, 47
'Adventurers', *passim*; term explained, xi
Agreement for the Voyage, the, quoted *passim*; discussed, xv, xvi
Agulhas, Cape, 5
Albatrosses, 3
Aldworth, Thomas, 118, 125, 130, 134
Algoa Bay, 5
Amboina, Amboyna, island, 44, 82, 140, 145
Amsterdam, xliii, xliv, lx
Amuck, 'playing' (=running), 94
Anaukpetlun, King of Burma, xxvii, 54*n*, 91, 92, 118
Andaman Islands, 109, 110
Anderson, John, quoted *passim*; title, 149
Angoche Islands, 6
Antheunis, Lucas, *passim*; identity and early life, xlv–xlix; in London, xiii–xix; chief merchant on the *Globe*, *passim*; on the Coromandel Coast, xlvi, 10–21; in Patani, 40; in Siam, xxv, xxxiii, 43, 45–52, 66, 141; in charge of Masulipatam, xxxiii, xlv, xlvi; return to London and later life, l, li; his private trade, l; his legal and moral position, lviii–lxi
Aor Islands, 32
Api, Raja, *see* Naresuen
Appajī, 115
Appa Kondayya, 124, 127
Apparel, trade in, *passim*; described, xix–xxi; on the Coromandel Coast, 17, 18, 117, 139; in Bantam, 27, 28, 77, 112, 144; in Patani and Siam, 37, 41–44, 52, 58, 66, 69–71, 73; in Macassar, 43, 87; in Borneo, 76
Arakan, kingdom, xxvi, xxvii, xxxvii, xxxviii, xlix, 14, 54, 55
Arbocas de Palimbam, 31
Armagon, seaport, xxxv
Aroa Islands, 106
Artisans, position of, xxii
'Assalan', Jewish merchant, xxxix
Astley, Thomas, xxviii*n*, lxv
Atmachan, Governor of Masulipatam, 111, 115, 120, 133*n*
Ava (Awa), xxvi, 91, 118
Ayuthia, capital of Siam, xxiii, xxv, xxvii–xxix, 45–47, 52*n*, 56, 57

Bābā, Hājī, 14
'Baddaga', *see* Vadagar
Bahār, unit of weight, *passim*; size of, lxix
Baixos da Judea, 6
Bajin, island, 32
Balai, Ballaia, term explained, 34
Balaos (boats), 70
Bali, island, 76
Ball, George, 145
Banda Islands, lv 44, 82, 88, 89
Banda, the, 23
Bandara, Dato', 94
Bangade Laa, Banga Dala, *see* Binnya Dala
Bangkok, 45; Bight of, 41*n*, 49
Bangsall, term explained, 114
Banjarmassin, 33
Banka, island, 31
Bantam, kingdom and seaport, *passim*; commercial position, xxiii, 27; English factory at, xi, 84, 127; the *Globe's* first visit, xxxii, 23–29; second do., 140–147; customs at, 23, 24; interest at, 25; private trade at, 61, 144; news from, 76, 77, 83, 84

Bantam, the, xlix, 23, 32, 43, 132
Barber, Frauncys, 43
Barbosa, Duarte, quoted, xx*n*
Barrawas, or Barwas, cape, 99
Bastinado, the, xxii, lxviii*n*
Batavia, xxiii; *and see* Jakatra
Batu Pahat, river, 105
Bayinnaung, King of Burma, xxvii, 52
Baylie, John, 144
Beggars in London, lii
Begin ende Voortgangh, quoted *passim*; title, 149
Bengal, Bay of, xi, xiii, xxxv, xl, 132
Benzoin, xxiv, lxiii, 79, 80, 116
Berbukit, seaport, 77, 81, 102
Berdaun Island, 103*n*
Besar, Dato', 34, 72, 94
Best, Thomas, 127, 142
Betilles, muslin, 66
Binnya Dala, 57, 119
Bintang, island, 31, 81, 87, 100–102
Birds, at Cape of Good Hope, 3
Birds' heads, trade in, 86
Bisshopp, Rychard, 125
'Black King', the, *see* Naresuen
Bocarro, Antonio, quoted, 55*n*
Bockholt, —, 97
Bona Esperanza, Cape, *see* Good Hope, Cape of
Bongsu, Raja, 63*n*, 81, 102
'Bonnetts', term explained, 109
Boom Island, 30
'Bordello', term explained, 59
Bordolongh, seaport, 70, 72, 95
Borneo, island, 26, 33, 44, 73, 98
Boteler's Dialogues, quoted *passim*; title, 149
Both, Pieter, Governor-General, 69, 82, 84, 85, 89
Bouwstoffen, quoted *passim*; title, 149
Boves, Andrew, quoted, 54*n*
Brāhmans, 134, 137
Brani Island, 100
Brazil, country, 2*n*
Brazil, dye-wood, *see* Sappan
Brett, Thomas, 43, 87, 88, 142
Broach, city, 125
Broadcloth, 13
Brothers' Islands, the, 108
Brouwer, Hendrik, 4, 145
Browne, Robert, *passim*; his service at Bantam, xvi; chief merchant on the *Globe*, xvi; on the Coromandel Coast, 10–16; illness and death, xxxiii, 10, 11, 13, 16; his estate, 16, 27; his private trade, lvii, 27
Buffaloes, 63, 86
Bulls, wild, 63
'Bulster', term explained, 89
Bulus, Cape, 100, 104, 105
Buncasey, seaport, 41
Burma, kingdom, *passim*; described, xxvi; ruin and recovery, xxvii, 53–55, 119; relations with Siam, xxvi, xxvii, 52–55, 90, 91, 119; trade with Masulipatam, 119, 129, 130
Busebullerau, Governor of Masulipatam, lxvii, lxviii, 111, 115, 129–139
Butang Islands, 107
Buton Island, 88

'Cake', term explained, 30*n*
Calendar of State Papers, quoted *passim*; title, 149
Callopa, merchant, 117, 137, 138
'Calynders' (pedlars), 70
Cambodia, kingdom, xxiv, 43, 55, 57, 58, 72, 73, 80, 142
'Campa', or 'Campon China', 41, 76
Canary Islands, 2
Candi, or Candy, unit of weight, *passim*; size of, lxix
Cannibals, 109
Canton, seaport, xxiv
Cantoor, term explained, 8*n*
'Cape merchant', term explained, 67
Capital for the Voyage, xv, xviii, xxx, 78–80
Caravel, or Carvel, *passim*; term explained, 2*n*
Cardamoms, 80
'Cargazon', term explained, 25*n*
Carimon, island, *see* Kerimun
Carseys, *see* Kerseys
Carvallo, Pedro do, 107
Cassas, muslin, 66
Caule, *Caull*, etc., see *Qaul*
Celebes, island, *see* Macassar
Celytones (boats), 9
Ceram, island, 83
Ceylon, xl, xli, 7, 8
Ceylon, the, xlix
'Chambers', term explained, 82

Chareboute, —, 31
'Chatties', 33
Chauncey, George, factor on the *Globe*, xxiii; left at Bantam, xxiii, 28, 29; on the *James*, xxxiii, 112; returns to the *Globe*, xxxiii, 118; on the Coromandel Coast, 121, 122, 126, 134–139; posted to Macassar, xxxiv, 145; death, xxxiv
Chay root, 71
'Cheremandall', *see* Coromandel Coast
Chhāpa-dalālī (local dues), 14
Chiengmai, state and town, xxiv, xxvi, xxvii, 43, 55, 58, 67, 73, 74, 86, 91
China (country), trade of, xxiii, xxiv, 27, 60, 73, 86, 120, 145; china (commodity), *see* Porcelain
Chint, or chintz, xx, 117
Christian, Edward, xxxii, 140, 143
Christ's Hospital, lii, liii
Chulias (pedlars), 70
Churcheman, Bartholomew, 72
Cinnamon, 146
Clove, the, 23, 83
Cloves, 83, 88
Cobb, Richard, 110, 111, 116
'Cobion', term discussed, 108
Cochinchina, 146
Cocks, Richard, 4*n*, 146
Coen, Jan Pietersz, xxxvi, 60*n*, 84*n*
Cœurdoux, Father R., quoted, xx
Cokayne, George, 71*n*, 141
Commissions for the Voyage, quoted, *passim*; discussed, xvi–xviii
Comorin, Cape, 7
Concord, the, Dutch ship, see *Eendracht*, the; English ship, 140, 145
Condamaa, *see* Kondamma
Cooper, Raphe, 97, 142
Copan, Siamese coin, *passim*; value of, lxix
Copper, 145
'Corge', term explained, xix
Coromandel Coast, *passim*; products and trade, xix–xxii; administration, xxii; projects for trade with, xiii–xix; establishment of the Dutch on, xxxviii–xlii; the *Globe's* first visit, 6–21; second visit, 111–139; currency, weights and measures, lxix, lxx; customs duties, 13–20, 113
Corrientes, Cape, 6
Coteels, Matheo, lxi, 30
Cotobaxa, *see* Qutbshāh
Cotton cloth and clothing, *passim*; trade in, explained, xix–xxii; on the Coromandel Coast, 17–20, 116, 127; in Bantam, 27, 28; in Patani and Siam, 41, 42, 58; for Europe, 78, 79; *see also* Apparel
Council of the *Globe*, the, 15, 52, 65
Court Minutes, quoted *passim*; title, 149
Cozucke, Sophony, 76
Crabs, 7
Creese (dagger), 64, 96
Currency, Note on, lxix
Customs duties—at Petapoli, 13; at Masulipatam, 14–20, 113; at Bantam, 23, 24; at Patani, 34–37; in Siam, 47

Dabhol, seaport, 21, 132
Dalgado, quoted *passim*; title, 149
Damask, 27, 64, 73
Danzig, xliv
Dariyā Khān, 120, 125
Darling, the, 83, 87–90, 141
Datapa, merchant, 138
Dato', term explained, 34
Davis, John (of Limehouse), 111–114, 116
de Brito, Philip, xxvii, 55, 91, 118, 119*n*
Deccanis in Golconda, 18*n*
de Haze, Hans, 132, 138
De Jonge, J. K. J., quoted *passim*; title, 149
de Labistrate, Jan, 67–69
Delft, the, xxxviii, xxxix, xlii
de Maire, Matchys, 32
Demak, seaport, 77
Denton, Adam, factor on the *Globe*, xxxiii, 45, 61*n*, 72, 73, 112; transferred to the *James*, xxxiii, 118; later movements, xxxiii, xxxiv, 141
der Goes, the, 21, 68, 119, 121, 125
Deroutes, name explained, 104
der Veer, the, 23
de Vries, Diricke, 146
Devyne, Florence, xiv
de Weert, Sebalt, xl
Diamond trade, the, 26, 27
Diaper, 64
'Divisions', xxxi

Dogs, 40, 82
Dopattas, 66
Downes, John, 62
Downs, the, 1
Dragans, 71, 76
Dragon, Foulon (Hans), 33
Dragon, the, xvii, 4*n*, 143
'**Droughthe**', term explained, 7*n*
Drunkenness on the *Globe*, xviii, 51, 60, 61, 122, 123, 125, 126
Duels, 125
Duncan Passage, the, 109, 110
Dutch, the, *passim*; formation and activities of the E.I. Co., xii; its legal position, lviii–lx; commercial policy, xxxv, xxxvi; activities at the Cape, 4, 5; on the Coromandel Coast, xxxviii ff., 8–12, 67–69, 127, 132, 136–138; in Japan, 35, 64, 145; in Java, xxiii, 23, 24, 64; in Patani and Siam, 32–36, 64, 75, 95; in the Spice Islands, 69, 82, 84, 85, 89; relations with the English Co., xxxv, xxxvi; wars with Spaniards and Portuguese, 21, 67–69, 84, 85; with Achin, 77, 97, 98; attitude towards Private Trade, lv, lvi, 44; service of Antheunis and Floris under, xxxviii–xlix
Dutchmen in English service, xiv, xlv, lx, lxi
Dysentery, xxxii, 30, 31, 38, 40

Eastern markets, character of, xix, xxi, 71
East India Company, Dutch, *see* Dutch, the
East India Company, English, *passim*; trading methods, xi–xiii; formation of Joint Stock, xiii, 140*n*, 141; arrangements for seventh Voyage, xiii–xviii; its financial results, xxx; admission of aliens, xviii; employment of foreigners, lx; attitude to Private Trade, lv–lviii, 27; relations with Dutch Co., xxxv, xxxvi
Ebert, William, on the *Globe*, xxxiv, 93; factor at Patani, xxxiv, 96, 97; at Bantam, 140–142; returns to the *Globe*, xxxiv; in London, xxxiv, lii
Eendracht, the, xl, xlvi, xlviii, xlix, 71
Eight Degree Channel, the, 7*n*
Ekathotsarot, King of Siam, xxvii, xxviii, 52–56
Elbing, town, xliii, xliv
Elephants, 12, *34; white, xxxviii, 54
Emmesworth, Thomas, 25
Empan, shipowner, 43
Engano, island, 22, 140
English Factories, quoted *passim*; title, 149
Enkhuizen, seaport, 32
Enkhuizen, or *Little Enkhuizen*, the (pinnace), 43, 82, 85; (ship), 146
Entertainments, Court, 63, 87
Equator, the, crossed, 2, 7, 22, 140
Eredia, quoted *passim*; title, 149
Erpenius, xlii*n*
Essington, Thomas, factor on the *Globe*, xxxii, and *passim*; on the Coromandel Coast, 14; appointed captain, xxxii, 38; in Siam, 43, 45–52; quarrels with John Johnson, 49–52; differences with Peter Floris, 92, 93; at Narasapur, 113–121; illness and death, 121; character, 121, 122; private trade, 122
Evans, Symon, xxxiii, lxiii, 14, 28
Evidence, law of, 19*n*
Expedition, the, 5*n*
Eyloff, Lodewyck Ysaacx, xlviii
Eyloff, Pieter Ysaacx, xxxviii, xxxix, xlviii, xlix

Factors, terms of employment of, xvi, xlix, lvi, lviii; wages of, lvi, 28, 29, 96, 97
'**Factory**', *passim*; term explained, xi
Farmān, term explained, 115
Farms of administration, xxii, 15–17, 115, 120
Festivals, 134
'**Feysons**', 3
Finch, William, 21
Firando (Hirado), seaport, xxv
Fire, danger from, at Patani, 35, 36, 94, 95; in Bantam, 76, 84
First Letter Book, quoted *passim*; full title, xiv, 149
Fish-skins, 64
Fiskaal, term explained, 97
Floods in India, xxxviii, xxxix, 128, 129; in Patani and Siam, 41, 46, 63, 67

Floris, Peter, *passim*; his identity, xxxvi–xxxviii; family and early life, xliii–xlv; Dutch service, xxxvi–xliii, 54, 129; in London, xvff.; chief merchant on the *Globe*, *passim*; on the Coromandel Coast, 8–21, 111–139; at Bantam, 23–29, 140–147; at Patani, 32–98; return to London, illness and death, l–lii; his funeral, lii, liii; his estate, xliv, li, lii; his Journal, text, 1 ff.; described, lxii–lxviii; his handwriting, xliii; his character, liii–lv; his private trade, lv–lviii; his legal and moral position, lviii–lxii; his relations with the Dutch, xviii, lxi, 10, 11, 30, 34, 69, 98, 117, 128, 136–138; his relations with authorities at Pulicat, 9–13; at Masulipatam, xxii, lxvii, 14–20, 113–116, 120, 129–139; at Bantam, 24, 25; at Patani, 33–38
Florissen, Jaques, xliii, xliv
Flux, the, *see* Dysentery
Formosa, island, xxiv
Foster, Sir William, quoted, xxxvi*n*, xli
Franckx, Cornelis, 118

Galle Point, 7, 8
Gambling, xviii, 60, 61
Gamboge, xxiv, 80
'Gentives', term explained, 134
Gĕtah (gum or resin), 80
Ginseng, *see* Ningin root
Girdles, xix, 28; price of, 144
'Glasses', term explained, 109
Globe, the, *passim*; equipment and despatch, xviii; voyage summarised, xxi–xxiii, xxx; results of Voyage, xxx–xxxvi; tonnage, xviii, 79; leaks in, 92, 107, 109, 114; sheathed, xxx, 46, 118, 123, 126; in danger, 6, 47, 48, 103, 104, 109, 131; numbers of crew, xviii, xxxii, 140, 143; mortality, xxxii, xxxiii, 29–32, 38, 39, 40, 48, 121; discipline, 49–52, 59–61, 92, 108, 116, 122, 125, 133
Goa, seaport, 119, 121
Gobars, 83
Godāvari, river, 110–130
Golconda, city, xxxvii, xxxviii, 68, 120, 121, 128
Golconda, kingdom, xxi; administration, xxii, 14–20, 114, 129–139; death of the King, 18
Golconda, Relations of, quoted *passim*; title, 150
Good Hope, Cape of, 3–5
Gottfried, Johan Lodwyck, lxv
Gouda, the, 4
'Gouvernesse' (Lady-Governor) of Pulicat, 10–13
Governor of E.I. Co., the, *see* Smythe, Sir Thomas
Governors, position of, xxii, 15–17, 120; conduct of, lxvii, 14–20, 24–26, 114, 115, 120, 129–139
Gran Canaria, island, 2
Gravesend, xviii, lx, 1
Green Lion, the, see *Groene Leeuw*, the
Greete, Hugh, 76
Greyhound, the, see *Hazewind*, the
Grimston, John, lii
Groene Leeuw, the, 113
Groote Sonne, the, xlvi–xlviii
'Guessing', term explained, 5*n*
Gujarāt, xx, xli, 42, 77, 84
Gums, xxiv, 80
Guns, ships', 113, 120
Gurney, John, 111–118, 141

Habshis in Golconda, 18*n*
Hadsie, Nachoda, 86
Hājī Bābā, 14
Half Moon, the, 23
Hanthawaddy, district, 53
Harvey, G. E., quoted *passim*; title, 150
Hascan, Nachoda, 76
Hāsta, unit of measurement, *passim*; size of, lxx
Hazewind, the, 33, 35, 64
Hector, the, 8, 23, 83
Hippon, Anthony, captain of the *Globe*, xvii, and *passim*; on the Coromandel Coast, 8–21; illness and death, xxxii, 38; quality of discipline, 60; his private trade, lvii, 61
Hirado, *see* Firando
Hitu, seaport, 83
Hobson-Jobson, quoted *passim*; title, 150
Hollandia, the, xl
Hope (*Hoop*), the, 81, 85, 97, 98
Horn, Cape, 4*n*
Houtman, Meerten, lxi, 43*n*, 66

Hūglī, river, xxxv
'Hull, to', term explained, 3*n*
Hunte, John, 31
Huyts, Samuell, 48
Hyderābād, 128*n*, 129*n*

Ibrahim Gujarātī, 43, 89
Ijzerman, J. W., quoted *passim*; title, 150
Ilhas dos Naos, As, 105
Impalement, 118, 119*n*
Imperial Gazetteer, the, quoted *passim*; title, 150
'In', used in special sense, 14*n*
Indĕra Muda, Raja, 44, 76, 88
India, Western, xiii; *see also* Dabhol, Goa, Gujarāt
Indigo, 78, 79, 115, 125, 127, 130
Inland Sea, the, 70*n*
Interest, rates of: in London, xxx; in Bantam, 25; in Patani, 75, 76
Intharaja, King of Siam, xxviii, 46, 47, 56, 57
Irens, Simon, *see* Evans, Symon
Iron, xxxix, 78, 115, 116, 144
Irrawaddy, river, xxvi
Itimād Khān, *see* Atmachan
Ivory, 86

Jacobsen, Lambert, 32
Jacobson, Phillip, lii*n*
Jagarāja, 124, 127
Jagoma, etc., *see* Chiengmai
Jakatra, xxiii, xxxvi, 23, 24, 147
Jambi, xxxvi, 44, 76
James, the, in the Straits, xxx, 77, 83; at Masulipatam, 111–118; at Pulicat, 124; at Bantam, 132, 140; at Patani, 132; homeward voyage, xxxi, 145
Jangadas (rafts), 13, 136
Jansen, Evert, 33
Jansen, or **Janssen, Hendrick**, lxi, 34, 66, 69, 82, 85, 86
Jansen, or **Janssen, Lucas**, *see* Antheunis, Lucas
Jansen, William, 95
Jantana, Point, 100, 101
Japan, *passim*; trade with Bantam, 145; with China, xxiv, xxv; with Patani and Siam, xxiv, 35, 64, 65, 74; English in, xxxv, 83, 146; *and see* Adams, William
Japanese in Patani and Siam, xxviii, 36, 56

Jara Island, 106
Java, *passim*; *and see* Bantam, Demak, Jakatra, Surabaya
'Jockcrommewaye', *see* Phya Naiwai
Johnson, John, master's mate on the *Globe*, xxxiii; appointed master, xxiii, 39; his misconduct, 49–52, 61; removed from office, 51; refuses enquiry, 65; sent to Bantam, 95; later movements, 142; returns to England as passenger, 145
Johore, kingdom, *passim*; war with Achin, 77, 81, 97, 98; with Pahang, 41, 73; restoration of the capital, 102; Dutch trade with, 23, 85
Johore, river and estuary, 81, 97, 102; Point of, *see* Jantana; Strait of, 100, 102
Joint Stock, First, xiii, 140*n*, 141
Joosten, Jacob, 74
Jortan (Surabaya), seaport, 44, 76
Josef, History of (manuscript), xli, xlii
Jourdain, John, liv, lv, 89, 90, 127, 141–146. His Journal, quoted *passim*; title, 150
Journal of the Voyage, the, *passim*; the manuscript described, lxii–lxv; its significance, xi; its handwriting, xliii, lxii; its evidential value, liii; the translator, lxii–lxiv
Judis, Simon, *see* Evans, Symon
Junk Ceylon, island, 108
Jury, trial by, 65

Kedah, seaport, 42, 44, 67, 69, 106, 107
Keeling, William, xiii
Kĕlings or *klings*, 70
Keppel Harbour, 100–103
Kerimun Island, Great, 100, 104, 105
Kerseys, 13, 64
Kindt, Samuel, xlv, xlvi
'King's Ship', the, 111–116, 132
Kistna, river, 128
Komatīs, 116, 134
Kondamma, Lady-Governor of Pulicat, 10–13
Kondapalli, fortress, 17
Krakatoa Islands, 22
Kundur Island, 105
Kwala Buca, 63, 95

Lac, 'lacquer', xxiv, 74, 79, 80, 116
Laksamana, Dato', 34, 81, 94
Lancaster, Sir James, xii. His *Voyages*, quoted *passim*; title, 150
'Langerys', 108
Lanshan, kingdom, xxiv, xxix, 43, 55, 57, 58, 67, 91
Lanzarote Island, 2
Laos, country, 58
Last, unit of measurement, lxx
'Latun', 145
'Lawnes', *see* Cotton cloth
Lead, xviii, xxiv, 13, 19
Leaden Hall, lii
Leeuw met Pijlen, the, 4, 64, 132, 137
Lemaire, Isaac, 4, 5
Lemaire, Jacob, 5
Lemaire Strait, 4*n*
'Lent', *see* Ramadhān
Letters Received, quoted *passim*; title, 150
l'Hermite, Jacques, 30*n*
Liefde, the, 35*n*, 74*n*
'Lieger', term explained, 25*n*
Ligor, state and seaport, xxiii, 55, 72, 73
'Lincange', *see* Nanking
Linga Island, 31
Lingua, *passim*; term explained, 17*n*
Linschoten, John Huyghen, quoted *passim*; title, 150
Lion with Arrows, the, see *Leeuw met Pijlen*
Little Enkhuizen, the, see *Enkhuizen*, the
Littlewood, Robert, purser on the *Globe*, xxxiv, 28*n*, 93; factor at Patani, xxxiv, 96, 97; his death, xxxiv, 142
Lizard, the, xxx, 1
Loans, Forced, xxii, lxvii, 115
Local duties, xxii, 14
Log of the *Globe*, the, lxiv, lxv
Longitude, calculated from variation, 2*n*
Lontor, island, 88
Looking-glasses, 64
Luang Prabang, *see* Lanshan
'Lucas', Mr, or Sr, *see* Antheunis, Lucas
Lucipara Island, 30
Lugor, *see* Ligor
Luhu, seaport, 83
Macao, Portuguese settlement, xxiv, 75
Macassar, seaport, xxxiv, 42, 43, 44, 82, 83, 87–90, 142, 145
Mace, 88
Mackian, island, 83
MacLeod, N., quoted *passim*; title, 150
Madagascar, 6*n*
Madeira Islands, 1
Madras, xxxv, 13*n*
Maha Thammaraja, King of Ayuthia, xxvii, 52, 53
Malabar Coast, xxiii
Malacca, seaport, xlvii, 42, 86, 105, 120
Malacca, Straits of, xxx, xlvi, 100, 105–107
Malay apparel, 37, 42, 70, 71
Maldive Islands, 7
'Malick Tusar', 120, 129
Malim, term explained, 69
Mancock, *see* Bangkok
Mandarins, term explained, 46
Mangas de veludo (birds), 3
Manillas, the, *see* Philippine Islands
Manoembing, mountain, 31
Manrique, Sebastien, quoted, 55*n*
Maps, errors in, 8
Marieko, fortress, 84
Marlowe, Edmond, 111, 116, 117, 140
Martaban, province, xxvii, 57*n*, 119*n*
Marten, or Martin, Nathaniel, lxiv, lxv, 61, 74, 86, 122
Martial Law, xvi*n*, xvii
Mas, silver coin, *passim*; value of, lxix
Masulipatam, *passim*; Dutch factory established, xxxviii; Floris' Dutch service at, xxxvi–xliii, 54, 129; the *Globe's* first visit, xxi, 14–21; second visit, 111–139; permanent factory established, xxxv; Governors of, 14, 111, 120, 133*n*; their conduct, xxii, lxvii, 14–20, 114, 115, 120, 129–139; products and trade, xx; customs and local duties, xxii, 14–20, 113; currency, weights and measures, lxix
Masulls, *passim*; term explained, 8*n*

Matelieff, Admiral, xlvi, xlvii
Matthias, Emperor, 85
Maund, unit of weight, *passim*; size of, lxix
Maurice (Mauritius), Prince, 11
Meander shoal, 103
Measures, Note on, lxx
Mekong, river, 98*n*
Menam, river, xxiii, 45, 46
Mergui, seaport, 42*n*
'**Mesapatania**', *see* Masulipatam
'**Meskita**', term explained, 94
Methwold, William, quoted *passim*; title, 150
Mexico, Viceroy of, 84
Michelborne, Sir Edward, 36*n*
Middelburg, lx
Middleton, David, 5, 23, 26, 146
Middleton, Sir Henry, commanding sixth Voyage, in London, xliv; at Table Bay, 5, 25; in the Red Sea, 21, 23, 77, 130; at Bantam, 76, 77, 112; death, 84
Mijl, Dutch unit of distance, lxx
Mīr, honorific prefix, 19*n*
'**Miriabeck**', 138
Mīr Jumla, Chief Minister of Golconda, 14–17
'**Mīr Masunim**', *see* Mīr Mu'min
Mīr Muhammad Razâ, 131, 134, 135
Mīr Muhammad Tâhir, 68, 138
Mīr Mu'min, 18, 129
Mīr Sadar-ud-dīn, 14–20, 111
'**Mīr Sumela**', *see* Mīr Jumla
Misardarens, 66
Mocha, 21, 84*n*, 111
Moginkwal, 6*n*, 7
Mollynauks, 3
Molucca Islands, 23, 42, 43, 69, 84, 85, 143, 147
Mon (race), xxvi, 53
Monopolies, xxv, 11, 13, 46, 47, 66
Monsoon, *passim*; term explained, 12*n*
Moore, Hugho, 32
Mortality on the Voyage, xxxii, xxxiii, 29–32, 38, 39, 40, 48, 121
Moulmein, province, xxvii
Mozambique, channel and seaport, 6, 7
Muhammad, King of Golconda, 18
Muhammad Amīn, 18
Muhammad Amīn, Mirza, 14*n*
Muhammad Qulī, King of Golconda, 18
Mullineux, Matthew, 8
Mundy, Peter, quoted *passim*; title, 150
Mūsi, river, 128
Muskets, 133, 136
Muslin, see *Betilles*, *Cassas*

'**Nachoda**', term explained, 25
Nagasaki, seaport, xxiv
Nandabayin, King of Burma, xxvii, 53, 54
Nanking, city, xxiv, 64
Narasapur, seaport, xxxii, 111–122, 125, 126, 128–131
Naresuen, King of Siam, xxvii, 52–55
'**Narsinga**', King of, 11; *and see* Vijayanagar
Nasarchan, 33, 45
Natal, 6
Navette, *passim*; term explained. 9*n*
Neblet (or Noblet), **Willem Jansen**, 32, 43
Negapatam, seaport, xl, 8, 42, 67
Neira, island and fortress, 88, 89
'**New Strait**', the, 100–103
Ningin root, 4, 5
Nizâmpatam, *see* Petapoli
Noblet, Jansen, *see* Neblet
North Sentinel Island, 110
Nuremberg wares, 64
Nutmegs, 88, 89

Obâjamma, Queen, 10, 124, 126, 132
'**Officers**', term explained, 39
Okyā, designation, 47
Ólafsson, Jón, quoted, lx*n*, 125*n*
'**Old Strait**', the, 100, 101, 103
Oliva, or **Olyva, Raphael**, 137
Ondya, *see* Ayuthia
Orangkaya, term explained, 34
Orissa, country, xxxv
Ortatan, market, 88
Osiander, the, xxxii, xxxiii, 140, 143, 145, 146
'**Overseers**', *passim*; term explained, lii*n*
Oysters, 106, 107, 108, 110

Pagell, term explained, 14
Pagoda, gold coin, *passim*; value of, lxix

Pahang, kingdom, and King, of, *passim*; war with Johore, 41, 73; dispute with Patani, 72, 73; the King visits Patani, 81, 82, 85–87
'Painted' cloth, xix–xxi
'Painters', xx, and *passim*
Palembang Strait, 31, 77
Palewares, term explained, 111
Palm, or palmite, trees, 103, 104, 110
Palmer, Job, 113, 125
Pangĕran, the (Governor of Bantam), 24–26
Pasan, *see* Pahang
Patani, kingdom and seaport, *passim*; described, xxiii; commercial conditions, xxv, 41, 42, 60, 70; conduct of officials, xxv, 34–38; trade with China, xxiv, 60, 73, 86; with Japan, xxiv, xxv, 35, 36, 64, 65; the *Globe* at, 32–40, 59–72, 91–98; the *James* at, 140; Dutch shipping at, 32, 33, 35, 64, 82, 95, 97; fires, 35, 94, 95; floods, 63, 67; thefts, 39, 40; outbreak of slaves, 94, 95; customs duties and charges, 34–37; rate of interest, 75, 76; currency, weights and measures, lxix
Patani, Queen of, *passim*; described, 62; her commercial activities, xxv, 75, 92; receives the merchants, 34, 62, 63, 87, 96; her entertainments, 63, 87; goes hunting, 62, 63; her quarrel with Pahang, 72, 87
Patani, Tanjong (=Cape), 32*n*
Patronymics, Dutch, xxxvi*n*
Pattas, 70, 71
'Paunde', term explained, 130
Peacock, Tempest, 146
Pedra Branca, islet, 31, 99–102
'Peece' (coin), value of, xxxiv
Pegu, kingdom, *see* Burma; city, xxvi, xxvii, 53–55, 74*n*, 119
Pemba Island, 7
Penang, island, 106, 107
Pender (or Ponder), George, 48
Pepper, xxiii, 37, 64, 86, 117, 127; price of, 25, 79, 132, 144
Peppercorn, the, 83
Persians in Golconda, 18
Persons (or Parsons), John, appointed factor, xxxiv, 29; at Patani, 33, 40; sent to Macassar, 43; news of, 83, 87–90; at Bantam, xxxiv, 142, 145; on the *Thomas*, xxxiv
Petapoli (Peddapalle), seaport, *passim*; products and trade, xx; Dutch factors at, xlvi–xlix; the *Globe* at, 13, 18; customs duties, 13
Phetchaburi, town, 57*n*
Philippine Islands, xxiv, 69, 85
Philpot Lane, li, lii
Phismachan, Okyā, 47, 66
Phongsawadan, the (chronicle), xxviii, xxix
Phra Klang, 47*n*
Phya Naiwai, xxviii, 56
Picul, unit of weight, *passim*; size of, lxx
Piece-goods, xix–xxi, and *passim*
Pieters, James, 92
Pigeons, Cape, 3
'Pilon', term explained, 54
Pinnace, *passim*; term explained, 9*n*
'Pintadoes', xx, *and see* Apparel
Pirates, 36*n*
Pishwā, designation, 18*n*
Plurbier, —, 72
Popenis, *poupenys*, etc., 20, 66
Porcelain, xxiii, 64, 73, 108, 116, 121
Porto Santo, island, 1
Portuguese, the, *passim*; in China, xxiv, 75; on the Coromandel Coast, 9, 67, 68; in Macassar, 88; in Malacca, 42, 86, 105; in Syriam, *see* de Brito, Philip; trade with Siam, 42; relations with the Dutch, 21, 67–69, 84, 85
Pound, weight of Dutch, lxix
'Poupenys', see *Popenis*
'Prauwes', praws, etc., *passim*; term explained, 62
Presents to officials, in Bantam, 24; in Masulipatam, xxii, 15, 115; in Patani, 33, 37; in Pulicat, 12; in Siam, 43, 66
Priaman, seaport, 25, 27
Primeiro Islands, 6
Printed cloth, xx, 117
Private Trade, *passim*; discussed, lv–lviii, 44; on the Coromandel Coast, 16, 117; in Bantam, lvii, 26, 61, 144; in Borneo, 26; in Patani, lvii, 62; practised by Antheunis, lv–lviii; by Browne, lvii, 27; by Essington, 122; by Floris, lv–lviii; by Hippon, lvii, 61

Profit of the Voyage, xxx, xxxi
'Protests', 137
Prussia, East, xliii, xliv
Puket, island, *see* Junk Ceylon
Pulau Ai, or Wai, island, 89
Pulau Bajin, island, 32, 99
Pulau Capas, island, 32, 99
Pulau Condore, island, 98
Pulau Panjang, island, 76
Pulau Parselar, 105, 106
Pulau Pinang, island, 31
Pulau Pisang, island, 105
Pulau Pon, island, 31
Pulau Tingi, island, 31, 99
Pulau Tuju, island, 31
Pulicat, *passim*; products and trade, xx, xxi; the *Globe* at, xxi, 9–12; Dutch factory at, 9; captured by Portuguese, 67; rebuilt and fortified, 116, 117, 132; site offered to the English, 124, 127; Queen of, *see* Obājamma; 'Gouvernesse' of, *see* Kondamma
Punishments, 125, 133
Puntu Gorbangh, 94
Purchas, The Rev. Samuel, quoted *passim*; his methods of work, lxiv–lxvi; title, 150
Pyrard de Laval, François, quoted *passim*; title, 150

Qāfila, term explained, 67
Qaul, *passim*; term explained, 10*n*
Qutbshāh, style of Golconda dynasty, 18

Rachado, Cape, 105
Ramadhān, 94
Ratans, 40, 86
Razadarit, King of Pegu, 119*n*
Reals of eight, *passim*; value, lix
Recado, *passim*; term explained, 11*n*
Redang Islands, 32, 59, 99
Red Sea, the, xiii; *and see* Mocha
Reis, Portuguese monetary unit, 55*n*
Restanten (remnants), term explained, xxxix
Reynst, Gerard, Governor-General, xxxvii, l, liv, lxi, 132
Reys-Gheschrift, quoted *passim*; title, 150
Rice, xxiv, 55, 72, 77, 116
Rio Formoso, river, 105
Rochester bridge, 129
Romenia, Cape, 100, 101
Rooden Leeuw, the, 137*n*
Rotterdam, xlvii, xlix, li
Rotterdam, the, 147
Royal Letters, to Patani, 33; to Japan, 86; to Siam, 34, 43; from Vijayanagar, 124, 126
Rudolph, Emperor, 85
Ruyll, Jan Gerritsz, xxxviii

Sabander, see Shāhbandar
Sabon, island and strait, 105
Sabrangh, the, 32, 62
Sack (of pepper), lxx
St Dionis Backchurch, Church of, lii
S. Helena, island, 132, 145
S. Thomé, xiii, 9, 67
Salalas, salalus, 71
Saldana Bay, *see* Table Bay
Saletters, Salettes, 101, 102
Salmon, Nathaniel, xxxiii, 143
'Salte hills', 128
'Salte Island', *see* Krakatoa
Samaritan, the, 146
Samuell, Thomas, 74
Sand brought by rain, 2
Sandalwood, 84
Sangerims, see *Jangadas*
Sanqua, Nachoda, 80, 81
Sappan, dye-wood, xxiv, 74, 116
Sarassas, 28
Saris, John, 69*n*, 83, 86. His Voyage, quoted *passim*: title, 151
Sarong, 27*n*; and see *Tapés*
Sashes, xix; *and see* Girdles
Satin, 64
Satow, Sir Ernest, quoted *passim*; title, 151; his criticism of Floris, xxviii, xxix
Sayers, John, *see* Saris
Schey, Raja, 94
Schismachan, *see* Phismachan
Schott, Apollonius, 84
Schouten, J., quoted *passim*; title, 151
Sea Adventure, the, 146*n*
Segertsz, Pieter, lxi, 30
Sĕlat Tĕbĕrau, strait, 100, 101
Sĕmbilan Islands, (*a*), off Singapore, 100; (*b*), off Perak River, 106; (*c*), off Junk Ceylon, 108
Sĕmbilan Strait, 100, 103, 104
'Serpent Master', the, 113

Seven Islands, the, 31
Shāhbandar, *passim*; term explained, 9*n*
Shan States, xxvi, 53*n*
Sheppard, William, 112, 143, 144
Siakai, Raja, 63
Siam, kingdom, *passim*; described, xxiii, xxiv, 52–58; relations with Burma, xxvi, xxvii, 52–55, 91, 92; internal troubles, xxviii, 56–58; commercial conditions, xxv, xxix, 43, 47, 52, 58, 66, 73, 74, 91, 141; trade with China, xxiv, 73; with India, 42, 52, 58; with Japan, xxiv, xxv, 64, 74; visits of the *Globe*, 45–52, 72, 91; Dutch factory, 46; English factory, 46; closed, xxxv; customs duties, 47; currency, weights and measures, lxix
Silk, xiii, xxiii, xxiv, 27, 35, 64, 73, 86, 145
Silk fabrics, 27, 35, 64, 73, 80
Silver, 64, 65, 145
Singapore Island, 100, 102
Singapore Straits, xxx, 83, 100–104
Singora, state and seaport, xxiii, 73, 86, 95
Sinki Strait, 100, 103
'Sinnar', the, 45
Sirnora, Orangkaya, 34, 72, 94
Sitterbangsa, Raja, 94
Skinner, John, master's mate on the *Globe*, *passim*; his courage, 48; appointed master, xxxiii, 52; in charge of the *Globe*, 123; his misconduct, 60, 61, 122, 126; transferred to the *Osiander*, xxxiii, 143
Skins, trade in, xxiv, 5, 64, 74, 86
Skirts, see *tapés*
Slaves, Javanese, 94, 95
Smith, Arthur, 31
Smith, Thomas, 39, 61
Smythe, Sir Thomas, xiv, li, lii, 1, 29, 43, 112, 141, 146
'Sockle', term explained, 88
Solomon, the, xxxiii, xxxv, xlv, xlvi, lxviii, 83
Solor Island, 84
Sombah datang, *benaga*, *datching*, *muson*, terms explained, 37
Songtham, King, *see* Intharaja
'Soulathd', term discussed, 118
Spalding, Augustine, 23–29, 44, 112, 143
Spaniards, the, 84, 85
Spice Islands, the, xxxv; *and see* Amboina, Banda, Molucca Islands
Spice trade, xii, xiii, 64, 78, 83, 88, 89
Stammell cloths, 64
Steel, 83
Stego, Idan, 50
Stone, Mr, lii
Storms, off Table Bay, 3; off Natal, 6; in Gulf of Siam, xxxii, 47–49; near Singapore, 104, 105; near the Andamans, 109; off Narasapur, 131
Sukadana, 26, 76, 83
Sumatra, 22, 30, 31, 140
Sunda Strait, 22, 140
Surabaya, seaport, 44, 76
Surat, Suratta, seaport, 21, 118, 130, 134
Suttee, 132
Syriam, seaport, xxvii, 55, 91, 118

Table Bay, 3–5, 25
Table Mountain, 3
Tael, unit of currency, *passim*; value of, lxix
Taffeta, 27, 64, 73
Takekoshi, Y., quoted *passim*; title, 151
Talaing (race), *see* Mon
Talapois, 56
Tanga, coin, 55
Tangu, *see* Toungoo
Tapés (skirts), *passim*; term explained, xix, 27*n*; price of, 61, 117, 144; *tapéchinders (-dos)*, 117, 144; *tapés kitchill*, 27; *tapésarassas*, 28; *tapé* girdles, 27, 144
Tashrīf, *passim*; term explained, 113
Taure, *Tauri*, 68
Tavoy, province, xxvii
Tegnapatam, seaport, 8, 67, 119
Telingāna, country, 18
Telugu language, the, xlii, xliii
Tembaga shoal, 102
Tenasserim, state and town, xxiii, xxvii, 14, 42, 43, 55, 119
Teneriffe, Peak of, 2
Ternate, island, 84
Terpstra, Dr H., quoted *passim*; title, 151
Ter Veer, the, xlix
Texel, the, 132

Thévenot, Melchisedech, lxv
Thieves, 39, 40
Thomas, the, 23, 146
Thomasine, the, 146
Tical, silver coin, lxix
Tidore, island, 84
Tigers, 41
Timarāja, 127
Tin, xxiv, 106
Tingall, Nachoda, 25
Tioman Island, 32, 98, 99
Ton, unit of measurement, lxx
Toungoo, province, xxvi, xxvii, 54, 91*n*
Trade winds, 2
Trades Increase, the, 5*n*, 76, 83, 84
Train-oil, 5
Trang, seaport, 42, 43, 44
Tristan da Cunha Island, 3
Tselitones, *see* Celytones
Tsulias, see *Chulias*
'Tuffetaphaties', 64
Tunny fish, 145
Turbans, xix, 66

Unite (coin), *see* 'Peece'
Unxa, *see* Pegu
'Upperwaters', term explained, 41

Vadagar, 18
Valentyn, F., quoted *passim*; title, 151; value of his work, xl, xlix
van Berchem, Wemmer, lxi, 68, 113, 117, 121, 136–138
van den Broeck, Abram, 82, 85, 86
van der Aa, Pieter, lxv
van Dijk, L. C. D., quoted *passim*; title, 151
van Elbing, Hans Willemsz, xliii, xliv, 1, 128, 141
van Elbing (Elbinck, etc.), **Pieter Willemsz**, *see* Floris, Peter
van Hastwell, Daniell, lii*n*
van Henseden, John, 95
van Leeuwen, Dirck, xlvi, xlviii
van Neijenrode, Cornelis, 43, 95
van Ravesteyn, Pieter Gilliesz, lxi, 128
van Santvoort, Melchior, 74, 86
van Soldt, Paul, xxxviii, xxxix, 129*n*
van Vliet, J., quoted *passim*; title, 151
van Wesick, Jan, lxi, 10, 11, 67*n*
Varellas, the, locality, 98
Variation, used to calculate longitude, 2*n*
Vellore, 12*n*, 124, 126, 139
Velvet, 27, 64, 73
Venkata, Venkatādri (with suffixes), *see* Vijayanagar, King of
Venkatādri, son of Busebullerau, lxvii, 113, 133–138
Vijayanagar, King of, xxi, 11, 12, 124, 126, 133
Voyages, separate, *passim*; nature of, xi; first Voyage of E.I. Co., xii; second, xii; third, xiii; fourth, xiii; fifth, xiii; sixth, xiii; *and see* Middleton, Sir Henry; seventh, *passim*; eighth, see *Clove*, *Hector*, *Thomas*, the; ninth, see *James*, the; tenth, 140; system discontinued, xiii

Warellas, *see* Varellas, the
Wars, *passim*; Dutch and English, xxxv; Dutch and Portuguese or Spaniards, 21, 84; Achin and Johore, 77, 81, 97, 98; Burma and Siam, 52–54, 91, 92; in Europe, 85; Johore and Pahang, 41, 73; Siam and Lanshan, etc., 43, 57
Warwijk, Admiral, Voyage of, xl, xli
Wax, 35, 64, 74
Weights, Note on, lxix
Welden, Richard, 88
Wencatadra, *see* Venkatādri
Wengali, 126, 127
Whales, 48; whaling, 4*n*, 5
'White King', the, *see* Ekathotsarot
White Lion, the, 132
Willem, father of Floris, xliii–xlv
Wood, W. A. R., quoted *passim*; title, 151
Woodall, John, li
Woollen cloth, xviii, 13, 19

'Xenga', *see* de Brito, Philip

Yarn, cotton, 58, 67, 71, 78, 79, 83, 115, 146

'Zalelchor Chan', 14
Zanzibar, island, 7
Zeeland Chamber, the, lx
Zelandia, the, 145, 147

CAMBRIDGE: PRINTED BY W. LEWIS, M.A., AT THE UNIVERSITY PRESS